Small Groups

Small Groups

An Introduction

A. Paul Hare, Herbert H. Blumberg,
Martin F. Davies, and M. Valerie Kent

PRAEGER

Westport, Connecticut
London

Library of Congress Cataloging-in-Publication Data

Small groups : an introduction / A. Paul Hare . . . [et al.].
    p.   cm.
    Includes bibliographical references and indexes.
    ISBN 0–275–94896–X (alk. paper)
    1. Social interaction.   2. Small groups.   I. Hare, A. Paul
    (Alexander Paul), 1923–   .
    HM291.S577   1996
    302.3'4—dc20   96–15329

British Library Cataloguing in Publication Data is available.

Library of Congress Catalog Card Number: 96–15329
ISBN: 0–275–94896–X

First published in 1996

Praeger Publishers, 88 Post Road West, Westport, CT 06881
An imprint of Greenwood Publishing Group, Inc.

Printed in the United States of America

The paper used in this book complies with the
Permanent Paper Standard issued by the National
Information Standards Organization (Z39.48–1984).

10 9 8 7 6 5 4 3 2 1

Copyright Acknowledgment

Every reasonable effort has been made to trace the owners of copyright materials in this book, but in some instances this has proven impossible. The authors and publisher will be glad to receive information leading to more complete acknowledgments in subsequent printings of the book, and in the meantime extend their apologies for any omissions.

Contents

Figures and Tables

FIGURES

TABLES

Introduction

A. Paul Hare

How does one begin an introduction to a book which is itself an introduction? Should there be an introduction to the introducer? If this is needed, see "Notes about Ourselves" at the end of this volume.

While we are asking questions, why write another introduction to the social-psychological literature on interaction in small groups? You will find a number of introductory texts on your library shelves. Homans (1950), *The human group*, has become a "classic" (and was reprinted in 1992, with an introduction by Paul Hare to Homans's work). For a short account of early research, Olmsted's (1959) book *The small group*, or the second edition (Olmsted and Hare, 1978), would be a good place to begin.

For many years, Cartwright and Zander's *Group dynamics* (1953, 1960, 1968), summary chapters combined with readings, was the most popular introduction to the field. Shaw's text, *Group dynamics: The psychology of small group behavior*, also revised through three editions (1971, 1976, 1981), next became the major text in the field. Some time has passed. More research has been published, and social psychologists have come closer to providing theoretical perspectives that can show the relationships between much of the data, although there is still no single overall theory to which all would subscribe.

The present introduction is a selection of the major themes that are reflected in research on social interaction in small groups. We draw mainly on our previous handbooks of small group research (Hare, 1962, 1976; Hare, Blumberg, Davies, & Kent, 1994) and our collections of readings (Hare, Borgatta, & Bales, 1955, 1965; Blumberg, Hare, Kent, & Davies, 1983) which review the literature from 1898 through 1988. For more recent material, we have checked major journals and books, and especially searched for the work of persons who have been frequent contributors to research in this area.

We continue to use the definition of a small group that was set out in the introduction to our handbook (Hare, Blumberg, Davies, & Kent, 1994, p. 1). A group is usually considered as "small" if it has from 2 to 30 members. However, even larger groups can have "small group" characteristics. Collections of a small number of persons who happen to share the same physical space without having a common task would not be considered a group. The characteristics that differentiate a group from a collection of individuals are that the group members (1) have shared values that maintain an overall pattern of activity, (2) acquire or develop resources or skills to be used in their activity, (3) conform to norms that define roles to be played and have a sufficient level of morale to provide "cohesiveness," and (4) have a specific goal with the coordination, usually through leadership, to combine the resources and the roles to accomplish the goal.

The organization of the chapters in our text is similar to that in the earlier handbook and selection of readings. Progressively more sources of influence are brought "on stage"—although the chapters can in fact be read independently. In Part I, on the situation and the person, we present research on the influence of the physical situation and of the personalities and social characteristics of the group members—in two chapters by Martin F. Davies. Part II, on the influence of others on the individual, consists of chapters on the presence of others and conformity by M. Valerie Kent. Part III, on group structure, includes a chapter on roles and relationships by A. Paul Hare and a chapter on leadership by M. Valerie Kent. Part IV, on group process, has chapters on social interaction by Martin F. Davies and group decision making and choice shift by Herbert H. Blumberg. Part V, on interactive modes, has chapters that combine several topics. One chapter covers competition, cooperation, and conflict resolution, and a second chapter summarizes research on bargaining, coalitions, and games. Both chapters are by Herbert H. Blumberg. The final section, Part VI, on the group and the situation, moves up one system level. The focus for the previous chapters has been on the individual in the group. Here it is on the group in the larger setting. One chapter is on the group in the context of an organization, by A. Paul Hare. The last chapter, by Martin F. Davies, discusses the relationships between groups.

On occasion, a report of research may have relevance for more that one chapter and will be cited separately in each context. This book is eclectic in approach, but one perspective that is highlighted in several chapters is the "SYMLOG" view of social interaction, associated with Bales and his colleagues.

In addition, a particular group process may play a part in the subject covered in different chapters. This is especially true for "conformity." The process of conformity appears in Chapter 4 mainly as a function of the exposure of an individual to the opinions of others. Subsequent chapters examine the effects of group structure and social interaction on conformity. Chapter 8 discusses conformity-like effects as they influence group decision making and choice shift.

At the end of the text we add some suggestions for further reading. The references are primarily to collections of readings or surveys, with some additional references for each of the chapters.

We would like to thank Joseph McGrath, Julie Raven, and David Cleeton for their helpful comments on a late draft of this work. We thank the staff of Greenwood Press and also Rainsford Type for their helpful and expeditious handling of this project.

This volume completes a trilogy that has, as it were, been several decades in the making. As noted above, classic readings and a handbook have already been available. We hope that, now in addition, readers will find this text enjoyable and useful.

PART I

The Situation and the Person

CHAPTER 1

The Physical Situation

Martin F. Davies

The physical situation in which an individual or group is located consists of: the *ambient environment*—such as noise level and temperature; the *human environment*—such as the number of people present and their spatial arrangement; and *material aspects* of the environment—such as room design, architecture, fixtures, and fittings.

These three aspects of the environment can influence behavior in various ways, but Darley and Gilbert (1985) suggest that the single most important influence of the physical situation is its *perceived purpose*. For example, the sorts of behavior associated with a classroom—and expected of its occupants—are different from the sorts of behavior associated with a factory assembly line or a barroom.

Although social psychologists usually speak of the "situation" as having some sort of direct influence on social behavior, environmental psychologists prefer to view the physical situation in terms of how it *facilitates* or *hinders* behavior. People do not simply exist in environments, they select "optimal" environments or try to change their existing environment so as to maximize their well-being and the fulfillment of their plans and goals. Often, however, people are unable to attain such optimal environmental conditions, in which case they must try to adapt to the existing less-than-ideal situation.

This chapter is based partly on M. F. Davies (1994), "Physical situation," in A. P. Hare, H. H. Blumberg, M. F. Davies, & M. V. Kent, *Small group research: A handbook* (Norwood, NJ: Ablex, pp. 11–39). Reprinted with permission from Ablex Publishing Corporation.

ENVIRONMENTAL STRESS

When environmental conditions are such that a person's adaptive and coping resources are strained or taxed, the environment is not only less than optimal, it is also stressful. Examples of environmental *stressors* include noise, heat, cold, pollution, and crowding or density (crowding and density are reviewed in a separate section of this chapter under "Human Spatial Behavior"). Stressors that are intense, prolonged, unpredictable, and uncontrollable are particularly distressing and debilitating. First of all, unpredictable and uncontrollable stressors make heavy demands on attentional capacity because of the effort required to "tune out" the distracting aspects of the stimulus or to monitor the threatening aspects of the stimulus. Prolonged exposure to such stressors results in *cognitive fatigue* and a depletion of attentional resources that persists even after the stressful experience has ended (Cohen, 1978). Second, exposure to unpredictable and uncontrollable stressors can lead to *learned helplessness* (Seligman, 1975)—people come to believe that their inability to cope with a specific stressful situation is indicative of a general inability to cope with life-tasks and events, resulting in motivational, emotional, and cognitive deficits.

Noise

The cognitive-fatigue hypothesis suggests that unpredictable, uncontrollable noise should lead to a reduction in people's sensitivity to social cues. In one study, Mathews and Canon (1975) arranged for an assistant of the experimenters to drop a box of books on a city street. In one condition, the assistant's arm was in a plaster cast; in the other condition, there was no plaster cast. The incident was staged either under noisy conditions (a nearby power mower) or quiet conditions. When the street was quiet, passers-by were much more likely to help the assistant with an arm cast than without a cast. Under noisy conditions, not only was there less helping overall, but passers-by were also no more likely to help the assistant with the arm cast than the assistant without the cast, because passers-by were less likely to notice the arm cast.

The role of *perceived control* in moderating the after-effects of noise stress was highlighted by Sherrod and Downs (1974). Subjects worked on a task under one of three noise conditions. In one condition (low stress), subjects were exposed to soothing sounds; in a second condition (high stress/low control), subjects were exposed to distressing sounds which could not be terminated; in a third condition (high stress/high control), subjects were also exposed to distressing sounds but could turn off the noise if they wished. After completion of the task and on their way out of the laboratory, subjects were asked by a second experimenter for help in a research project. Subjects who had been exposed to the soothing sounds volunteered the most, subjects exposed to the uncontrollable distressing sounds volunteered least, and subjects exposed to controllable distressing sounds showed an intermediate amount of helping.

Temperature

It might seem intuitively plausible that unpleasantly hot temperatures should result in more negative feelings and behavior. Early studies by Griffitt (Griffitt, 1970; Griffitt & Veitch, 1971) in laboratory settings did indeed find that subjects liked a fictitious stranger (described in a dossier) less under hot and humid conditions than under normal conditions. However, some studies have not found that high temperatures lead to disliking of a stranger. Kenrick and Johnson (1979) argued that the presence of others can reduce the unpleasant experience of stressful situations, leading to more attraction to a stranger in stressful conditions—called a *shared stress* effect. If the stranger is physically present, there is greater liking under stressful than under comfortable conditions; but if the stranger is not physically present (as in the fictitious stranger paradigm), there is less liking under stressful than comfortable conditions.

It might also seem plausible that high temperatures should lead to greater arousal, activity, and energy, and hence to greater aggressive—even violent—activities; everyday sayings exhort you to: "keep your cool, man!" and "don't get hot under the collar!" But, in a number of laboratory studies, Baron (Baron & Bell, 1976) found a *curvilinear* relation between temperature and aggressive behavior. Up to a certain point, an increase in temperature increased aggression. Beyond this point, however, further increases in temperature led to reductions in aggression, apparently because the motivation to aggress was supplanted by other motivations—such as how to escape or avoid the unpleasant conditions.

Extending this to situations outside of the laboratory, Baron and Ransberger (1978) predicted that occurrences of collective violence were more likely when the weather was moderately hot rather than extremely hot. Support for this curvilinear relationship was obtained by analyzing the incidence of 102 riots in the United States between 1967 and 1971 and the weather conditions prevailing at the time (see Figure 1.1).

However, Carlsmith and Anderson (1979) argued that Baron and Ransberger had failed to take into account how many days there were at particular temperatures. If it turned out that there were more days in a year at moderately hot temperatures than at very hot temperatures, then there would simply be more *opportunities* for riots to occur at moderately hot temperatures. The appropriate analysis, therefore, would be to test whether there are *relatively* more riots at moderately hot than at cooler or hotter temperatures. When Carlsmith and Anderson did this analysis, they found strong evidence for a *linear* rather than a curvilinear relation—the hotter

Figure 1.1
Violence and the Long, Hot Summer

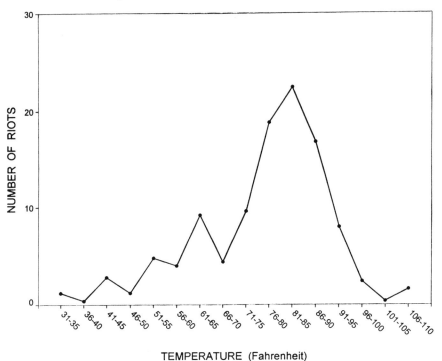

TEMPERATURE (Fahrenheit)

Source: Baron, R. A., & Ransberger, V. M. (1978). Ambient temperature and the occurrence
of collective violence: The "long, hot summer" revisited. *Journal of Personality and Social
Psychology, 36,* 351–360. Copyright © 1978 by the American Psychological Association.
Reprinted with permission.

it got, the more likely the occurrence of a riot. (Obviously, however, there
does come a point, beyond naturally occurring temperatures, at which it is
just too hot to engage in any activity.)

Other Stressors

Some research has been done on air or atmospheric *pollution.* For example, Rotton, Barry, Frey, and Soler (1978) looked at the effects of atmospheric pollution on liking an attitudinally similar or dissimilar fictitious
stranger. In one study, they found—contrary to predictions—that liking a
similar stranger was greatest in a polluted atmosphere (ammonium sulfide)
compared to a neutral (no odor) condition. This suggested a *shared stress*
effect (previously discussed in the "Temperature" section). In a second
study, subjects were told they were alone in the lab and would not meet

the (bogus) stranger. This had the effect of producing the expected relation between a stressful condition (air pollution) and disliking a stranger as well as disliking the environment. As with lab studies on temperature and aggression, Rotton, Frey, Barry, Mulligan, and Fitzpatrick (1979) found a curvilinear relation between pollution level and aggression, suggesting that anger and aggression increase until the point comes where people prefer to avoid the polluted conditions rather than aggress.

Generally, however, little is known about the effects of air pollution on social behavior (Evans & Jacobs, 1981). If it operates like other stressors, then unpredictable, uncontrollable, and intense pollution should lead to: impaired task performance, learned helplessness, attentional deficits and insensitivity to the needs of others, and negative mood and feelings.

HUMAN SPATIAL BEHAVIOR

Psychologists have investigated how humans space themselves around the environment. Human spatial behavior consists of: *territories*—the occupancy, marking, and defense of places or objects; *personal space*—the interpersonal distance at which people prefer to converse and interact; *spatial arrangements*—the ways in which people space themselves in a group environment; and *crowding*—the stress and negative feelings experienced when there are felt to be too many people in a particular place.

Privacy

An important concept underlying ideas about spatial behavior is privacy. The most influential approach to privacy is Altman's (1975) *boundary-regulation* model shown in Figure 1.2. According to Altman's model, people try to achieve an optimal level of social contact or stimulation—a desired level of privacy. If, at a given point in time, there is too much social contact, a person may feel crowded or intruded upon. If there is too little social contact, the person will feel lonely or isolated. In order to increase or reduce the amount of social contact to achieve the desired level of privacy, Altman suggests people use various *privacy-regulation* or interpersonal control mechanisms. These mechanisms include verbal, nonverbal, as well as spatial behaviors.

People can regulate the amount of social stimulation and contact they receive by exerting control over particular places in the environment—*territories*—where control is exerted by deploying markers and signs, either explicit ("keep out!") or implicit (leaving a scarf on a library seat). In casual encounters, people can regulate the amount of stimulation they receive from others by varying the openness/closedness of their self-boundary (or in the case of groups, the group-boundary). This can be achieved through *interpersonal distancing* (sitting or standing close to or far from other people),

Figure 1.2
Relationships between Privacy, Territory, Personal Space, and Crowding

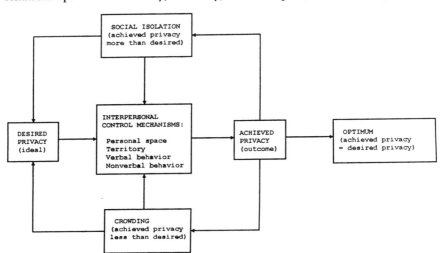

Source: Altman, I. (1975). *The environment and social behavior.* Monterey, CA: Brooks/Cole.
   Reprinted with permission of the author.

nonverbal behavior (more open or closed postures, more or less eye contact), and verbal behavior (talking more or less, or talking about more or
less intimate topics). In group settings, desired levels of privacy can be
achieved by selecting suitable *seating positions,* such as central positions
for high levels of stimulation or peripheral positions for low levels. Finally,
crowding can be viewed as the *consequence* of failing to achieve an optimal
level of privacy; when the density of people is such that a higher-than-
desired level of social stimulation occurs, people feel crowded (Taylor &
Altman, 1983).

Territories

In territories, boundaries are regulated by the marking of a place to indicate ownership and occupancy. Altman (1975) classified territories into
three types: primary, secondary, and public. *Primary* territories—such as
bedrooms, apartments, family homes—are owned and exclusively occupied
on a regular and long-term basis by individuals and groups. There is a high
degree of control over access to such territories, ensuring a high degree of
privacy for personally important or intimate activities. *Secondary* territories
are places used by groups on an intermittent basis, such as local clubs and
bars, meeting rooms, work premises, communal areas of student dormitories, and apartment buildings. The group members do not own such
places on a legal basis, but they still claim rights and restrict access to such

Figure 1.3
Effectiveness of Territorial Markers

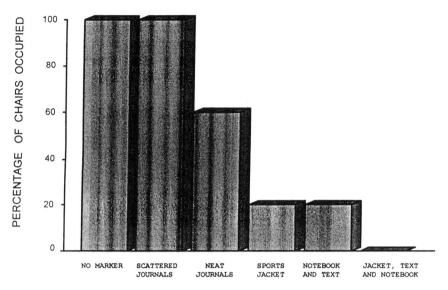

Source: Sommer, R., & Becker, F. D. (1969). Territorial defense and the good neighbor. *Journal of Personality and Social Psychology, 11*, 85–92.

places. For example, residents of an apartment building may confront non-residents (intruders) in communal areas of the building; regular patrons of a bar may discourage use of it by outsiders. *Public* territories—such as restaurant tables, park benches, or library seats—are not owned by the occupants, and are used only for a short time. There is usually little control over access to such places, and there is little privacy.

In public territories, people often use territorial "markers" to reserve their places. These markers are usually artifactual and symbolic. In a crowded library, Sommer and Becker (1969) observed that a marked chair was less likely to be occupied the more personalized markers were used to reserve it, as shown in Figure 1.3. However, if, for some reason, another person *does* invade or intrude upon a "marked" space, there is not much evidence that people are willing to defend the territory or confront the invader (Becker, 1973).

In secondary territories, an individual's rights are more variable and un-certain, since they are situated somewhere between the common access of public spaces and the exclusive ownership of primary territories. Conse-quently, there are more likely to be conflicts over the use of secondary territories. Newman (1972) analyzed crimes in public-housing projects and found that crimes against the person often occurred in secondary territories such as hallways, stairwells, and elevators. Residents considered these areas too difficult to defend and came to treat them as public territories. Newman suggested that such areas could become *defensible spaces* by making appropriate architectural alterations: allowing easier surveillance of the high-risk areas by residents, and building smaller residential units so that there would be a small number of users who would be able to recognize one another and spot intruders.

Primary territories are not only the most central arenas of people's lives, they can also be said to constitute extensions of the self—especially homes (Cooper, 1974). Consequently, people personalize their primary territories, particularly if they feel attached to them. Hansen and Altman (1976) discovered that university dropouts displayed fewer signs of personalization of their college rooms (e.g., posters and pictures) than nondropouts. Sebba and Churchman (1983) identified four different areas of family homes. There were *individual* areas such as studies and single bedrooms; *shared* areas were used by subgroupings within the family, for example, bedrooms shared by two or more children; *jurisdiction* areas were used by all the family, but the rights tended to reside in one member; and *public* areas were used by all the family (living rooms, lounges, hallways, bathrooms).

Personal Space

The study of personal space and interpersonal distance has proved to be an enormously popular research topic. Hayduk (1978) defined personal space as the area individuals maintain around themselves into which others cannot intrude without arousing discomfort—a sort of "portable" territory that people carry around with them.

A number of theories or models of interpersonal spacing have been developed. Argyle and Dean (1965) proposed that in any interaction there are various "approach" forces that pull people together (such as need for affiliation or contact) and "avoidance" forces that push people apart (such as fear of social embarrassment or rejection). Argyle and Dean suggested that for a particular interaction there is an appropriate level of intimacy between interactants. Greater eye contact, more open postures, warmer voice tone, more intimate topics of conversation, and closer interaction distances all contribute to increasing the intimacy of the encounter. If the level of intimacy is either lower or higher than the desired or appropriate level, then the interactants may modify one or more of these verbal and nonverbal behaviors to achieve the desired level of intimacy. Interactants use *compensatory* means of regulating deviations from the desired level of intimacy. If it is felt that the interpersonal distance is too close, this increased intimacy can be compensated for by either gazing less at the other, adopting a more closed posture, or changing to a less intimate topic. Similarly, if one person feels the other person is introducing too intimate topics

Figure 1.4
Patterson's Arousal Model of Interpersonal Intimacy

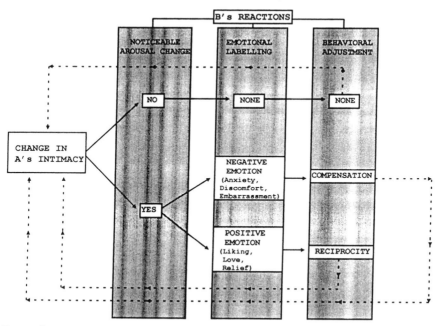

Source: Patterson, M. L. (1976). An arousal model of interpersonal intimacy. *Psychological Review*, *83*, 235–245. Copyright © 1976 by the American Psychological Association. Reprinted with permission.

into the discussion, this can be compensated for by reducing eye contact, closing up the posture, or moving further away.

However, Patterson (1976) proposed a theory that predicts *reciprocal* as well as compensatory changes, as shown in Figure 1.4. Patterson argued that changes in intimacy level produce changes in *arousal* that accentuate existing feelings. This arousal may be felt as a negative emotion (anxiety, discomfort, embarrassment) or as a positive emotion (liking, love, relief) depending on the setting, the other person, or the relationship. If one person increases the intimacy of the encounter and this produces negative feelings in the other person, the other person will compensate and try to reduce the arousal by lowering the intimacy level. But, if a positive feeling is produced, the other person will attempt to maintain or increase the intimacy level by a *reciprocal* reaction. Thus, compensation is more likely in interaction with a stranger than with a friend. A friend is less likely to induce anxiety, and, assuming a "friendly" interaction ensues, increases in intimacy are likely to be reciprocated.

Hayduk (1983) located 27 studies that found significant sex differences in personal space, 54 that obtained mixed evidence, and 29 studies that found no sex differences. Some studies find that personal space is greatest between two males, followed by one male and one female, with the shortest space between two females. However, quite a few studies find one or the other of these differences to be reversed. Hayduk argued that it is unlikely that there are simple biological sex differences in personal space. One view, for example, is that large male spaces and small female spaces simply serve to reinforce traditional sex roles—that males are active and dominant, and that females are intimate and submissive (Frieze & Ramsey, 1976). Ickes and Barnes (1977) suggest that some of the apparent sex differences in spacing may be due to body size. Using "nearest-point-of-body" measures, they found no sex differences in spacing. However, when distance between "body-midline" was used, male-pair distances were larger than female-pair distances because of greater male body size.

Hall (1966) described Arabic, Mediterranean, and Latin American cultures as being "contact cultures," where touching and close interpersonal distances are common, whereas North American and North European cultures are "noncontact cultures," where touching and close interpersonal distances are not common. However, support for Hall's analysis is not unanimous. Shuter (1976) found large differences in interpersonal spacing across different Latin American countries which are all supposed to be contact cultures.

Hall's analysis of personal space suggested that interpersonal distance is heavily dependent on the particular setting, interaction, and relationship. *Intimate* distances (0–1.5 feet) are appropriate for intimate, private activities, such as lovemaking. *Personal* distances (1.5–4 feet) are appropriate for conversations between friends. *Social* distances (4–12) are appropriate for casual encounters between strangers. And *public* distances (over 12 feet) are appropriate for a speaker addressing an audience.

Spatial Arrangements

Research by Sommer (1969, 1983) concluded that most people prefer particular seating arrangements for different types of interpersonal activities (see Figure 1.5). For casual conversations, people prefer to sit at right angles in one corner of a table, or face to face, so that there is physical proximity and visual contact. In cooperating situations, people prefer to sit side by side, so that it is easy to share things. In competing situations, people choose distant face-to-face arrangements which reduce intimacy and stimulate a competitive "eyeball-to-eyeball" orientation. In coacting situations (individuals working separately at a task), distant seating arrangements— such as opposite corners of a table—are chosen since the minimal eye contact does not distract attention from the task.

Some of the findings on seating preferences may be explained in terms of privacy. Koneya (1977) discussed seating arrangements from the point

Figure 1.5
Seating Preferences at Rectangular Tables

PERCENTAGE CHOOSING SEATING ARRANGEMENTS

	Conversing	Cooperating	Coacting	Competing
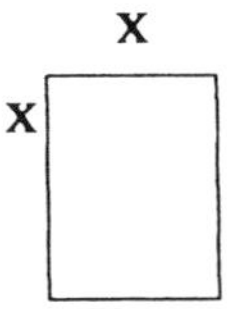	42	19	3	7
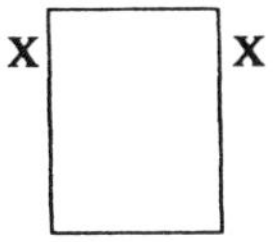	46	25	32	41
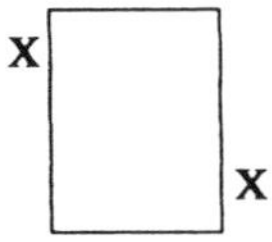	1	5	43	20
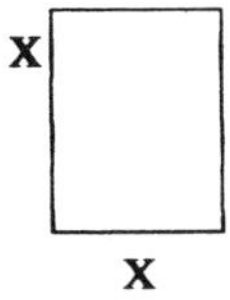	0	0	3	5
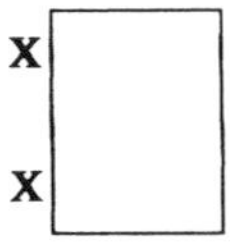	11	51	7	8
	0	0	13	18
TOTAL %	100	100	100	100

Source: Sommer, R. (1969). *Personal space: The behavioral basis of design.* Englewood Cliffs, NJ: Prentice-Hall.

of view of *privacy regulation*. Seat locations in a group affect participation rates and visual accessibility of group members, resulting in more or less social stimulation and contact. Seating choice may therefore indicate desired level of privacy: central for greater stimulation, peripheral for less stimulation.

An important regulator of social interaction is eye contact. Osmond (1957) suggested that certain sorts of seating arrangements encourage conversation and interaction by increasing the possibility of eye contact (*sociopetal spaces*), whereas other arrangements discourage conversation (*sociofugal spaces*). For example, in waiting areas, rows of seats which face away from each other are sociofugal, whereas rows of seats which face each other would be sociopetal (as long as the distance between the rows is not so great as to make conversation difficult). Holahan (1974) investigated the effects of sociofugal, sociopetal, mixed sociofugal and sociopetal, and freely chosen seating arrangements on social interaction in psychiatric hospitals. Sociopetal and mixed seating facilitated social interaction, whereas sociofugal and free seating inhibited it. Type of conversation was also affected by seating arrangements.

The importance of eye contact in small groups was shown by Steinzor (1950) who found that people seated around a circular table tend to communicate with others sitting across the table, who are more visually accessible, rather than with others sitting next to them. Similarly, it has often been observed that the leader of a group takes the most prominent position, such as at the head of a table, and that people who take prominent positions are perceived as leaders (Strodtbeck & Hook, 1961). Lecuyer (1976) found that leaders in rectangular arrangements took a position at the head of the table and participated more in group discussion than ordinary members, but this did not occur for leaders in a circular arrangement, where there is no dominant position. In the rectangular arrangement, leaders spent more time on task activities, whereas in the circular arrangement, leaders spent more time on socio-emotional activities.

Crowding

Early studies of animal behavior (Calhoun, 1962) suggested that overcrowding might lead to a variety of pathological conditions in humans. However, Freedman (1979) claimed there was little reliable support for the view that lack of space is harmful either to humans or animals. Studies of human populations have found little evidence of a relation between household density and social pathology when account is taken of important factors, such as socio-economic status, ethnicity, and so on (Gove, Hughes, & Galle, 1979).

Research on prison populations (Cox, Paulus, & McCain, 1984) does indicate a link between density (total number of inmates, and number of inmates per cell) and pathology (higher suicide and death rates, greater illness complaints and psychiatric conditions). Of course, prisons are not designed for congenial lifestyles, and, unlike households, apartments, or student dormitories, crowding in prisons is usually long term, intense, and inescapable.

Definitions have been a problem in research on crowding and density. Stokols (1972) pointed out the difference between *density* (a physical quantity) and *crowding* (a psychological state). High density may be a necessary but not a sufficient condition for crowding to occur; that is, feeling crowded depends on individual, social, and situational factors in addition to conditions of high density.

A number of theories have been developed to account for when and why high density will lead to feelings of crowding. Early accounts of crowding were divided into those that emphasized "output" processes (behavioral constraint/social interference) and those that emphasized "input" processes (information or cognitive overload).

Behavioral Constraint. This theory suggests that people will feel crowded when density results in interference or inhibition of ongoing activities (Schopler & Stockdale, 1977). Thus, Stokols, Rall, Pinner, and Schopler (1973) found that people felt more crowded in competitive than in cooperative groups; in competitive groups, there is more interference and inhibition than in cooperative groups. Likewise, Heller, Groff, and Solomon (1977) found that high density led to interference in group performance only when a high degree of physical interaction between group members was required in group activities. When physical interaction was minimal, high density did not lead to interference and crowding.

Information Overload. With increasing levels of environmental stimulation, greater demands are made on a person's attentional capacity. This can have adverse effects on current tasks and activities. Thus, Saegert (1973) reported that customers in a department store recalled fewer details of the store under high-density than under low-density conditions. McCarthy and Saegert (1978) found that residents of high-rise apartments came into contact with more people in communal areas of the building than did residents of low-rise apartments, with the consequence that the high-rise residents felt greater social overload, unwanted social contact, and negative feelings associated with crowding.

Arousal-Attribution. This theory suggests that high density produces increased levels of physiological and psychological arousal such as high blood pressure and heart rate. This increased arousal may be due to close interpersonal distances (Evans, 1978) or fear of being physically harmed in some way (Paulus, 1980). Whether such arousal is experienced as a feeling of being crowded depends on whether the *cause* of the arousal is attributed to density or not. If the arousal is attributed to density, then people will feel crowded; if it is attributed to nondensity factors, then people will not feel crowded.

Worchel and Teddlie (1976) varied spatial density (room size), interaction distance (close or far), and presence/absence of visual distractors (pictures hanging on the wall). Feelings of crowding were greatest with high density, close interpersonal distances, and no visual distractors. However, feelings of crowding were significantly reduced when picture distractors were present. Worchel and Teddlie argued that the arousal caused by close interpersonal distances was attributed solely to room density when no distractors were present; but when picture distractors were present, attention was diverted away from room density, felt arousal was attributed in part to the picture distractors, and so feelings of crowding were reduced.

Perceived Control. Currently, the most inclusive explanation of the link between density and crowding is in terms of perceived control; when density results in a reduction in perceived control, people experience feelings of crowding. Schmidt and Keating (1979) claim that all the major theories of crowding can be interpreted in terms of perceived control. For example, when high density interferes with ongoing activities (behavioral constraint), resultant feelings of crowding may be due to perceived loss of control rather than to the interference or restriction per se. And, as noted earlier under "Environmental Stress," Cohen (1978) argued that the cognitive fatigue induced by information overload is particularly acute for unpredictable and uncontrollable stressors. Reviewing the literature on field studies of crowding, Epstein (1981) concluded that the adverse effects of high density are greatest when level of control and social cooperation are lowest. Crowding appears to be most severe in prisons, intermediate in dormitories, and least in family residences—a progression in keeping with increasing degrees of personal control.

In one study of the effects of perceived control and crowding, Rodin, Solomon, and Metcalf (1978) had a group of experimental confederates enter an elevator along with a naive subject. In one condition, the subject was maneuvered away from the elevator control panel (low control), whereas in another condition, the subject was maneuvered next to the control panel (high control). As can be seen in Figure 1.6, subjects who stood next to the elevator control panel felt less crowded and judged the elevator to be larger than subjects standing far from the control panel.

Paralleling the findings on behavioral control, there have been a number of studies on the beneficial effects of *informational* control on crowding. Giving people information about the causes, consequences, and feelings associated with a stressful experience has been found to reduce unpleasant reactions. Therefore, the more information a person has about crowded situations, the less stress should occur. Thus, Langer and Saegert (1977) found that people felt less uncomfortable and less crowded when they were

Figure 1.6
Perceived Control and Crowding in an Elevator

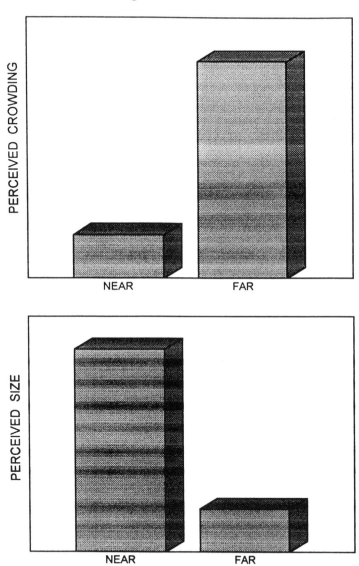

DISTANCE FROM CONTROL PANEL

Source: Rodin, J., Solomon, S. K., & Metcalf, J. (1978). Role of control in mediating perceptions of density. *Journal of Personality and Social Psychology, 36,* 988–999. Copyright © 1978 by the American Psychological Association. Reprinted with permission.

told before entering a crowded supermarket about the likely feelings they would experience.

Long-term exposure to high density conditions can lead to *learned help-lessness* particularly when crowding stress is unpredictable and uncontrollable. Baum, Aiello, and Calesnick (1978) found that residents of long-corridor dormitories experienced more frequent unwanted contact with unfamiliar neighbors and felt more crowding than did residents of short-corridor dormitories. Initially, the long-corridor residents showed evidence of attempting to reassert control, but over a longer period, they became withdrawn and exhibited symptoms of loss of control and learned helplessness.

THE BUILT ENVIRONMENT

In addition to ambient factors and human spatial factors, architectural aspects of the environment can affect social behavior in a number of ways, for example, by making places pleasant or unpleasant for interaction, by helping or hindering behavior, or by increasing or decreasing privacy.

Urban Overload

Milgram (1970) suggested that the experience of living in cities is one of sensory or information overload, including noise, bright lights, and crowds of people. To cope with this, city dwellers filter out a lot of environmental stimulation, and thereby become less attentive to, and less inclined to interact with, other people (the vast majority of whom are likely to be total strangers, unlike a rural village where everyone knows everyone else).

In support of this *urban incivility* effect, it has been found that the larger the town or city, the lower the levels of eye contact between strangers (Newman & McCauley, 1977), the lower the likelihood of accepting a handshake (Milgram, 1977) or helping another person (Amato, 1983). However, Korte, Ypma, and Toppen (1975) failed to find the expected differences in helping between Dutch cities and towns, rather they observed differences as a function of environmental input level (sound level, traffic count, pedestrian count, and building count). For areas of low input level in both cities and towns, there was greater likelihood of helping a stranger. Goldman, Lewandowski, and Carrill (1982) also found no urban-nonurban differences in helpfulness, but they did find less helping in the business areas of both cities and small towns than in the residential areas; people in the business areas were—not surprisingly—too busy to help!

In a review of urban-rural differences in helping behavior, Steblay (1987) concluded that there was consistent evidence that helping behavior is more likely in nonurban than in urban contexts, and that this was due not to subject variables (urbanites having less helpful attitudes than their country cousins) but to situational factors (the environment is more likely to facilitate helping in rural than in urban areas). On this basis, urbanites who move to the country should become more helpful, and rural dwellers who move to the city should become less helpful.

Residential Design

As discussed previously under *"Territories,"* residences vary in their defensible space (Newman, 1972), particularly for secondary territories of apartment buildings, and, within family homes, particular areas differ in their privacy and territorial exclusivity (Sebba & Churchman, 1983). Residents of high-rise compared to low-rise apartment buildings feel crowded, less safe, and experience feelings of low control and low privacy due to the prevalence of unwanted social contact in the communal areas (secondary territory) of the building (McCarthy & Saegert, 1978). Similarly, Wilcox and Holahan (1976) found that there was less involvement, cohesion, and emotional support among student residents of high-rise than low-rise university dormitories.

In a series of studies of university dormitory design, Baum and Valins investigated the effects of living in corridor-style versus suite-style dorms. In both types of dorm there were about the same number of students living on each floor, and room sizes and room designs were comparable. However, they differed in that each corridor-style dorm housed 34 students in double bedrooms on either side of a long corridor, whereas the suite-style dorm housed only six students in a suite of three bedrooms situated around a central lounge area. Students in corridor-style dorms experienced more unwanted contact with unfamiliar neighbors and felt more crowded than students in suite-style dorms (Baum, Aiello, & Calesnick, 1978). They were also less likely to seek social contact, spent more time away from the dorm, and avoided the communal dormitory areas (such as lounges)—all to avoid unwanted social contact (Baum & Valins, 1977).

When they were away from the dormitory environment, corridor-style residents showed signs of withdrawal in their social interactions—such as reduced eye contact and lower interpersonal intimacy (Baum, Harpin, & Valins, 1975). After the first weeks housed in corridor-style dorms, it seemed that such coping strategies were successful; in laboratory games, the students showed evidence of asserting control (greater competitiveness). However, over a longer period, the corridor-style residents showed evidence of a failure to cope and showed signs of a loss of control and learned helplessness (Baum, Aiello, & Calesnick, 1978). By a simple architectural intervention—simply separating the one long corridor into two halves by creating a central lounge area—Baum and Davis (1980) found that some of the problems associated with corridor-style living were alleviated.

SUMMARY

The physical situation in which an individual or group is located consists of the ambient environment (noise, temperature), presence of others (density, spatial arrangement), and material aspects (architecture, room design). These environmental factors influence behavior in various ways, by facilitating or hindering ongoing activities, but perhaps the single most important influence of the physical situation is its perceived purpose.

An environment becomes stressful when an individual's or group's resources are not sufficient to cope, and this can lead to cognitive fatigue or learned helplessness. Excessive noise can reduce a person's sensitivity to social cues. An increase in temperature can move people to become angry and violent, unless the temperature is so high that they only wish to escape the heat.

The analysis of human spatial behavior includes: territory (occupancy, marking, and defense of an area), personal space (preferred interpersonal distance), spatial arrangements (positions of individuals in a group), and crowding (the feeling that there are too many people in a place). All of these variables can be seen to reflect an individual's concern for privacy, and an attempt to maintain an optimal level of social contact or stimulation.

Territories can be classified as primary (homes or other areas used on a long-term and exclusive basis), secondary (social or work areas used on an intermittent basis), and public (areas open to anyone on a short-term basis). In public places, such as libraries, individuals may place personal objects as "markers" to define their territory as areas they are willing to defend. Conflicts are more likely in secondary areas, since people's rights are more variable and uncertain. In residential areas, crimes are less likely in places that appear to be defended.

Personal space is the distance at which a person prefers to interact with another person. In the United States, situational factors may determine whether the interpersonal distance is intimate (0–1.5 feet), personal (1.5–4 feet), social (4–12 feet), or public (over 12 feet). For a particular interaction there is an appropriate level of intimacy, indicated by the amount of eye contact, openness of posture, warmth of tone of voice, intimacy of conversational topic, and closeness of distance between persons. If the level of intimacy is either lower or higher than the desired or appropriate level, the individuals may modify one or more of these variables.

Seating arrangements vary with the type of task and the degree of closeness desired, with closer seating indicating greater intimacy. For casual conversation, sitting at right angles or face to face is preferred; for cooperation, sitting side by side; and for competition, sitting face to face. Persons occupying central seats that are close to and in full view of others are better able to maintain eye contact with other group members. Leaders tend to take more prominent seats, and persons who do take prominent positions are perceived as leaders.

Feelings of being crowded can result from having a large number of people in a space in relation to its size. People are more likely to feel crowded when the density of people in a place interferes with their activity, reduces their perception of control, and produces an overload of information. Long-term exposure to high-density conditions can lead to learned helplessness particularly when crowding stress is unpredictable and uncontrollable.

Architectural design in cities, apartments, homes, offices, and classrooms can affect social behavior by making places pleasant or unpleasant, helping or hindering behavior, or increasing or decreasing privacy. High-density cities, apartments, dormitories, and workplaces produce adverse effects in individuals and groups if they result in prolonged unwanted social stimulation or reduced privacy.

CHAPTER 2

Personality and Social Characteristics

Martin F. Davies

Groups are more than mere aggregates of human units. The characteristics of each group member can have a significant influence on group functioning. Personal attributes, such as age, sex, personality, and abilities, affect how group members relate to and interact with each other. In addition, particular combinations of group members can affect individual and group functioning through group composition effects; for example, a group composed of highly dominant individuals will function differently from a group composed of individuals varying in dominance.

PERSONALITY CHARACTERISTICS

Over the years, a large number of personality traits have been investigated; Mann (1959) found that over 500 different personality measures had been studied in group research alone. Researchers have looked at the relationships between personality traits to see if there is some underlying structure that might represent basic personality dimensions. Cattell (1947) discovered sixteen main factors. Norman (1963), however, found only five (surgency, agreeableness, conscientiousness, emotional stability, and culture); while Peabody and Goldberg (1989) identified three major factors and three minor ones.

Since the 1960s, a significant development in group research has been

This chapter is based partly on M. F. Davies (1994), "Personality and social characteristics," in A. P. Hare, H. H. Blumberg, M. F. Davies, & M. V. Kent, *Small group research: A handbook* (Norwood, NJ: Ablex, pp. 41–78). Reprinted with permission from Ablex Publishing Corporation.

the SYMLOG theory of personality and group dynamics (Bales & Cohen, 1979; Hare, 1989). In this theory, there are three principal interpersonal dimensions: Upward-Downward (Dominant versus Submissive), Positive-Negative (Friendly versus Unfriendly), and Forward-Backward (Accepting authority versus Nonacceptance of authority). This three-dimensional scheme is depicted in the SYMLOG Cube in Figure 2.1.

The Upward-Downward Dimension

Typically, people who are dominant, assertive, or outgoing are more likely to participate in group interactions, influence group decisions, and lead group activities; whereas people who are depressed, anxious, or emotionally unstable are less likely to participate, influence decisions, or lead the group, and may interfere with the functioning of the group (Haythorn, 1953). Similarly, people who are high in self-esteem are more likely to take part in group interaction than those low in self-esteem.

An interesting variation on the theme of dominance and assertiveness is Machiavellianism (Christie & Geis, 1970). Machiavellians (high "Machs") are able to manipulate interpersonal encounters so that they influence and control social situations for their own ends. Rather than using "obvious" ways to dominate others, high Machs use more subtle approaches. They are able to remain cool and detached when others are getting hot and bothered; they are skillful at influencing other people and are themselves resistant to social influence. In group interactions, high Machs exert their influence by intervening at critical phases of discussions (Bochner, di Salvo, & Jonas, 1975).

In one study, three-person groups composed of one high Mach, one medium Mach, and one low Mach played a bargaining game (Christie & Geis, 1970) which involved the group members agreeing on how to divide up ten $1 bills between any *two* of them. When two players made an agreement which the third player could not break, the game was over and the money was shared out between the two according to the agreement they had made. High Machs won the most money and low Machs won the least. In addition, high Machs were always in the winning pair and never ended up as the losing singleton.

Another advantage that high Machs have in influencing others is that they make more convincing liars (Geis & Moon, 1981). Because of their ability to influence others, it might be expected that high Machs would be more likely to become leaders. However, what little evidence there is suggests this is not the case (Gleason, Seaman, & Hollander, 1978).

The Positive-Negative Dimension

People who are sociable and affiliative are more likely to engage in social interaction and their interactions are more cooperative, warm, and friendly,

Figure 2.1
The SYMLOG Cube

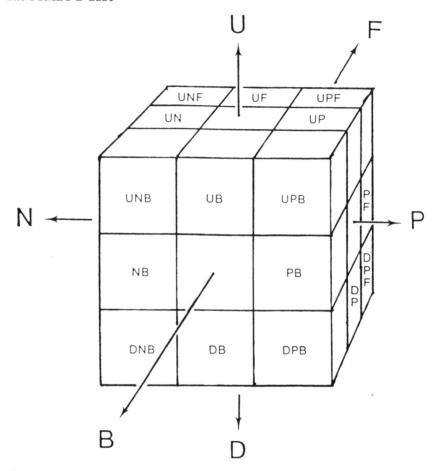

Directions in the Physical Space Model

Metaphorical names for the physical directions coordinated with names
for describing the Value directions for Individual and Organizational Values.

U	=	"Upward"	= Values on Dominance
D	=	"Downward"	= Values on Submissiveness
P	=	"Positive"	= Values on Friendliness
N	=	"Negative"	= Values on Unfriendliness
F	=	"Forward"	= Values on Acceptance of Authority
B	=	"Backward"	= Values on Non-Acceptance of Authority

Source: Bales, R. F. (1988). A new overview of the SYMLOG system: Measuring and changing
behavior in groups. In R. B. Polley, A. P. Hare, and P. J. Stone (Eds.), *The SYMLOG
practitioner: Applications of small group research* (pp. 319–344). New York: Praeger.
Reprinted with permission of Greenwood Publishing Group, Inc., Westport, CT.

resulting in more positive group atmospheres, high morale, and high cohesiveness in the group. Part of this positive effect may be that such people disclose more information about themselves which engenders trust in other group members. People who are socially sensitive are more likely to be accepted by other group members: as well as enhancing the effectiveness of the group, their social sensitivity and insight may result in them becoming leaders (Stogdill, 1948).

People who are shy are reserved in social interaction. One might think that shy people are low in sociability. However, Cheek and Buss (1981) found that shyness and low sociability are not the same thing. Sociability is defined in terms of affiliating with others—*preferring to be with other people* rather than alone. Shyness, however, is a person's *reactions to being with others*—tension, concern, feelings of awkwardness, and inhibition. Comparing people's scores on sociability and shyness measures, Cheek and Buss found that, although there was a negative correlation between the two, they seemed to be tapping separate dimensions. In addition, they observed people in social interactions and found that shy people were more inhibited, tense, and anxious than non-shy people. However, this was true only for people who were *shy and sociable* rather than for those who were shy and unsociable. Shy-sociable people talked least, engaged in the least eye contact, and were rated by observers as most tense and inhibited. Cheek and Buss suggest that shy-sociable people are strongly motivated to be with others but find themselves too fearful and tense to engage satisfactorily in social interaction. This conflict between a need for affiliation and an inability to interact socially makes shy-sociable people even more tense and inhibited. Shy-unsociable people are not particularly keen to be with others and are therefore less concerned about their inadequate performance in social interaction.

The Forward-Backward Dimension

People who are not accepting of authority tend to behave in unexpected and unpredictable ways. This can upset the functioning of the group. Although other group members may initially attempt to persuade a deviant group member to conform to the group, persistent disagreement with the majority leads to rejection (Schachter, 1951). By contrast, acceptance of authority facilitates group functioning by greater conformity to group norms and working to accomplish the group's goals and tasks. People who accept authority are likely to emerge as leaders (Stogdill, 1948). However, *successful* leadership may require innovation and change (Hollander, 1958) rather than slavish conformity to accepted rules and norms.

An extreme form of acceptance of authority is authoritarianism (Adorno, Frenkel-Brunswik, Levinson, & Sanford, 1950). Authoritarians respect power and authority, and when in a position of power or authority they act in a domineering and directive manner. However, when they are in subordinate positions, their acceptance of the power or authority systems makes them act in a submissive and conformist way. Authoritarians prefer a highly centralized group structure and they tend to be punitive toward people who do not conform. Not surprisingly, the leader of a group of authoritarian people behaves in a more autocratic way than the leader of a group composed of nonauthoritarian people (Haythorn, Couch, Haefner, Langham, & Carter, 1956).

A number of studies have investigated the implications of authoritarian punitiveness in mock-jury trials. For example, Bray and Noble (1978) found that authoritarian jurors and juries reached guilty verdicts more often and imposed more severe sentences. In addition, jury deliberations produced a shift toward greater severity of punishment in high authoritarians, but a shift toward greater leniency in low authoritarians, as shown in Figure 2.2.

Personality Composition

Groups with members who have compatible personalities are likely to be happier (more cohesive), more efficient, and more productive than groups with incompatible members. One reason for this is that, in incompatible groups, interactions among group members are disrupted or inhibited resulting in detrimental effects on task and socio-emotional activities. One problem is deciding what makes for compatible personalities. On the one hand, people with *similar* personalities may be compatible, such as a group composed of all extraverts. On the other hand, it could be that people with *different* personalities are more compatible—for example, a group composed of a mixture of dominant and submissive individuals. From studies of interpersonal attraction, the evidence seems to support the notion that "birds of a feather flock together" rather than the notion that "opposites attract."

Studies of groups have found little consistent evidence to suggest that certain personality types are more or less compatible. One reason for this is that in a group there are a number of different roles to be played, so that an individual with a particular type of personality can find a suitable role in the group. One exception to this concerns differences in need for affection (Schutz, 1958). Schutz conducted one study where some groups were composed entirely of "personal" people (who preferred close, intimate relations with others) or entirely of "counterpersonal" people (who preferred to keep others at a distance), whereas other groups were composed of a mixture of the two types. The compatible groups (all personal or all counterpersonal) were found to be more productive than the incompatible groups (mixtures of personal and counterpersonal). The incompatible

Figure 2.2
Authoritarianism and Jury Decisions

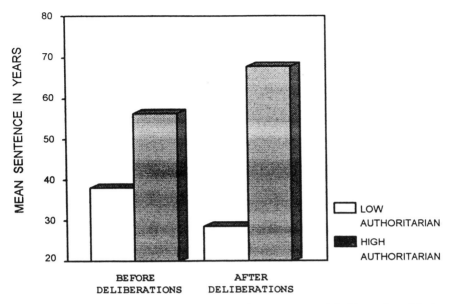

Source: Bray, R. M., & Noble, A. M. (1978). Authoritarianism and decisions of mock juries: Evidence of jury bias and group polarization. *Journal of Personality and Social Psychology, 36,* 1424–1430. Copyright © 1978 by the American Psychological Association. Reprinted with permission.

groups would have been hampered by their difficulty in establishing a harmonious level of interpersonal relationships.

Altman and Haythorn (1967) investigated needs for achievement, dominance, and affiliation. They predicted that groups which were homogeneous with respect to need for affiliation would be more compatible than heterogeneous need-affiliation groups. In line with Schutz's findings, homogeneous need-affiliation groups were found to be more effective. However, contrary to expectations, groups who were homogeneous with respect to need for achievement performed worse than heterogeneous need-achievement groups. Also contrary to expectations was their finding that groups who were homogeneous with respect to need for dominance performed better than heterogeneous need-dominance groups. To confuse the picture still further, Hill (1975) found that *incompatible* groups were more productive than compatible groups, and he suggested that a moderate amount of tension within groups, rather than complete group harmony, may result in greater productivity and effective group functioning.

There may not therefore be a straightforward link between personality composition, compatibility, and group functioning. The type of task, the

Figure 2.3
Group Productivity, Group Structure, and Motivational Orientation

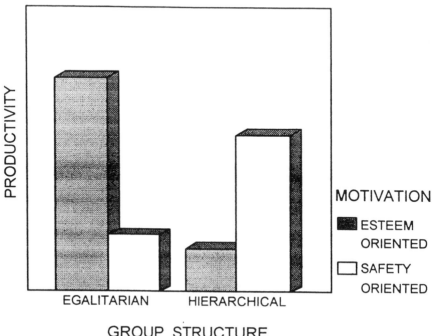

Source: Wilson, J. P., Aronoff, J., & Messé, L. A. (1975). Social structure, member motivation, and group productivity. *Journal of Personality and Social Psychology, 32,* 1094–1098. Copyright © 1975 by the American Psychological Association. Reprinted with permission.

type of group, and situational factors may need to be taken into account. For example, Wilson, Aronoff, and Messé (1975) examined the relationship between personality composition and group productivity as a function of group structure. They formed homogeneous three-person groups composed of either safety-oriented or esteem-oriented individuals, and had them work under either a hierarchical or an egalitarian social structure. They argued that safety-oriented individuals prefer hierarchically organized social structures, whereas esteem-oriented individuals prefer democratic and egalitarian social structures. It was predicted that group productivity would be affected by the congruence between motivational orientation and group structure. In line with predictions, Wilson, Aronoff, and Messé found greater productivity when esteem-oriented individuals worked under egalitarian conditions and when safety-oriented individuals worked under hierarchical conditions, as shown in Figure 2.3.

SOCIAL CHARACTERISTICS

Social psychologists have studied a variety of social variables. These variables include age, sex, race or ethnic group, occupation, physical attributes, birth order, and so on, and the findings have been many and complex. This apparent complexity in the findings on social variables, however, can be simplified if the variables are viewed as indicators of *status*.

Status Characteristics and Expectation States

When people are brought together in groups, differences in influence and participation quickly appear; group members talk more or less and lead the group with varying degrees of success (Bales, 1950). Berger, Cohen, and Zelditch (1966) suggested that these inequalities are due to differences in "performance-expectation states"—beliefs about the likely task ability of each group member. An important part of group interaction involves sorting out each member's likely contribution to the group, and task ability is a key element of this contribution. Early on in the formation of groups, the members make judgments about each others' relative task abilities based on existing information, so that a picture of the performance expectations of each group member is built up. It is differences in performance expectation states that lead to the observed pattern of unequal influence and participation; those who are judged to have high ability are encouraged to contribute more to the group, whereas those of low perceived ability are discouraged.

Some of the information about performance expectation states comes from the group interaction, when initial impressions of each group member are being formed. However, relevant information also comes from external status characteristics—attributes that people bring with them to the group, such as age, sex, race, occupation, and so on. These characteristics determine performance expectations even before interaction has begun. Berger, Fisek, Norman, and Zelditch (1977) distinguish between *diffuse* characteristics like age, sex, and race—whose contribution to performance expectations is unlimited—and *specific* characteristics like occupation—whose contribution to performance expectations is more specific, depending on the match between the particular occupational skills (e.g., accountancy) and the particular group task skills required (e.g., decision making).

There are two important points about expectation-states theory. First, the pattern of influence and activity in a group is likely to be heavily determined from the start by stereotypical beliefs rather than by direct evidence of ability. In accordance with the self-fulfilling prophecy, when group members have formed their expectations about each other based on status cues, subsequent group interaction is likely to provide behavioral confirmation of these expectations as the group members act in a fashion consistent with their expectations. Thus, a middle-aged male manager is likely to be more influential than a young female clerk regardless of actual task ability. Second, the effects of different social characteristics may not be due to the particular characteristics per se but to their status value; for example, apparent sex differences in group performance may not be due to biological sex differences but to attributed status differences.

One way of increasing status and influence in a group might be simply to behave in a dominating or assertive manner. However, this approach can lead to status or dominance struggles in groups. Katz (1970) found that giving blacks assertiveness training did produce some increase in participation in mixed-race groups, but it also resulted in hostility and aggressiveness. In terms of expectation-states, the assertiveness training may have increased blacks' expectations about themselves, but did not increase whites' expectations of blacks. Thus, a status struggle or conflict ensued. Similarly, women who act in a dominant fashion in mixed-sex groups find themselves in status conflict with males (Meeker & Weitzel-O'Neill, 1977). Ridgeway (1982) suggested that members' perceived motivation toward the group may be an important determinant of the influence and status they attain in task-oriented groups. People who enter a group with low status can use the communication of group-oriented motivation ("we orientation") in combination with reasonably competent task performance to overcome the status inequality and improve their influence in the group. In experimental confirmation, it was found that females in male-dominated groups achieved fairly high influence and status when they appeared to be group-oriented, but very low status when self-oriented ("me orientation"). As expected, males in female groups achieved high influence regardless of their motivation.

Sex and Sex Roles

Sex differences in interpersonal and group behavior have been explained in the following ways:

Biological differences. Men and women behave in different ways because of innate biological differences.

Sex-role socialization. Men and women behave differently because they are subject to differing sex-role influences during their upbringing.

Status differences. Men and women are influenced by differences in status attributed to them in social situations.

Currently, explanations in terms of status differences have provided better accounts of group behavior than explanations in terms of sex-role or socio-biological differences.

Social Interaction. The findings on sex differences in social interaction (see reviews by Anderson and Blanchard, 1982; Baird, 1976) show that males are typically task-oriented and engage in instrumental behaviors (e.g., giving opinions or information), whereas females are typically expressive and engage in socio-emotional behaviors (e.g., agreeing and being friendly).

With respect to amount of participation in *groups*, men appear to talk more than women (Aries, 1976; Kelly, Wildman, & Urey, 1982). This may simply reflect the fact that the priority of most groups is the attainment of task goals (rather than expressive or socio-emotional activities) and men are more likely to engage in task-oriented activities. In *dyadic* interaction, however, there is some evidence that, at least in same-sex dyads, women talk more than men (Ickes & Barnes, 1977). This may be because, in such brief unstructured interactions with strangers, there is little explicit task-oriented activity; much of the time is devoted to socio-emotional activities ("getting acquainted").

Intimacy and Disclosure. Given that females engage in more socio-emotional and expressive behavior, it would be expected that their inter-actions would involve greater intimacy and "self-disclosure" (Jourard, 1971). This has been confirmed in same- and mixed-sex dyads of strangers (Reis, Senchak, & Solomon, 1985). Somewhat surprisingly, Hacker (1981) reported no sex differences in self-disclosure in same-sex *friendships*, and that men were more confiding than women in mixed-sex friendships. With respect to sex roles, Grigsby and Weatherley (1983) found that masculinity was negatively related to self-disclosure intimacy, but that femininity was not related. Stokes, Childs, and Fuehrer (1981) found that androgynous subjects (those scoring highly on *both* masculinity and femininity) reported more self-disclosure than other sex-role types. These results suggest that intimate self-disclosure requires both assertiveness (associated with the traditional masculine role) and sensitivity (associated with the traditional feminine role).

Nonverbal Behavior. Similar findings have been found in studies of nonverbal behaviors. In same-sex dyads, females show greater involvement and "immediacy" in their encounters than males, such as orienting their bodies more directly toward each other, gazing and gesturing more, as well as talking more (Ickes & Barnes, 1977). Sex-role orientation also has a significant influence on immediacy and involvement in both same-sex dyads (Ickes, Schermer, & Steeno, 1979) and mixed-sex dyads (Ickes & Barnes, 1978). Males and females who were stereotypically sex-typed (masculine/feminine) showed least involvement and had the most difficulty in inter-action—less gazing, gesturing, smiling, laughing, and talking—and, at the end of the encounter, these "sex-typed" pairs expressed the least satisfaction and liking. These findings suggest that interactional involvement requires both traditionally "masculine" (instrumental) and "feminine" (expressive) capacities; with both instrumental and expressive skills, social interaction is more rewarding.

Women appear to be better at encoding and decoding nonverbal cues (Hall, 1984), possibly due to the capability of a less powerful group (women) to predict the behavior of a more powerful group (men). Henley (1977) argues that perceived power and status differences underlie observed sex differences in nonverbal behaviors.

Aggression. Sex-role socialization in Western society encourages males to be assertive and aggressive, and females to be unassertive and unaggressive. Eagly and Steffen (1986) took the view that aggression can be seen as behavior governed by the norms associated with sex roles. The male role comprises norms encouraging many forms of aggression. However, the expectation of *chivalry* attached to the male role may temper aggression toward the weak and subordinate. By contrast, aggression is not part of the female gender role, since nurturing and caring qualities are incompatible with aggression. Eagly and Steffen (1986) found that men do indeed aggress more (but not so much toward weak targets) and receive more aggression than women, but the differences were not as great as expected. The sex differences were more pronounced for aggression that produces pain or physical injury than for aggression that produces psychological or social harm. Women reported more guilt and anxiety as a consequence of aggression, they were more vigilant about the harm aggression may cause, and were more concerned about retaliation.

Helping. Eagly and Crowley (1986) also employed sex-role theory to account for sex differences in helping; the male role fosters helping that is heroic and chivalrous, whereas the female role fosters helping that is nurturant and caring. They noted that research on helping has not been representative of helping in natural settings. Experimental studies of helping have involved almost exclusively brief encounters between strangers and not long-term relationships within families, small groups, or organizations. Such conditions would favor male-role helping over female-role helping. This led to the prediction that studies of helping should show more male helping than female helping, and females receiving help more often than males. In accordance with the male-role idea, men were found to help women more than men, and women were especially likely to receive help when an audience of onlookers was present (increased pressure on men to conform to a chivalry norm). It was also found that men helped more when they felt themselves to be competent and comfortable engaging in the helping behavior. This shows that the helping behavior of males and females can be determined by the sex-typed skills needed for effective helping.

Conformity and Influence. Reviews by Cooper (1979) and Eagly (1978) did not find strong evidence for sex differences in influenceability, although sex differences were found to exist in some situations, notably, group pressure situations such as in the Asch conformity paradigm. One possible reason for greater influenceability in females than in males is that the sort of tasks typically involved in conformity studies favors male rather than fe-

Figure 2.4
Sex Differences in Conformity

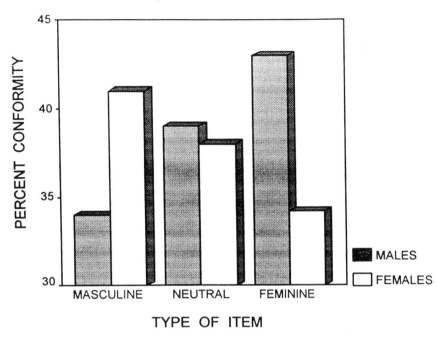

TYPE OF ITEM

Source: Sistrunk, F., & McDavid, J. W. (1971). Sex variable in conforming behavior. *Journal of Personality and Social Psychology, 17,* 200–207. Copyright © 1971 by the American Psychological Association. Reprinted with permission.

male expertise and interests. Sistrunk and McDavid (1971) tested this idea by having males and females make judgments about issues that were either familiar to men ("masculine" items, such as identifying a particular type of wrench), familiar to women ("feminine" items, such as recognizing the difference between types of needlework), or familiar to both men and women ("neutral" items, such as identifying pop stars). As can be seen from Figure 2.4, females conformed more than males when judgments involved masculine items, but males conformed more than females when judgments involved feminine items, and there were no sex differences in conformity when the judgments concerned neutral items.

A second explanation for sex differences in conformity is that women tend to be more oriented toward interpersonal goals in groups than men. Women may therefore conform more than men in order to maintain group harmony and cohesiveness, consistent with their sex-role orientation. However, Eagly, Wood, and Fishbaugh (1981) did not find that concern for group harmony accounted for greater female conformity. If anything, their results indicated that sex differences in conformity might be better described as a tendency toward *nonconformity* in men rather than conformity in women. This is consistent with findings (Ridgeway, 1981; Wahrman & Pugh, 1974) that nonconformity in men is likely to lead to more influence in groups, whereas women must exhibit initial conformity in order to be influential.

Sex differences in conformity might be better explained by expectation-states theory. Women are assigned lower status than men, so that they are expected to have lower task ability and competence and should therefore defer to higher status members. Higher status members—typically men—are allowed (and indeed expected) to exert more influence and to be less influenceable than lower status members.

Leadership. It is often noted how few women are found in important leadership positions in society. The popular sex-role stereotype is that leadership in mixed-sex groups is not a suitable role for females, and that males make more effective leaders (Bartol & Butterfield, 1976; O'Leary, 1974). However, comparatively little research has been done on sex differences in leadership; the vast majority of research has involved all-male groups. In laboratory studies of mixed-sex discussion groups, males usually take the lead (Nyquist & Spence, 1986). Gender differences in leadership effectiveness may be due more to self-fulfilling beliefs than to actual sex differences in leadership ability or behavior. If group members do not believe women make good leaders, then they will be more resistant to being led by a female (Cohen, Bunker, Burton, & McManus, 1978), and the woman leader herself may also hold the same belief, so that she will be less confident in her leader behavior (Lenney, 1977; O'Leary, 1974). In addition, apparently successful leadership by women is attributed to luck, whereas successful leadership by men is attributed to ability (Rice, Bender, & Vitters, 1980).

Expectation-states theory suggests that, in the absence of any other status cues, females are accorded lower status than males because it is assumed that they have less task ability or competence than males. Those of low status (low perceived task ability) are not encouraged by other group members in their attempts at influence, leadership, or other active task behaviors. For females to be elected leaders in mixed-sex groups, they must somehow overcome their low status by demonstrating their value to the group. This could be done directly by engaging in more task-relevant activity and influence but, first, there would be resistance to this from other group members and, second, there would be status conflict with the male members (Meeker & Weitzel-O'Neill, 1977). Ridgeway (1982) suggests that one way for females to overcome their status disadvantage is to demonstrate a group-oriented motivation (rather than an individualistic orientation) at the same time as engaging in task activities. Females' influence can also be increased by interventions designed to enhance their task skills and subsequently demonstrating their ability and competence in group interaction (Pugh & Wahrman, 1983). (See also, the discussion of gender, near the end of Chapter 6.)

Group Performance. Wood (1987) noted that sex differences in group productivity are likely to occur if the particular group task suits the interest, experience, or ability of one sex more than the other. For example, women tend to be better than men at a variety of verbal tasks, whereas men tend to be better than women at a variety of quantitative, motor, and visual-spatial tasks (Maccoby & Jacklin, 1974). Second, men may be better motivated than women at problem-solving tasks (Meeker & Weitzel-O'Neill, 1977). Some factors, however, may uniquely affect *group* rather than *individual* performance, such as the way men and women interact in same-sex groups. As previously discussed, men's style is instrumental and task oriented, whereas women's style is expressive and socio-emotional. Thus, it might seem plausible that men's greater task activity should facilitate task completion, whereas women's greater socio-emotional behavior should inhibit task completion. On the other hand, Wood argues that positive socio-emotional behavior can improve performance by increasing group cohesion and involving all group members in the task. The effect of sex, then, may vary with type of task depending on whether task performance is facilitated by active task behavior or positive socio-emotional behavior.

For example, Wood, Polek, and Aiken (1985) had same-sex groups work either on discussion tasks, which required group members to reach consensus on an issue, or on production tasks, which required the generation of ideas. The content of the tasks was carefully selected so as not to favor the interests and expertise of either sex. It was expected that the greater task-oriented behavior of males would lead to better performance by all-male groups on production tasks, while the greater positive social behavior of females would lead to better performance by all-female groups on discussion tasks. As can be seen from Figure 2.5, male groups produced a greater number of solutions than female groups on the production tasks, but female groups produced more creative solutions than male groups on the discussion tasks.

Wood (1987) concluded that, taken overall, men's performance was superior to women's performance on both individual and group tasks, and that sex differences are attributable to factors such as task content favoring men's interests and abilities. Specific group-level factors—in particular, interaction style—were found to be implicated in these sex differences. For tasks requiring a high level of task-oriented activity, males were superior to females in both individual and group performance. Contrary to expectation, however, the male superiority was only slightly greater for group than for individual performance, suggesting that men's interaction style contributes only a little to successful group performance. By contrast, for tasks requiring a high level of social activity, men outperformed women in individual performance, but showed no superiority in group performance.

Figure 2.5
Sex Differences in Group Performance

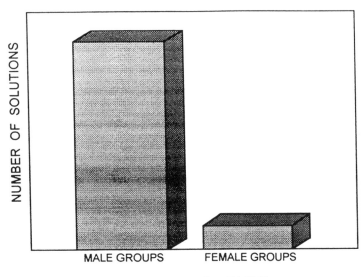

NUMBER OF SOLUTIONS

MALE GROUPS   FEMALE GROUPS

PRODUCTION TASKS

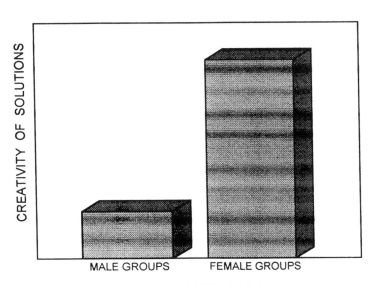

CREATIVITY OF SOLUTIONS

MALE GROUPS   FEMALE GROUPS

DISCUSSION TASKS

Source: Wood, W., Polek, D., & Aiken, C. (1985). Sex differences in group task performance. *Journal of Personality and Social Psychology, 48,* 63–71. Copyright © 1985 by the American Psychological Association. Reprinted with permission.

This implies that *women's* interaction style facilitates group performance in socio-emotional activities.

With respect to the sex *composition* of groups, Hoffman (1965) suggested that mixed-sex groups are more effective than same-sex groups because of the differing skills brought to the task by men and women. Hare (1976), however, argued that same-sex groups are more efficient than mixed-sex groups because same-sex groups spend less time on socio-emotional activities. Shaw (1981) suggested that both these conclusions may be correct; mixed-sex groups may be more effective than same-sex groups when task solution requires differing perspectives, but mixed-sex groups can be less efficient if the presence of members of the opposite sex distracts from task performance. Wood's (1987) review turned up few findings relating to sex composition and group performance. What findings there were provided slight evidence that mixed-sex groups outperform same-sex groups.

SUMMARY

Personal attributes, such as age, sex, personality, and abilities, affect how group members relate to, and interact with, each other. Psychologists continue to search for those personality traits that are important in accounting for behavior. One scheme for understanding personality suggests there are three major dimensions: Upward-Downward (Dominant versus Submissive); Positive-Negative (Friendly versus Unfriendly); and Forward-Backward (Accepting authority versus Not accepting authority).

Dominant, assertive, or outgoing people participate more in group interactions, influence group decisions, and lead group activities. Machiavellians use more subtle approaches in influencing others; they can remain cool and detached, they intervene at crucial phases in group discussions, and they make convincing liars.

People who are friendly are sociable and affiliative. They are more likely to engage in social interaction, and their interactions are more warm and cooperative, resulting in more positive group atmospheres. Friendly people disclose more information about themselves which creates trust in other group members. Shy people are not simply low on sociability; they may want to be with others but they feel tense and awkward in the presence of other people. Shy-sociable people seem to suffer the most because of a conflict between a need for affiliation and an inability to interact socially.

People who do not accept authority behave in unexpected and unpredictable ways. This can upset the functioning of the group. Individuals who do accept authority promote effective group functioning by conforming to group norms and working to accomplish the group's goals and tasks. Such people are likely to emerge as leaders. An extreme form of acceptance of authority is authoritarianism. Authoritarians respect power and authority, and when in a position of power they act in a domineering and punitive way. However, when they are in subordinate positions, their acceptance of the power or authority systems makes them act in a submissive and conformist way.

Groups with members who have compatible personalities are likely to be happier, more efficient, and more productive than groups with incompatible members. People with similar personalities tend to be more compatible. However, a moderate amount of tension may lead to greater productivity than complete harmony. In addition, the relation between compatibility and group productivity depends on the nature of the task and the structure of the group.

Inequalities in participation rates develop quickly in a new group, and they seem to be the result of differences in "performance expectation states" (beliefs about the task ability of each group member). Persons who are judged to have high task ability are encouraged to contribute more. These early estimates of ability are based on social status characteristics that are external to the group, such as age, sex, race, and occupation. Once the status of a person has been determined, behavior related to that status will tend to follow. Thus, high-status persons will be more dominant, and low-status persons will be more submissive. Positions in the hierarchy can be altered by increasing the task ability of low status persons.

In problem-solving groups, males are typically active and task-oriented, whereas females are typically positive and expressive, involving intimacy and friendliness. In nonverbal behavior, females show more involvement and immediacy in their encounters, as indicated by gaze, body posture, and gesture. Males are more likely to be concerned about maintaining their personal space, are more aggressive, and more likely to give help than to receive it. In Western society, assertiveness, competitiveness, dominance, and power are all characteristics associated with the male role, and the higher status of males allows them to be more nonconformist and assume leadership positions more often.

PART II

The Influence of Others on the Individual

CHAPTER 3

Presence of Others

M. Valerie Kent

The idea of studying the effects of the presence of other people may appear straightforward. Certainly the feeling that the presence of other people makes a difference to us is very familiar. There is, however, no single kind of feeling, nor is there a simple effect. What happens will depend on whether the other is friendly, neutral, or hostile—and on whether they are an audience or a coactor doing the same or a different task. The others may be part of a group—the major aspects of group interaction are addressed in later chapters. The present chapter considers, in terms of three research areas, what happens when another person is simply present.

First, there is *social facilitation*—the effects of performing with another person present, whether as audience or coactor. Here, the focus is on whether performance is enhanced or impaired.

Second, there is *social inhibition*—the suppression of behavior because of the presence of others. Both helping behavior and aggression will be discussed.

Third, there is *affiliation*—seeking the presence of others when faced with behavior under stress.

SOCIAL FACILITATION

For many people, performing in front of other people is terrifying (Borden, 1980) and they may feel they would have done better if not observed. For others, the excitement of an audience may generate a sense of exhilaration and their performance is enhanced. This may not just vary among individuals. It may be that any one person will feel differently depending on the task (adding up numbers, playing a piano concerto, learning to drive a car). Equally, the kinds of other people present, the reason for their being there, and how they are behaving may also make a difference.

Perhaps for all these reasons, research on what became known as *social facilitation* (Allport, 1924) produced conflicting results over several decades. In some studies, performance improved when others were present, while in others people did worse, or no effects were found. Differing types of presence were noted as having different consequences (Dashiell, 1930) but no overall theoretical framework was proposed until Zajonc (1965) reviewed the literature. He used the concepts of Hull-Spence learning theory to explain performance—essentially that arousal enhances the performance of dominant responses. He argued that the conflicting findings of earlier research could be accommodated within the same theoretical framework if one made the fundamental assumption that the presence of others is arousing. Thus, once aroused because of the presence of others, performance of well-learned or easy tasks would be enhanced because the appropriate responses would be dominant. Learning new tasks, or performance of complex tasks, would be impaired because errors would be dominant.

Zajonc proposed that this was a general theory, applying to species other than humans: arousal is heightened by the presence of a conspecific. Evidence of this was found in a variety of species, including cockroaches (Zajonc & Sales, 1966). The simple elegance of the idea was appealing and generated much research. Thirty years later, the picture is no longer simple, but the processes are becoming more clear.

Drive Theories

Zajonc made the assumption that the presence of others increases drive/arousal. There has been dispute about the reasons for the increase: whether it is due to mere presence, socially learned evaluation apprehension, or the distracting effects of others. See Geen (1989) for a review of the literature.

Mere Presence. Zajonc himself believes that the heightened arousal in the presence of a conspecific (compresence) is a result of evolution—being prepared to respond. The predictions of his theory have been confirmed in a meta-analysis of 241 social facilitation studies; Bond and Titus (1983) found the effects in terms of impaired or enhanced performance were weak but highly significant. However, they found that mere presence itself accounted for less than 3% of the variance. Guerin and Innes (1982) found that social facilitation effects occurred only if the subject was aware of the presence of an audience but, because they were seated behind the subject, it was not possible to watch or monitor them. This lends some support to the evolutionary readiness view, but apparently mere presence is not always sufficient to produce an effect. In a review, Guerin (1986a) concluded that while mere presence effects exist, other processes also operate to produce social facilitation, among them socially learned responses.

Socially Learned Drive. Very soon after the publication of the theory, the idea that mere presence led to increased arousal was challenged. Cottrell, Wack, Sekerak, and Rittle (1968) tested this by comparing the effects of two types of presence: a blindfolded other or an attentive observer. Finding that the blindfolded other did not have effects on performance, they argued that this confirmed their view that arousal increases only when the person is worried about evaluation by the other. This *evaluation apprehension* is a learned source of drive, acquired through past experience of rewards and punishments from others. Arousal would not increase in the presence of just any conspecific, but only those whose evaluations are believed to be important.

Distraction-Conflict. A third view is that arousal increases in order to cope with the distracting effects of the presence of others while one tries to perform the task (Sanders, Baron, & Moore, 1978). Coactors working on the same task are more distracting than those working on another task, because watching them may provide useful information. Subjects in the distraction-conflict condition of Sanders et al.'s experiment showed greater social facilitation effects. See also Sanders (1981a, 1981b).

Arousal

Comparatively few studies actually measure arousal. It is normally invoked as an intervening variable and is assumed to have increased if the predicted behavioral effects are found. Measurement of arousal can be difficult, and the act of measurement may itself affect performance. The difficulties of doing so in social facilitation studies are discussed by Moore and Baron (1983), who also present studies where various arousal measurement techniques have been used.

Field Studies

This area lends itself to field studies, but the findings are as disparate as those produced in the laboratory. Krantz (1979) found, when observing in a cafeteria, that obese people ate less when accompanied, whereas non-obese people ate more when in the company of others. Michaels, Blommel, Brocato, Linkous, and Rowe (1982) studied expert and novice pool players. The experts improved with an audience, while novices deteriorated, fitting the "classic" social facilitation predictions.

Worringham and Messick (1983) compared people's performance when running alone or encountering a confederate looking either toward or away from them. They concluded that evaluation apprehension best explained the increased performance in the observed condition.

Cognition and Social Facilitation

Along with a general move away from simple learning theories elsewhere in psychology, doubts have been expressed about Zajonc's theory being too drive-based, not taking into account cognitive processes. Glaser (1982), in a wide-ranging critique of Zajonc's approach, suggested that the subjective meaning of the situation should receive attention, arguing that the simple incorporation of Hull-Spence learning theory was inappropriate when it had been abandoned in psychology generally. Manstead and Semin (1980), like many other researchers, found it difficult to replicate Zajonc's findings. After a series of experiments, they felt that the effect they found when they were able to demonstrate it was better explained in a non-drive way. Their formulation is very like that of Sanders in that they believe the presence of others to be distracting. However, rather than invoke drive as an intervening variable, they use the concepts of cognitive psychology, suggesting that distraction leads to extra demands on attention and possibly attentional overload (Schneider and Shiffrin, 1977). They argue that this leads to a focusing on simple tasks when otherwise the attention might wander. For complex tasks, overload of attention would impair performance. Thus, classic social facilitation findings could be explained without recourse to the concept of arousal.

Baron (1986) has also concluded that social facilitation effects may be explained by the attentional consequences of distraction caused by the presence of others. He adds that such an explanation would accommodate findings of social facilitation where complex cognition might be implausible, such as in cockroaches.

Another cognitive view was explored in an ingenious study by Bond (1982), who believed that the social facilitation was the result of embarrassment. Rather than giving subjects either easy or difficult lists to learn, he gave subjects lists where easy items were embedded in a difficult list, or difficult items were embedded in an easy list. Arousal theory would predict that within a list, the presence of others would have a differential effect on difficult and easy items. People should do well on the easy task and perform badly when the task is difficult. Bond predicted that, if a more self-presentational embarrassment view is correct, people will do better when they perform in the presence of others if easy items come first, because they will feel good and go on to do the more difficult items well. If difficult items come first, embarrassment will lead to the poorer performance of even the easy items in the list. This is what Bond found.

If cognitive factors are involved, not only attentional but also in terms of self-presentation, then it should be possible to mimic the effects of the presence of others in other ways. Using the standard technique in self-presentation research, Innes and Gordon (1985) found that performing in front of a mirror showed a similar negative effect on performance to that produced by the presence of an inattentive other.

Another suggestion is that the presence of others inhibits us from doing those things which help our performance—talking to ourselves, counting on our fingers, and so on. Guerin and Innes (1982) noted that these were reduced when others were watching. Berger, Carli, Garcia, and Brady (1982) found the presence of others inhibited overt practice, and Yarczower and Daruns (1982) found social inhibition of children's facial expressions, that is, they controlled their facial expressions in the presence of others.

If self-awareness is involved, then it is possible that some of the contradictory findings in the research literature arose because people in the alone condition do not really feel alone. Indeed, in many studies, subjects have been alone all but for the presence of the experimenter (Geen & Gange, 1983)! Perhaps social facilitation effects arise as soon as a subject takes part in an experiment. Markus (1978) tried to separate these effects by having subjects change their clothes, having to get dressed or undressed in either familiar or unfamiliar clothes. She found that the mere presence of others enhanced dressing in familiar clothes but interfered with dressing in unfamiliar clothes. Markus (1981) suggested that it was important to establish if mere presence was sufficient to produce social facilitation effects and to eliminate the subject's sense of being in an experiment.

In a modification of Markus's approach, Schmitt, Gilovich, Goore, and Joseph (1986) asked people to type into a computer, giving an easy or difficult task (their name or a complicated identification code), before the real experiment supposedly started. In one condition the other person wore blindfold and earmuffs, in another an "evaluative experimenter" was present, and in the third the subject was alone. Schmitt et al. found that mere presence was sufficient to elicit social facilitation.

It is perfectly possible that mere presence is indeed sufficient, but that as both Sanders (1983) and Guerin (1986a, 1986b) have suggested, other processes may add to the effect. Rather than being competing theories, many researchers suggest that several of the explanations may be valid, each applying in different situations or to different extents.

Social Impact Theory

An entirely different explanation was proposed by Latané, who sought to explain stage fright, social facilitation, helping behavior, and many other social phenomena in terms of his Social Impact Theory (Latané, 1981). The effect of others arises from their social impact, defined as a multiplicative function of their numbers, immediacy, and strength. Thus, the larger the audience the greater the impact, although each additional member contributes less to the overall effect. Impact will be greater if the audience is important, thus encompassing the idea of evaluation apprehension within the notion of social impact. However, if a large number of people are performing together in front of an audience, the impact is distributed across performers. A fuller description of the theory is to be found in the section on social inhibition.

SOCIAL INHIBITION

The previous section considered the effect of the presence of others on carrying out a task, in terms of whether the person's performance is enhanced or impaired. In the next section a somewhat different idea is discussed. Rather than changing the quality of performance, the presence of others may affect whether the behavior occurs at all. In other words, other people may inhibit performance entirely. Work on social inhibition of behavior has looked at whether the others are merely present, as an audience or bystanders, or whether performance is inhibited in what is perceived as a group performance. This last effect, known as *social loafing*, refers to reduced effort made by people when they believe they are part of a group and their contribution to the output cannot be evaluated (Karau & Williams, 1995; Shepperd, 1995). Harkins (1987) has argued that social facilitation and social loafing are complementary rather than distinct research areas, and can be accommodated within the same paradigm. Harkins and Szymanski (1989) found that if it could be evaluated, performance on a simple task improved, via evaluation apprehension, whereas performance was impaired on complex tasks, via evaluation apprehension or distraction, or both. If, however, performance could not be evaluated, performance was worse on simple tasks. Harkins and Szymanski suggest that this is due to social loafing. They found improved performance on complex tasks and, to explain this, argue that people are less worried about failing when they know they cannot be identified—and they are therefore then more likely to attempt the complex task. Further discussion of social loafing can be found in Chapter 5, where the issue of believing oneself to be part of a group is more central.

This section concentrates on whether the presence of others inhibits behavior. The main research emphasis here has been on helping behavior, ever since the early studies of bystander "apathy" by Latané and Darley (1968, 1970), who found that intervening in an apparent emergency was less likely when other bystanders were present. They used several ingenious contrived emergencies, the best known being the "Lady in Distress" which has been used in many later studies. A female experimenter hands a questionnaire to the subject and withdraws to the next room to fetch something. She is heard to climb a ladder, fall, and cry for help. Subjects alone were most likely to help (70%), as were two friends together (70%). Two strangers helped much less (40%), and in the condition where a naive subject was in the presence of a non-intervening accomplice help was given in only 7% of cases.

In another study, when a person in a pseudo-group communicating over an intercom had an apparent epileptic fit, intervention was increasingly less likely the larger the number of other people believed to be present. This did not appear to be a social loafing effect, in that people were upset and asked afterwards about the victim's welfare. Evidence that it was not just a "not caring" effect also came from another of Latané and Darley's early studies, for they found that people were less likely to report smoke coming under the door while they filled in a questionnaire if someone else were present, especially if the others were unresponsive experimental accomplices. Helping oneself can also, it seems, be inhibited by the presence of others. In a study to see whether there was social inhibition in literally helping oneself to a leaflet promising a free hamburger, Petty, Williams, Harkins, and Latané (1977) found the presence of others to relate inversely to taking the leaflet, even though plenty of leaflets were available.

Several processes are likely to occur in the helping situation which may affect the likelihood of intervention (Kent & Blumberg, 1988/1992b). Latané and Darley saw them as a sequence, from defining the situation as an emergency, then deciding what needs to be done, who should do it, and how the help is to be put into effect. An alternative framework involves arousal and the assessments of the likely costs of intervention or non-intervention (Piliavin, Dovidio, Gaertner, & Clark, 1981).

Defining the Situation

People will not intervene if they do not see the situation as problematic. When other bystanders are present who themselves do not intervene (not necessarily experimenter's accomplices!), this provides information that the situation is not an emergency. This presumption arises because each thinks that if it were in fact a crisis, someone would be doing something. This does not mean that people are not wondering if there is a problem. Their non-intervention may be the result of pluralistic ignorance. However, they hesitate to act because of something akin to evaluation apprehension. They do not want to look foolish, interfering, or panicky to others, and lose face. Some support for this arises from findings that people who know each other are more likely to intervene.

Helping situations are not necessarily emergencies, especially in experiments. Although the "Lady in Distress" has been repeated (Staub, 1974; Abele, 1982), and others have used dramatic events such as choking (Gottlieb & Carver, 1980) or arterial bleeding (Shotland & Heinold, 1985), many helping studies use more minor events such as losing a contact lens (Murray & Vincenzo, 1976), dropping coins or pencils (Latané & Dabbs, 1975), or directing a lost commuter (Harada, 1985). Explanations of helping in emergencies may not be the same as those for more low-key help situations.

Shotland and Huston (1979) studied 1232 undergraduates to discover what situations were defined as emergencies. They found that emergencies were seen as a subclass of the consequences of an accident. The defining characteristic of the emergency was that the threatened or actual harm was seen to increase over time and that the victim would need outside help to deal with the problem. There was a high level of agreement on what situations were emergencies. Where people disagreed, it was because of differing perceptions of whether harm would increase over time. The authors also found bystanders were more likely to help in situations they defined as emergencies, particularly as a result of the perceived need of the victim.

However, as noted above, bystanders are prey to pluralistic ignorance: their mutual lack of intervention leads each person to conclude that there is no emergency or that intervention is inappropriate. Miller and Mc-Farland (1987) suggested that a further element in pluralistic ignorance is that people believe that embarrassment is a sufficient explanation for their own inaction but not for the inaction of others. In a series of experiments. they found, first, that people tend to attribute traits related to social inhibition to themselves rather than other people. When subjects were then given the opportunity for action which could have both beneficial and embarrassing consequences for themselves, they tended to avoid the embarrassing action while at the same time overestimating the percentage of other people whom they believed would take the embarrassing course of action regardless. In their third study, they put groups rather than individuals in the predicament of the second study. They found that all subjects refrained from the embarrassing action. At the same time, all of them believed that their own reasons for doing so were different from the reasons of the other people present.

Some studies have specifically manipulated the ambiguity of the situation. Solomon, Solomon, and Stone (1978) varied ambiguity by making the emergency heard only, or seen and heard at the same time. When the situation was only audible, subjects were less likely to define the situation as an emergency, were less certain that help was needed, and were more able to reduce the stress induced by the situation. As group size increased, the reduction in helping was more pronounced in the more ambiguous heard-only condition.

Solomon, Solomon, and Maiorca (1982) looked at the impact of several variables on helping in a field situation. Finding that urban dwellers were less likely to help than suburban dwellers, especially where the victim was poorly dressed and the situation ambiguous, they suggested that urban dwellers try to adapt to stimulus overload by ignoring "low-priority inputs such as low-status victims and ambiguous requests for help." This last view suggests that people may choose to ignore the needs of others when their own needs are pressing.

Further evidence of the importance of the subjects' perceptions of emergency situations comes from a study by Shotland and Straw (1976) in which a fight was staged between a man and a woman. If the subjects believed the fight was between "strangers," they were more likely to intervene. They also saw the woman as more in need of help, the fight more likely to be damaging, and the attacker as more likely to run away. However, if the subject had little information about the participants, they were more likely to be seen as married, lovers, or dating couples than as strangers, and intervention was less likely. This is reminiscent of the street attack on a young girl where residents failed to intervene—causing a public outcry and stimulating Latané and Darley's work on bystander "apathy."

Diffusion of Responsibility

It is clear that a reduction in helping is often found when the number of bystanders increases even when the situation is not ambiguous. For reviews of the relevant literature, see Latané and Nida (1981) and Mishra and Das (1983). One explanation has been put in terms of diffusion of responsibility. Here, the individual feels less personally responsible for helping since there are others present. Given that action seems to be needed, it may appear that someone else would be better to engage in the necessary behavior. Here, a weighing up of the rewards and costs of intervention might arise, not just in terms of whether or not the situation is risky, but also whether the person is best qualified to do what is needed. Diffusion of responsibility for helping is not quite the same as social loafing; in the former, people are not engaging in an action at all, in the belief, for whatever reason, that someone else will or should do it. In social loafing, effort on a shared task is reduced.

Social Impact Theory

A different argument for the effect of the number of bystanders comes from Latané himself who sees group size as one of the three elements of social impact theory. Jackson and Latané (1981) looked at door-to-door collections, and found support for the application of the theory to generosity and altruism. This was based on their finding that donations increased with social impact: the number of people soliciting for donations, their strength in terms of seniority and dress, and their immediacy in terms of nearness to the door. Conversely, when many people are receiving the message that help is needed, the social impact on any one of them is reduced.

Social Impact Theory was also the context of a study of the help-seeking behavior of victims (Williams & Williams, 1983). In keeping with the predictions of the theory, they found that the increased number and strength of bystanders was inversely related to the extent to which the victim sought help. The presence of a larger number of bystanders led to increased social inhibition of help-seeking behavior. In real life situations, such a change in victim behavior might affect the apparent indifference of groups of bystanders. (Help-seeking is a growing research area. See, for example, Fisher, Nadler, and Whitcher-Alagna, 1982).

However, as noted above, number of others present may operate through diffusion of responsibility, perceiving that there are others to whom the needy person could turn. Ahmed (1979) found motorists more likely to help on a lonely rather than a busy road, and Berkowitz (1978) found that female subjects worked less hard for a needy confederate if they believed they had two co-workers. Berkowitz argued that this was because of a reduced sense that the needy person was dependent on them alone. Since this was an apparent co-worker situation, social loafing effects may also have been present.

Other Factors

A rather different concept was introduced by Cacioppo, Petty, and Losch (1986), who suggested that diffusion of responsibility should be distinguished from confusion of responsibility. They suggest that when bystanders intervene, others who appear on the scene may perceive them as having been responsible for the victim's plight in the first place. Subjects, asked to take the perspective of a helper following an accident, reported that—as increasing numbers of bystanders arrived—they increasingly felt that they would be seen as responsible for the victim's plight. Other subjects in the study were asked to imagine that they were arriving at the scene of an accident, with varying numbers of others already present. The greater the number of people described as being at the scene, the more likely it was that these hypothetical onlookers would describe the person helping as the cause of the victim's harm.

Some studies have found that helping is not reduced or even increases in the presence of others. However, where this happens, as in Latané and Darley's original work, it seems to be when the bystanders are acquainted. Yinon, Sharin, Gonen, and Adam (1982) found that groups of passers-by in a public place in Israel were more likely to act on seeing a suspect package than were solitary passers-by. This was also influenced by whether the passers-by were local people or transient: not one transient when alone took any action. Overall, they argued that the situation provoked the norm of social responsibility rather than responsibility diffusion. Also, deGuzman (1979) found more help was given to a lost commuter by pairs of bystanders, and that more help was given for the most dependent people.

Harari, Harari, and White (1985) found that the white male undergraduates in their research were more likely to intervene in rape simulated in a natural setting if they were in groups, rather than alone; 80% of interventions were direct rather than calling the police. Again, the undergraduates in real groups seem to be more responsive than those in "mere presence" situations.

Rutkowski, Gruder, and Romer (1983) also suggest that the group-size effects typical of bystander research, namely that the presence of greater numbers of others inhibits helping, only arise because the bystanders are unacquainted. They, too, suggest that the norm of social responsibility may come into play when people are in high-cohesive groups, since they found highly cohesive groups to be more helpful—but low-cohesive groups to be less helpful—than individuals. Misavage and Richardson (1974) compared help given by subjects who were alone, or in either noninteracting or interacting groups. They concluded that group interaction serves to focus rather than diffuse responsibility to help.

Sometimes responsibility may be assigned by the victim. Moriarty (1975) found people more willing to intervene when a radio was stolen from a beach blanket if they had promised to look after it. Austin (1979) also found willingness to stop a theft was greater if there was prior verbal commitment. Valentine and Ehrlichman (1979) found that if a victim gazed at a bystander, females were more likely to help female victims but males were less likely to help male victims. They suggest that males and females may interpret gaze differently. Valentine (1980), studying female subjects, again found gaze important. It increased helping in both alone and passive confederate conditions. Where the victim did not look at the subject, bystander effects were noted. Thus, again, there is some evidence that the behavior of the victim may have some impact on helping in emergencies—and that the victim's lack of engagement may perhaps explain non-intervention in some experimental studies.

A more cognitive explanation was proposed by Wegner and Schaefer (1978), who conducted a study in which both the number of bystanders and the number of victims was varied. They concluded that the group size effect was the result of the effects of the presence of other people upon self-focused attention.

It may well be that the presence of other bystanders may in some cases alert the individual to the need for help. This was manipulated by Abele (1982) who used the lady in distress situation. In addition to finding that help was less likely from individuals more concerned to complete the questionnaire, she also found that a startled expression from the confederate increased intervention, while passive behavior seemed to inhibit intervention. Rather similarly, Borges and Penta (1977) found that help for someone lying on the ground and moaning was much more likely in the presence of an experimental confederate saying "Do you think we should do something?" Without such a confederate present, there were no group-size effects.

It appears, however, that actual interaction is not necessary; even anticipating future interaction with the others who are present can overcome the bystander effect. This would suggest that interaction is not simply a question of providing information to disambiguate the situation. Gottlieb and Carver (1980), using a version of the original Latané and Darley epileptic fit experiment, arranged an intercom discussion during which one person apparently choked. Subjects believed either that they were the only other person in the discussion or that they were one of six people. For each condition, half the subjects believed that they would interact with each other in the future. Those who believed in future interaction helped rapidly, and in this condition the group-size effect was not significant. Where future interaction was not expected, subjects were slower to help in the larger "group."

Ambiguity was varied in two studies by Harada (1985) by having the victim ask for help or not. In both, evidence for both normative and informational influence was found. The effect of ambiguity was most evident in the situation where the person was acquainted rather than unfamiliar with the other bystander. Again, we see that it is not merely the presence of the other which has an effect. It depends on which other, whether the situation is clear, whether future interaction is expected. It may also depend on individual as well as situational differences.

HELPER VARIABLES

Sex Differences

As noted above, Valentine found that gaze from the victim increased the helping of females by females but reduced that of males for males. Rather than looking at gender, Tice and Baumeister (1985) measured sex-role orientation on the Bem Sex-Role Inventory. Highly masculine subjects were least likely to help the victim of an apparent choking fit, which they suggested was due to a fear of potential embarrassment and loss of poise. No effects were found for femininity or actual gender.

In a study of real-life bystanders, Lay, Allen, and Kassirer (1974) confirmed that responsive bystanders tended to be alone; they also found males more likely to intervene than females. The role of gender differences in helping is not entirely clear and may depend on the person's perceived competence in the required behavior and the degree of risk involved, as well as their ability to assess the situation. Gender differences in helping are reviewed by Eagly and Crowley (1986) in their meta-analysis of relevant studies. (See also Chapter 2 of this volume.) On the whole, there do not appear to be gender differences in the effect of the presence of others on helping, which is the focus of the present chapter.

Competence

People may vary in their ability to define a situation as one in which help is needed. Past experience of emergencies may help in defining the situation and in evaluating appropriate action. Those with no past experience of emergencies may tend to feel that someone else would be better at intervening, may overestimate the costs or risks, or underestimate the rewards of helping.

When a simulated murder was staged in university classes, only two of the 213 subjects intervened, although fourteen went for help once the "murderer" was out of sight. Of the two who intervened, one was a football player and the other a probation officer (Schreiber, 1979).

The sense of competence to intervene was also identified by Huston, Ruggiero, Conner, and Geis (1981) in their study of 32 people who had intervened in a violent crime to help the victim, compared to a matched group of non-interveners. They found that the interveners had themselves been more exposed to crime. However, neither humanitarian nor antisocial impulses explained their intervention, rather, it was their sense of capability to deal with the situation, based on both their superior strength and their training, which led to their action.

AGGRESSION

The effect of the presence of others on aggressive behavior has been studied from the point of view of anonymity or deindividuation (Kent & Blumberg, 1988/1992a). The argument is that where people feel less identifiable, they will feel free to engage in behavior from which they would normally refrain. In terms of aggression, this is taken to be especially the case where the other people are encouraging aggressive actions. This is often studied by having an experimenter ask the subject to give an electric shock to another person (an accomplice) (Milgram, 1974).

Deindividuation may be accomplished by anonymous responding, by the wearing of uniforms or masks. The most famous study was carried out by Haney, Banks, and Zimbardo (1973), who asked student subjects to play the role of prisoners or guards in a very realistic simulated prison study, carried out over what was to be two weeks. The experiment was stopped after one week, because the "guards" had become brutal and the "prisoners" passive or conniving, although people had been randomly assigned to these roles.

A laboratory study of delivery of electric shock found that identifiable people in bright light, wearing name badges, and in normal clothes gave fewer and briefer shocks than deindividuated people in all-encompassing uniform hoods and robes, without name badges, in dim lighting (Zimbardo, 1970).

Dunand, Berkowitz, and Leyens (1984) found that the presence of an active confederate while a subject was watching aggressive movies was associated with increased aggression later, compared to alone or passive confederate conditions. They used social facilitation and social inhibition to explain their findings.

It should not be assumed that deindividuation necessarily leads to aggression. Deindividuation led to increased prosocial behavior where the robes which subjects were given to wear were described as nurses' hospital gowns rather than as being from Ku Klux Klan members (Johnson & Downing, 1979).

Studies of deindividuation are also relevant to the behavior of large groups and mass behavior; on the whole, they are not simply concerned with the presence of others but are concerned about the behavior of anonymous members of one group toward another. For example, Rehm, Steinleitner, and Lilli (1987) looked at aggressive play in handball teams when one side wore uniforms and the other did not. Those in uniformed teams were more aggressive. The effects may be due to reduced accountability (Prentice-Dunn & Rogers, 1989). It has also been suggested that there is reduced self-awareness, since in the deindividuated situation people do not think others are focusing on them, while at the same time people may have to attend to more in the environment rather than the self.

On the whole, this area of study has more to do with group or implied group behavior than the simple effects of the presence of others. However, the reader should be aware of the overlap between these issues.

AFFILIATION

In apparent direct contrast to the arousal theory of social facilitation, another line of research on the effects of the presence of others is concerned with the calming effects of having a companion.

Schachter (1959) first proposed the idea that "misery loves company," arguing that when faced with an anxiety-provoking event, the presence of another person reduces stress. He tested this on subjects told they were going to take part in a study where they would receive an electric shock. They were given a choice of waiting room—either with another person or alone. They chose to be with others. In refinements of the study, Schachter found that they preferred to be with others awaiting the same study rather than another: he suggested that misery prefers miserable company. This area has not received anything like the level of attention as other effects of the presence of others on behavior.

There are two lines of explanation for seeking the company of similar others when under stress. The first is social comparison, where the other person is a standard against which to evaluate attitudes, emotions, and behavior. An alternative view is that other people may help in appraising the situation, providing information, and helping to overcome the anxiety (Shaver & Klinnert, 1982). Subjects told to wait for a study involving an electric shock talked more to each other and spent more time discussing the impending experiment than did controls told to wait for another study (Morris, Worchel, Bois, Pearson, Rountree, Samaha, Wachtler, & Wright, 1976). It may be that both processes occur in different situations. Rofé (1984) found that in some instances people preferred to be with a very competent and intelligent other, while in other cases they preferred the presence of a warm and supportive companion. In a study of men about to have major heart surgery, Kulik and Mahler (1989) found that most preferred to share a room with someone who was recuperating from the same operation, rather than someone also about to undergo the same surgery. This again suggests that others serve to give reassurance.

The effects of others may not be confined to human friends, however. A study of the presence of female subjects' own pet dogs in a stressful experimental setting showed reduction in stress indicators and improved performance (Allen, Blascovich, Tomaka, & Kelsey, 1991). The presence of human friends increased stress levels. This latter finding would sit comfortably with the social facilitation research on the effects of the presence of others on performance.

Whatever our theories, they may also have to accommodate the findings of animal studies on affiliation. It appears that a calm companion can reduce fear responses in a number of species from chickens to humans (Epley, 1974). Epley and Cottrell (1977) found that the presence of a companion led to increased speed of escape from electric shock, suggesting a social facilitation effect. Had company been comforting, speed of escape would have been predicted to be slower. Epley suggests different effects may arise depending on whether the stressor is primary or acquired.

As in social facilitation studies, the possibility that the other serves simply as a distracter has been raised. Schachter eliminated this in his first studies, because people preferred some companions over others. However, an animal study by Moore, Byers, and Baron (1981) found that rats were calmed by the presence of an experienced rat in an open field situation, whereas a naive companion had no stress-reducing effect. The experimenters, having observed that the experienced rats engaged in more social interaction with the naive rats, set up an experiment to see if distraction was created by social interaction. They found that socially deprived rats with socially deprived but experienced companions had the highest levels of social interaction and the greatest fear reduction. They therefore concluded that distraction was the major factor in stress reduction by the presence of a companion. This work reflects the development of Baron's ideas on the

arousing role of distraction in social facilitation studies, leading to his later
comments (Baron, 1986) that distraction itself may explain social facilitation via its attentional consequences. He also favored the distraction explanation for the effects of the presence of others precisely because it could
accommodate both human and animal findings without having to attribute
higher cognitive functions to the latter.

A study of women who were about to give birth in a hospital gives
further support to the idea that the value of others lies in their ability to
act as distracters. They were asked if they wanted to wait alone, or with
other women who were also about to give birth. Most preferred to wait
alone. Further, when they were asked about what they would talk about
if they were with someone else, they said they would want to talk about
something that would distract them, rather than comparing their emotions
with someone facing the same sort of stress (Rofé & Lewin, 1986).

It is clear that while we are beginning to understand more about the
effects of the presence of others, the issues are not simple. Perhaps this is
hardly surprising, given the highly social and highly complex human animal.

SUMMARY

The presence of other people tends to enhance performance of simple or
well-learned tasks, and to impair the performance of complex or new tasks.
Several theories to explain this have been based on Zajonc's argument that
the presence of others increases arousal, which then favors the performance
of dominant responses. There is dispute over just why the presence of others
should be arousing, although it may be that the explanations are not mutually exclusive. Other researchers have favored non-drive explanations,
introducing more cognitive concepts such as attentional overload and self-
presentation. Again, there is no necessary incompatibility between the theories, but as yet it is not at all clear when which will apply.

Studies of social inhibition look at the suppression of behavior in the
presence of others. Research on helping has found that people in groups
are less likely to help in an emergency than they are when they are alone.
The effect is particularly marked if the other people are strangers rather
than friends or people with whom future interaction is expected. Social
inhibition of helping may be explained by pluralistic ignorance, responsibility diffusion, and by the costs of helping when others are present, for
example embarrassment or being seen as the cause of the harm.

The presence of others may also inhibit the control of aggressive behavior, through deindividuation. This sense that one is not an identifiable individual may be enhanced by anonymity, by a decreased sense of
self-awareness, and by the active modelling of aggression by the other person.

Seeking to affiliate, wanting the presence of others, has been regarded as a way of reducing stress, particularly if the others face the same stressor. This suggests that there are situations when the presence of others diminishes arousal, instead of increasing it as many social facilitation researchers have suggested. Rather little work has been done on affiliation, although some recent attempts have been made to integrate the literature by considering that stress may be reduced because the presence of other people affects attention.

CHAPTER 4

Social Influence

M. Valerie Kent

Conformity and compliance are familiar words. Sometimes they have negative overtones: dull, sheep-like, passive, unthinking. They are also used positively: helpfully fitting in, agreeable, not being difficult. In this chapter, some everyday words will be reconsidered in social psychological terms.

Conformity is not *being* like other people; it is about *change*—that is, *becoming like* others. The change may involve outward behavior (public conformity) or internal beliefs (private acceptance), or both. While pressure to change may come directly from others, it may equally be felt by a person even when there is no explicit request or demand to change. This is the result of the person's perception of the situation. Even when the pressure is only imagined, or someone changes in the wrong way, misunderstanding what is required, the resulting behavior is still due to social influence processes. Some studies focus on behavior change, while others look at enduring change. The latter may be similar to research on attitude change, but in social influence the social context of change is crucial.

INFLUENCE IN GROUPS

Norm Formation and Change

A norm is an expectation, shared by group members, about the validity of perceptions or interpretations of the world and about the appropriateness of behavior. In order to study the development of norms in the laboratory, Sherif (1935) gave people the opportunity to make novel judgments with or without the presence of others. He asked two or three subjects, who did not know his hypothesis, to judge out loud how far a pinpoint of light moved in an otherwise totally dark room. He was taking advantage of a visual illusion, the *autokinetic effect*, in which a stationary pinpoint of light appears to move.

Although he had not asked them to agree, subjects in groups made judgments which were more similar to each other than subjects who made judgments alone. This demonstrated *norm formation*, since there was no initial "right answer" for anyone, as there might be in real-life groups. It seems that people "adjusted" their judgments. When people were taken from the group setting and asked to repeat the task alone, they were still influenced by the norm, apparently believing it to be the right answer. This happened even for a longer term follow-up. Sherif was even thanked by one subject for providing the opportunity to repeat it alone, proving to himself he had not just been influenced by the other person! Norms help us to interpret reality. When we are unsure about physical reality, we turn to social reality—we use other people for information. Festinger (1954) called this process social comparison. It helps us to understand and behave appropriately. It can also lead to error or to inaction, as in the bystander apathy studies (see Chapter 3).

Jacobs and Campbell (1961) used confederates to create an exceptionally high norm for the autokinetic effect. They replaced, one by one, confederates and then the original subjects with new naive subjects, and were able to show the effects of the induced high norm through eleven "generations" of groups. Montgomery, Hinkle, and Enzie (1976) followed the Jacobs and Campbell procedure, using two levels of arbitrary norms in groups formed on the basis of California F-scale scores. Authoritarian groups perpetuated both norms across more generations, although the higher norm gradually declined. For low-authoritarian groups, both these arbitrary norms declined rapidly to levels normally produced by the illusion.

MAJORITY INFLUENCE

A line of research which has continued ever since was begun by Asch (1951), who believed that the level of conformity found in Sherif's studies was probably due to the ambiguity of a visual illusion. To test his view that people would be less influenced if there were a real right answer, he used judgments of a series of line lengths in the presence of confederates. Each time, they were to choose which of three lines matched the length of a standard. While giving the right answer most of the time, the confederates would every so often, on certain prearranged "critical" trials, unanimously give the wrong answer as each answered in turn. By having the confederates arrive early for the experiment, Asch was able to assign the second-from-last seat in a semicircle to the naive subject without arousing suspicion.

Asch had established that control subjects, alone, were right virtually all the time. On the critical trials, however, across all his experimental groups, he found that subjects conformed about 34 percent of the time. There were individual differences, with some conforming most of the time and some hardly ever. Afterwards, it was clear that some subjects really believed they were wrong, while others did what Asch called "conscious conforming" and did not privately believe what they had said in the group. The finding of two processes, both genuine perceptual change and falsification of perceptions, was also shown by Jennings and George (1984).

Contrary to his expectation, Asch had found that people sometimes changed their behavior and even their beliefs as a result of differing from a group. Why should this be? Why are some people more likely to conform than others? Why are only public actions affected some of the time, while at others people seem to change their underlying perceptions and beliefs?

Social Influence Processes

Sherif's study showed norm formation. There was no real movement of the light, so the subjects were mutually dependent on each other to make sense of the ambiguity. Although there was no explicit pressure on them to agree, the experiment made use of the expectation that judgments of distance must have an objective "right answer." The subjects did not know they were in a world of illusion and used each other's judgments in a social comparison process. It seems that internalized beliefs were affected, but some concern about the reaction of other group members, of appearing foolish, cannot be entirely ruled out.

In Asch's work, two processes are more clearly in evidence. Deutsch and Gerard (1955) conducted an elaborate experiment to look at the role of anonymous responding. They demonstrated both public conformity and private acceptance, according to situational variables. They proposed two types of influence, *normative* and *informational*.

In a similar vein, Jones and Gerard (1967) suggested that people can depend on others in the following ways.

Effect dependence. Others intervene in the effects or outcomes of a person's actions, e.g., if you do that, I will reward/punish/love/despise you (*normative influence*).

Information dependence. Other people are needed for information, e.g., if you do that, you may hurt yourself/pass your exams/find the North Pole (*informational influence*).

The two principles underlying social influence can be seen as: wanting to get the best outcomes from other people, perhaps in terms of being approved of or liked; and wanting to be right, to act on what appears to be good information. Wanting both to be right and to be liked underpin social influence processes, as confirmed by Insko, Smith, Alicke, Wade, and Taylor (1985).

These ideas were put slightly differently by Kelman (1958) in his discussion of three processes of social influence. These are listed below, with the type of power base of the influencer, in terms of the rather similar ideas of French and Raven (1959), which are discussed more fully in Chapter 6.

Compliance. The influencer controls rewards and/or punishments. Without surveillance to ensure compliance, the changed behavior will not last (*reward and/or coercive power*).

Identification. The person changes behavior in order to maintain a satisfying relationship with the influencer. This may mean the person wants to be liked, but not necessarily. It may be wanting to appear as a nice person, or as a "good" patient to the doctor. The behavior will last as long as the influencer seems to prefer it and the person wants to maintain this relationship (*referent power*).

Internalization. This occurs when the influencer is perceived to be credible, that is, both expert and trustworthy. It is a relatively enduring change which may last independently of the source, since it fits with other values and beliefs about what is right, valid, true (*expert power*).

Kelman pointed out that these were logically distinct but difficult to separate in practice. Any one situation might involve all three processes of social influence, and this can be seen in considering the Sherif and Asch experiments. Experimental variations may tend to stress one aspect of influence more than another, but the others cannot be absolutely ruled out.

Situational and Task Variables in Social Influence

Anonymity. Anonymity of response has proved to be a significant variable. Where it is effective in reducing conformity, it suggests that the underlying process of social influence is based on a concern for being liked or maximizing outcomes (gaining rewards or avoiding costs). In Deutsch and Gerard's terms, the situation gives rise to effect dependence rather than information dependence. Current studies of anonymity often use the word "deindividuation," suggesting a state in which the person does not feel accountable as an identifiable individual, and may thus feel released from the constraints of normative expectations. A well-known example is Haney, Banks, and Zimbardo's study of students acting the roles of prisoners and their guards (see Chapter 3).

Group Size. Since Asch's early studies, it has been clear that group size has an effect on conformity, but the effect is nonlinear. In current research it is more likely to be construed in terms of social impact theory or minority influence (see below). A study by Wilder (1977) varied the organization of the number of persons attempting to influence subjects, so that the subjects perceived them as a single group, as several separate groups, or as an aggregate of unrelated individuals. He found that varying group size as such had little effect on conformity. However, conformity increased as the number of separate individuals and groups increased.

This seems to explore an area similar to that studied by Petty, Cacioppo, and Harkins (1983) who looked at the effect on persuasion of using differing numbers of message sources and arguments. They found an interaction effect and suggested that the results could be explained in terms of the extent to which the subject is induced to engage in *cognitive effort*. That is, there was more persuasion if the procedure made people think about the message. Although their study was on persuasion rather than small group conformity, there seems to be room for cross-fertilization here. This is especially the case as they are suggesting that the numbers effect serves to enhance thinking about the message and genuine internalized change where the message is well-argued.

Task Competence. If people believe that others are better at the task than they themselves are, they may be vulnerable to informational influence. Campbell, Tesser, and Fairey (1986) suggest that it may be more complex than this. They studied the effects of several factors on attention to the stimulus, including group pressure, self-doubt, norm extremity, and the order in which norm extremity was presented. They found that attention to the stimulus was low where both pressure and self-doubt were absent, while there was moderate attention to the stimulus where both were present. There was high attention to the stimulus when only one of the two variables was present—pressure without self-doubt or self-doubt but no pressure. They suggest that different psychological processes are involved, confirming a study by Tesser, Campbell, and Mickler (1983), when conformity had also been found to be positively associated with self-doubt and negatively with attention to the stimulus. Social pressure increased conformity and was related to subjects paying little attention to the stimulus. As both self-doubt and pressure were found to affect attention to the stimulus itself, these findings partly support both Asch's work on majority influence and Moscovici's work on minority influence (see below).

Group Composition. More cohesive groups show greater conformity. Williams and Sogon (1984) found significant differences in conforming depending on whether the other members were friends or strangers. This is also an issue for Social Identity Theory (see below). See also Hogg (1992), who has refocused attention on the importance of the concept of cohesiveness.

Response Pattern. Sheehan (1979) used a consistent bias in the false responses, and halfway through the experiment switched subjects to responding first rather than last. He found that they anticipated the group response and demonstrated the effects of social influence even prior to the statement of the group norm for a particular item. This is consistent with the view of Social Identity Theory, discussed at the end of the chapter.

Individual Difference Variables and Social Influence

Personality. Personality variables can largely be cast into what would be predicted from either effect dependence or information dependence. It is more useful to approach the area with a conceptual framework rather than simply listing a catalog of personality correlates of social influence. Subjects may be more susceptible to influence if they have low self-esteem, low assertiveness, an external locus of control, or high need for social approval.

Yarnold, Grimm, and Mueser (1986) found, using the Asch paradigm, that Type B (noncoronary prone) subjects conformed twice as often as Type A (coronary prone) subjects. They suggested that this might be explained in terms of reactance, in that Type A subjects might be particularly sensitive to threats to their personal control and hence more resistant to social pressure to conform (see *reactance*, below).

Bauer, Schlottmann, Bates, and Masters (1983) looked at the relationship of both state and trait anxiety with subjects' imitation of a high or low status model. They found the high prestige model was imitated more, and the high trait anxious subjects were the most likely to do so. Female subjects high on trait-anxiety conformed more to a high prestige model than those low on trait-anxiety (see also Chapter 2).

Sex Differences. As in many areas of psychology, one approach to looking at the evidence is to undertake a meta-analysis of available and statistically comparable studies.

Eagly and Carli (1981) conducted a meta-analysis of social influence studies, looking also at sex of researchers and sex-typed communications. They found women more persuasible than men, and that women were more likely than men to conform in group pressure situations where they were also under the surveillance of the influencing agent. Contrary to earlier explanations for sex differences in persuasion, though, they did not find greater frequency of masculine rather than feminine task content in the studies. They did, however, find that sex difference in researchers was a determinant of the sex differences observed. Of the influenceability studies, 79 percent of researchers were male, and men found sex differences in the direction where women were more persuasible and conforming. Women researchers did not find sex differences. In a later review, Eagly (1983) proposed that the inequalities of status in natural settings may account for the differences in influence and influenceability between men and women. However, she pointed out that small stereotypical sex differences have also been found in laboratory settings where men and women should have equal status. She suggested that the expectancies about male and female social interaction, learned from unequal status encounters, affect the behaviors found in the laboratory. Nemeth (1983) also noted an interrelationship between status and behavior. She argued that both structural characteristics of groups (status distributions) and group process (changes in patterns of verbal and nonverbal cues over time) are reflected in the influence which occurs within small groups.

Interestingly, Eagly, Wood, and Fishbaugh (1981) found that males were significantly less likely than females to conform when under surveillance, and their conformity was also significantly less than for males or females without surveillance. This was interpreted as reflecting the independence of the male gender role and the greater likelihood that when males do not conform they may be influential, which is not so for female nonconformity. Eagly and Wood (1982) have also looked at inferred sex differences in status as an explanation of differences in yielding to influence.

In a laboratory study designed to examine expectation states theory, Pugh and Wahrman (1983) found that sex functions as a diffuse status characteristic. Unless there were experimental intervention, females in mixed-sex groups deferred to the judgment of males, and males refused to be influenced by the judgment of females. Ridgeway and Jacobson (1977) examined the effects on females' judgments of early or late nonconformity by a male or a female confederate. They used a game described either as a quasi-mathematical task or as a common game. There was greater conformity toward a male confederate and for a quasi-mathematical task, without interaction effects. As in Wahrman and Pugh (1972), no support was found for Hollander's (1958) view that conformity early on in group interaction enhances influence. Wahrman and Pugh (1974) found that a female confederate in a male group was more rejected the earlier she deviated in a series of trials. Cull (1976) found, using only male subjects, that male confederates induced greater conformity on perceptual tasks than did female confederates.

Some studies have specifically focused upon the influence strategies of males and females toward targets of either sex. Ridgeway (1982) found differential success for male and female confederates who tried to influence by using one of two message types. Females succeeded when using a style based on concern for the group, while the male was more influential when asserting the correctness of his view. In a self-report study where subjects indicated their preferred influence strategies, Offermann and Schrier (1985) found women claimed a greater likelihood of using Personal/Dependent and Negotiation strategies than men, while men reported a greater likelihood of using Reward/Coercion and Indirect strategies than women. Gender differences in strategy may reflect the learning of effective styles of intervention which may themselves maintain stereotypes. However, when Instone, Major, and Bunker (1983) found weak gender differences in social influence strategies in line with sex-role stereotypes, they argued that the gender-linked differences in influence strategy in fact reflected differences in self-confidence: females displayed lower levels of self-confidence than males.

Social Influence and Social Interaction

Focusing on the influencer in interaction introduces a new perspective. A study by Gilbert, Jones, and Pelham (1987) suggests that observers make different attributions from influencers about how and why the targets are being influenced. Observers tended to be more aware of other concurrent sources of influence on the target's behavior, whereas influencers made deductions based on their (experimentally varied) personal power. Cialdini, Braver, and Lewis (1974) found that influencers regard the people they influence as more intelligent and attractive than those who resist. Cialdini and Mirels (1976) found that this difference between influencers' perceptions of people who yield to them or resist was more marked for subjects who scored high on personal control.

BEHAVIORAL COMPLIANCE

Compliance with a Request

Many studies investigate *compliance with a request*. There are many occasions when an immediate short-term effect on behavior is all that is wanted, so that a petition is signed, a product bought, or medication taken. Once done, the act is irrevocable. The various stratagems which enhance compliance seem to be not unfamiliar to sales personnel. These include the "foot-in-the-door" (FITD), "door-in-the-face" (DITF), and "low-ball" techniques. Each will be briefly outlined below.

Foot-in-the-Door. The idea here is that if people can be induced to grant a small request, it will be easier to have them agree to a large one. Having first taken a small step, it may be easier to go much further. This is known as the foot-in-the-door technique (FITD). Freedman and Fraser (1966) found that women were more willing to have a large, ugly billboard in their garden if, two weeks earlier, they had agreed to sign a petition when asked by another researcher, even when on a different issue. Women who had not had the first request were less likely to agree to the billboard.

There appear to be two necessary elements in the FITD procedure. The initial request must be large enough to provoke the subject into thinking about its implications (Seligman, Bush, & Kirsch, 1976), and the person must feel there was freedom of choice about whether or not to comply. They also found that the initial request did not need to be about the same issue as the second request, although using similar issues had a cumulative effect.

One reason for the effectiveness of FITD may be that subjects experience a change in self-perception. After agreeing to the initial request, they perceive themselves as the sort of person who behaves in that kind of way, and hence compliance with the second, larger request is a way of confirming the changed self-image (DeJong & Musilli, 1982). An alternative view is that initial compliance provides an opportunity for subjects to discover that helping is not as threatening or negative an experience as they had expected, and this discovery makes them more willing to comply with a larger request (Rittle, 1981).

Those who refuse the initial request are less likely to comply with the larger one than those who did not receive the initial request at all (Snyder & Cunningham, 1975). FITD has not always proved effective in studies making large requests, such as for blood donation (Foss & Dempsey, 1979).

For a review and meta-analysis of 15 years of studies on the effectiveness of the "foot-in-the-door," see Beaman, Cole, Preston, Klentz, and Steblay (1983).

Door-in-the-Face (DITF). This term was coined by Cialdini, Vincent, Lewis, Catalan, Wheeler, and Darby (1975). Here, a very large request is made which the person is likely to refuse and, just before the door is slammed, metaphorically, a very much smaller request is made instead. This leads to greater compliance than just making the small request in the first place (Cialdini, Cacioppo, Bassett, & Miller, 1978; Mowen & Cialdini, 1980).

Pendleton and Batson (1979) concluded from studies of DITF that the effect could best be explained by the idea that the situation gives rise to concern about self-presentation. They conducted a study in which they compared subjects' self-ratings after refusal of a large or moderate request, finding that the latter group felt that they would be seen as less helpful, friendly, and concerned.

Fern, Monroe, and Avila (1986) have compared effects of FITD and DITF as reported in published research. While finding support for the greater effectiveness of FITD, the authors note that compliance rates vary, and that they depend on situational factors, the type of respondent, and the nature of the requests.

Lowball. Here, the technique used is to change the rules about the situation after the subject has agreed to an initial request. This is different from the foot-in-the-door approach in that, rather than following a small request with a large one, here the person finds that the promised advantages of compliance have been changed—having agreed to buy the car, you are told the low price naturally does not include the seats! The lowball effect may depend on commitment and a negative self-view resulting from changing a decision. It may also be that a sense of obligation is created (Burger & Petty, 1981). Deaux and Wrightsman (1988) have suggested that, having dealt with the stress of making the choice in the first place, people may be reluctant to reopen the decision and begin the stressful task of making a new choice.

That's-Not-All! This involves offering a product at a high price, not allowing the customer to respond for a few seconds, and then offering a better deal by either adding another product or lowering the price. Burger (1986) tested the technique in a series of experiments and compared the technique to DITF, finding "that's not all" to be more effective.

All these strategies may work for one-off compliance, which is all the salesperson needs. They may depend on people's self-image, wanting not to appear unreasonable to themselves or to the stranger who is actually acting unreasonably. These techniques are not so effective when people are aware of them, have time to reflect, or where their continuing commitment is needed.

Obedience

We may sometimes comply because we believe that the other person has power to reward or punish us; that is, we obey direct commands. In a famous series of experiments, Milgram (1963, 1965, 1974) sought to see if people would obey extreme orders in a laboratory situation. There were two roles to play in what was advertised as a study of learning. One participant was to act as teacher and the other as learner. They would be in adjacent rooms, the teacher asking questions and, if the learner was wrong, giving an electric shock. The severity of these shocks was to be increased steadily for each wrong answer. In fact, the draw was fixed, the learner was always the experimenter's accomplice. No shocks were ever delivered when the teacher pulled the levers, which were clearly labelled at 15-volt intervals from 0 to 450 volts: from "slight shock," through "Danger: severe shock," to "XXX." The accomplice acted the part, and as the level apparently increased, cried out, banged on the wall, begged that the shocks should stop, and at 450 volts, fell silent.

Many subjects protested but the researcher just told them that they must continue. Although psychiatrists before the study thought that perhaps 5 percent of people might deliver a "fatal" shock, 66 percent in fact did so. Naturally, subjects were distressed by what they believed they had done, and by what they had discovered about themselves. It is here that the ethical controversy lies. Although Milgram did debrief them, it is doubtful that such a study would pass a modern ethics committee. Nonetheless, it provided startling insight into people's willingness to be obedient. The subjects were not the all-too-familiar university students, but had responded to a newspaper advertisement for people to help with a study of learning. It was argued that perhaps the results were due to the expert power of a researcher at the University (it must be all right, he must know). However, even when carried out in a downtown office with a "postgraduate student," almost half the subjects gave the maximum shock. The setting made a difference but the effect was still considerable. It was stated earlier that it is difficult to disentangle compliance, identification, and internalization. In this experiment we can see that "authority" had an effect. How much greater it may be in the world outside the laboratory, where disobedience may affect one's own survival, safety, job security, or desire to be admired by the other!

The experiment was conducted with several variants. Where another person dissented (one of the researcher's assistants "objected"), obedience was reduced dramatically. This suggests that people did not want to continue, as is known from their reported remarks, but felt they had to. People also disobeyed if the researcher was not physically present to check on them.

Gilbert (1981) has argued that the procedure is similar to the foot in the door, where the initially mild and then gradual increase in shock levels provided no breakpoint where subjects could switch from obeying to disobeying.

It is often assumed that we are willing to obey if it hurts others (but not ourselves). However, an ingenious study by Martin, Lobb, Chapman, and Spillane (1976) asked secondary schoolboys to say what level of noxious sound (which could cause up to a 50 percent hearing loss) they were willing to administer to themselves. The experiment used a fake "sound generator" similar to Milgram's fake "shock generator," and the danger level of the stimulus was clearly displayed in front of the subjects. The results were very similar to Milgram's, indicating that the Milgram effect does not depend on injuring another, but reflects a more general human tendency to concede to authority.

Milgram himself had suggested that the situation led subjects to cast off their sense of responsibility for their actions in obeying a higher authority figure, but Mantell and Panzarella (1976) found that obedient subjects did not disown responsibility but instead came to define themselves as authority figures.

Geller (1978) carried out a role-playing replication of Milgram's study, successfully replicating both the obedience findings and the participants' experience of the situation. He discussed whether such simulations can in fact avoid the ethical issues aroused by the Milgram paradigm, since these subjects showed "realistic and stressful emotional responses (p. 219)."

In summary, obedience studies suggest that people may obey as a result of the perceived status or power of an authority figure, but not only because they are frightened of what the experimenter might do to them. They may also obey because they are trying to use the available information to make sense of a distressing reality.

AUTOMATIC PROCESSING

"Making sense of reality" suggests that we are doing a lot of rational thinking. We do a lot of what appears to be thinking, but we are constantly bombarded with so much information that we often use shortcuts, not really processing the information. Langer (1989) has argued that we often are in a state of "mindlessness." A small request for the time of day may lead to agreement. While this is also a form of influence, it is rather automatic. We are not much concerned about the power of the other or if they like us. We have simply learned a form of social interaction—a social script.

Abelson (1981) and Langer (1978) have argued that much behavior is scripted, and people follow their "script" for a social interaction without necessarily processing the information which might be relevant. Langer, Blank, and Chanowitz (1978) found that in a simple request to cut into a queue to use a photocopier, subjects would comply with a "placebic" explanation—please may I use the copier because I have to make copies—if the number of copies were small; but compliance for a large number (20) depended on the use of a realistic explanation. Thus, there is some evidence that "request plus explanation" may induce a "compliance script," and that the information will be properly processed only if there is a demand which threatens the subject's own position. Langer refers to the subject's state as "mindless."

Folkes (1985) partially replicated and extended the work of Langer, Blank, and Chanowitz (1978), but concluded that her subjects were in fact mindful, since there were different compliance rates in the request-plus-explanation format, depending upon the controllability of the explanation (e.g., "I feel really sick" or "I don't want to wait"). Folkes argued that her own four studies pointed to cognitive processing in social interaction rather than mindlessness. Langer, Chanowitz, and Blank (1985) responded that they saw no reason to change their position, as people are sometimes mindful and sometimes not. They also clarified "mindlessness," stating that it does not imply the absence of cognitive processing, but "the absence of flexible cognitive processing. Under such circumstances, individuals are neither reasoning well nor reasoning badly about the significance of the environment. They are not reasoning at all (p. 605)."

In a study of linguistic forms in dyads, Drake and Moberg (1986) refer to the use of certain forms which act as linguistic "palliatives and sedatives." The target may be palliated into compliance when there is in fact no sufficient inducement for behavior, or may be sedated into automatic compliance. On the other hand, where there are adequate inducements, language that violates power or social distance expectations may undermine compliance.

We can delude ourselves in other ways by automatic or *peripheral* (as opposed to *central*) processing (Petty & Cacioppo, 1986). It seems that we often use rules of thumb or shortcuts in information processing, known as *heuristics* (Chaiken & Stangor, 1987). Sometimes we imagine that we have thought things through; at other times we use shortcuts knowingly because we do not have enough information to go on. Chaiken, Liberman, and Eagly (1989) suggest, on the basis of their research, that we may accept information from someone who simply seems nice or looks like an expert, for example. This suggests that we may jump to conclusions about an influencer's credibility, which would then affect what we internalize. On important issues, we are likely to process the information more fully.

RESISTANCE TO INFLUENCE

Reactance

Sometimes people may be influenced to behave in a way that has been forbidden them, because they wish to restore their freedom of action. The psychological process underlying this is known as reactance (Brehm & Brehm, 1981). Since an influence attempt may well be seen as an attempt to limit freedom, the concept of reactance is relevant here. Heilman (1976) interpreted subjects' compliance with petition signing in terms of reactance—with less compliance if the influence agent was viewed as threatening, as having the power to implement the threat, and if the subject could remain anonymous.

Deviants in Groups

Some studies focus on deviance—the group's response to it, individual resistance to conformity pressure, and the group leader's problem in innovating, since this may be perceived as deviation from group norms.

Early studies of social influence focused on the impact of majorities on minorities. A classic example is Schachter's (1951) research into how groups treated deviants. He introduced paid accomplices into real-life boys' clubs, telling them beforehand to behave in one of three different ways. He found that accomplices who were asked to deviate persistently from the group's position in a discussion initially had a lot of communication directed at them. When they kept on disagreeing they were ignored, receiving a much lower level of communication than accomplices who immediately accepted or else slid toward the group's position. In later elections for posts in the clubs, persistent deviants were not chosen, but those who appeared to change their minds were included. This sort of research seemed to show the importance of conformity for the good functioning of a group, and the pressure and penalties associated with not conforming. However, as Brown (1988) has pointed out, Schachter discarded some groups from his analysis because the persistent deviant persuaded the rest of the group to his own extreme view—the minority influenced the majority. Schachter seemed to think that these groups had somehow not behaved normally.

Individual Resistance to Conformity Pressure

It would seem that the actual presence of a social supporter in a small group may not be necessary for resisting group pressure. If a person believes that an absent other would also resist social pressure when facing the same situation, conformity is reduced (Allen & Wilder, 1979). The notion of the reference group or reference person has a long history in the psychology of social influence. It seems not, however, to be considered in most contemporary studies. Concern is focused more on the factors which produce influence in groups, rather than on those distant drummers to whose tune the nonconformist or independent subject may be marching.

Status and Deviance

Nagata (1980) found that status affected dissent in four-person groups. High status members would conform more than a low status member if the norm benefited the group, but would dissent more if the group norm was detrimental to task achievement. High-assertive subjects were more likely than low-assertive subjects to resist conforming to low-status experimental confederates according to Williams (1984).

Deviants and Interaction

The verbal behavior of deviants in small decision-making groups has been studied by Bradley (1978), who found that as discussion went on, deviants' statements increased in emotionality and decreased in rationality. Deviants also initially increased and ultimately decreased in dominance over time.

The Group's Response to Deviants

Groups may respond unfavorably to deviants because of the consequences for the group's decision making. Miller and Anderson (1979) had groups of four naive female subjects and a female confederate discuss a case history of a juvenile delinquent in an institution, so designed that naive subjects would recommend release, against the confederate's position. There were three decision rules: majority, unanimity, or dictatorship. Under the latter two, the deviant could sometimes force her decision on the group. Under the majority rule, the deviant was only weakly rejected and the decision rules were perceived as fair. In the other two conditions, but especially under dictatorship, the deviant was strongly rejected and the decision was seen as unrepresentative, with unfair decision rules. These findings were confirmed in a study of male undergraduates (Miller, Jackson, Mueller, & Schersching, 1987). The deviant's apparent reasons for not conforming also affect group reaction. In a study by Levine and Ruback (1980), the deviant was represented as neutral for one of three reasons: indifference, ignorance, or ambivalence. The group consensus was at one end of a 9-point scale. Rejection depended on the apparent reason for the deviance rather than deviance itself.

Influential Deviance

Wahrman and Pugh (1972) found that male subjects accepted the influence of a deviant significantly more if the deviant acted differently from the group norms from the beginning of a series of 15 trials, rather than from trial 6 or 11. This study supported Moscovici's view of minority influence, rather than Hollander's concept of idiosyncrasy credit (see below and Chapter 6). However, when the confederate was female in a group of male subjects, she was rejected, the more so the sooner she deviated (Wahrman & Pugh, 1974).

In fact, Schachter, in discarding groups from the analysis of his early study on communication and deviants, failed to identify something which for the past 25 years has attracted much interest: how minorities affect majorities. If deviants were never influential, how could social change ever happen? Why would we not all end up uniform? It is not always good for groups to resist innovation and development. New ideas may be needed in order to survive.

MINORITY INFLUENCE

The many experiments carried out by Moscovici and his colleagues have shown how a minority can persuade the majority. The basic paradigm is rather like a reverse Asch experiment, in which two dissenting confederates, in a group with four naive subjects, agree that some of a series of blue slides, varying in shade and light intensity, are "green" (Moscovici, Lage, & Naffrechoux, 1969). The critical slides were labelled "green" by 8 percent in the minority pressure condition, against 0.25 percent for control subjects; 32 percent of people changed at least one judgment.

The influence effect was quite small when compared to Asch-type majority effects where there is generally conformity on about one-third of trials, but it was statistically significant and of theoretical importance.

Moscovici went on to vary the study. Sometimes the two deviants would agree with each other, at other times they would not. Sometimes they followed a "pattern," agreeing the wrong color for all slides with a similar light intensity. In general, he and his co-workers have found that influence is higher when there is a consensus between the deviants—they agree about the different answer. This suggests that people are trying to make sense of what the deviants are saying; it is as if the majority were thinking "there

might be something in this, since those two always agree." This effect is even stronger if the responses are patterned, that is, if the minority dissents for all the brighter slides or all the duller ones. Again, this suggests that the others are thinking that there is an underlying logical reason for the disagreement—that there is pattern and sense to it.

An intriguing finding is that minority influence has a greater impact on people's private beliefs than on their public behavior. People may be persuaded by the minority, but do not like to say so in front of the majority. In many studies of majority influence, subjects privately disagree with their publicly stated judgment. Conversely, minority influence produces change which is sometimes apparent in private rather than public statements (Maass & Clark, 1983). Furthermore, minority influence is often manifest not on direct measures but on related items—that is, the influence is demonstrated indirectly. Mugny (1984) found, using the Asch paradigm, that while a majority led to direct influence, indirect influence could be produced by a majority (if the subjects believed there was an illusion) or a minority.

The time may come when people who have been privately doubting admit to their new views, and minorities may be a catalyst for this. Moscovici uses the story of the "Emperor's new clothes" to illustrate this. A deviant minority is particularly effective in helping a doubting majority to shift where there is already a move toward change (Paicheler, 1977). The presence of a deviant minority in itself generates conflict; one way of resolving the conflict is for the majority to accept the minority view. In fact, any influence attempt creates conflict; the majority view will generate interpersonal conflict (Guillon & Personnaz, 1983), whereas the minority viewpoint may elicit cognitive conflict. This cognitive conflict may lead the majority to be more creative. Nemeth and Kwan (1985) found that after exposure to the blue-green situation, more original word associations to "blue" and "green" were given by subjects in the minority influence condition. Nemeth and Kwan (1987) confirmed, using an anagram task, the prediction made by Nemeth (1986) that exposure to minority viewpoints would lead to divergent thinking. Exposure to minority influence may also affect a person's own subsequent willingness to be deviant. Nemeth and Chiles (1988) found that subjects who had prior experience of being in a group where a consistent dissenter labelled blue slides as green were more likely to take a minority position themselves in a subsequent test, correctly saying slides were "red" against majority (confederate) pressure. Bradley, MacHamon, and Harris (1976) found that group members were significantly more likely than chance to use the very arguments which they had heard presented by lone deviants in earlier group discussions. It appears that the arguments of deviants may have an effect on subsequent discussions of the same topic.

Moscovici claims that the traditional emphasis on norm formation and majority influence entirely fails to cope with the fact that social changes happen, innovations are accepted. He refers to these earlier approaches to conformity as "functional," since conformity was assumed to serve the group's ends and deviance was negatively valued. He argues, to the contrary, that innovation and social change are vital for social groups, and that they are usually the product of minority influence. He discounts as totally inappropriate Hollander's (1958) attempt to explain innovation by the notion of "idiosyncrasy credits" accrued by leaders through conforming to group norms—if that were so, he says, then Lenin would first have had to become Tsar of all the Russias before attempting revolution (Moscovici & Paicheler, 1983).

Bray, Johnson, and Chilstrom (1982) had a confederate argue a minority position only on the last issue, in line with Hollander's view, and compared the effectiveness of this with the strategy of dissenting from the beginning, as proposed by Moscovici and Faucheux (1972). In fact, both procedures showed significant influence in comparison to a baseline control. Hollander's procedure was more successful than Moscovici's for males, especially where the confederate showed high competence. Female groups were less influenced overall, and were equally influenced by either method, irrespective of confederate competence.

In Moscovici's view, it is the behavioral style of the minority which serves to convince the majority that the "deviant" position must be correct. Majorities are convinced by minorities whose behavior suggests that they understand the causes of events. For this to work, the minority must be consistent, and, if more than one person, must also agree. The majority sees them as credible. Consistency may imply expertise. Galileo would not have been very convincing if he had suggested that perhaps everyone was right and the sun did go around the earth; he created doubt and conflict for people who had been previously certain and, in maintaining his argument, provided a new certainty.

Moscovici (1976) also argued that it is in fact the consistency of the confederates in the Asch experiment, not their majority, which leads to social influence, since a larger but non-unanimous majority is not as effective as a unanimous group of three. Equally, a group larger than three, even if unanimous, does not have a much greater effect. Looking at the size effects of the minority, Arbuthnot and Wayner (1982) found that a minority of one was less effective than a minority of two, or a minority of one who gained a convert. Nemeth, Wachtler, and Endicott (1977) examined the relative gains and losses of increasing minority size; it appeared from their data that, with increased size, the minority is presumed to be more competent but their presumed confidence is decreased. Effective influence was predicted by a combination of the two.

The minority's style also leads people to believe that they are honest and independent. Being prepared to speak out and suffer any consequences may convince others that you are sincere, with nothing to gain and everything to lose. Moscovici's minorities were paid accomplices, but real-life minorities often do suffer, and the attribution that they are trustworthy may sometimes be justified. Nemeth and Wachtler (1974) found that the dissenting accomplice who was seen to choose to sit at the head of the table for a group discussion was more influential than the dissenter who was seen to be assigned to that seat by the experimenter.

We can see that minorities can lead to informational influence. Because people want to understand, and to predict events and behavior, they may be susceptible to a minority group or individual whose style seems to reflect expertise and trustworthiness. Minorities are most effective when consistently different on a particular issue, while maintaining fairness and reasonableness in other respects. The rigidity of a minority might appear to be the same as consistency but it has different effects. Where the minority is perceived to be rigid and unwilling to negotiate with the majority, it may be dismissed as an outgroup irrelevant to the group's functioning and psycho-social identity (Mugny & Perez, 1991).

Moscovici says that minority influence generates conversion, whereas majority influence leads to compliance. However, the distinction does not seem clear-cut. Minority influence certainly seems to involve informational influence; people seeking to understand their world will only believe a minority which seems credible. This does not necessarily mean they are right. Chaiken's work on shortcuts in processing shows that, even with informational influence, we may process fairly automatically rather than thinking logically. Behavioral style itself may lead to shortcuts—as in the effect of choosing the head-of-table position in Nemeth and Wachtler's study, above. This kind of change may be peripheral and short-term rather than conversion.

Majority and Minority Influence: Dual or Single Process?

There is an ongoing and unresolved debate in the literature as to whether majority and minority influence should really be seen as distinct processes (dual process theory) or as part of essentially the same process.

If minority influence produces genuine conversion, it is, arguably, more effective than majority influence, which Moscovici (1980) says leads only to compliance. He sees the minority influence process as one of genuine cognitive or perceptual change.

A comparison may usefully be drawn with work by Petty and Cacioppo (1981, 1986) on their Elaboration Likelihood Model of persuasion, which distinguishes between enduring change via the central route, and temporary, superficial change via peripheral routes. Central routes involve elaboration—for example, thinking about the message and its implications. Peripheral processing focuses on the superficial aspects of the message and the context of its delivery, such as an attractive source. A range of factors affects the likelihood of thinking further about the material. It is hard to see that it should inevitably be the case that majorities can only produce transient change, while minorities only effect enduring conversion. Majorities may indeed worry or frighten us into complying, but they often convince us also—if everyone else is doing something different, this may make us think about the issues, perhaps deciding that the others are right.

Mackie (1987) has specifically addressed the debate on possible differences between majority and minority influence. She looked at the systematic and nonsystematic processing of persuasive communications emanating from minorities and majorities. In a series of four experiments, she used a very different type of exposure to group discrepancy from other studies. In the first two studies, she exposed subjects to a minority with which they agreed and a majority with which they disagreed. She found that subjects thought a lot more about relevant issues and were more likely to show long-term acceptance of the majority position with which they initially disagreed. She went on to show that simply giving consensus information about both minority and majority positions without any persuasive communication also led to a significant change toward the majority position. However, this was neither generalized nor mediated by the way in which the subjects thought about the issue.

Disagreement may itself serve as a useful cue; Mackie also found a slight shift to the minority when subjects were exposed to a minority view. In that it addresses the role of thought within the influence process, this work has much in common with contemporary analysis of attitude change processes mentioned above.

Social Impact Theory

Social impact theorists argue for a single process view of social influence. The social impact of sheer number may seem to favor majority influence, but a minority can also be effective if it has social impact, which is determined by strength and immediacy as well as simply number. Thus, for example, a high-status minority or one which is perceived to be competent will have more impact, as will a minority which is very immediate (close in space or time). The very consistency of a minority is seen as adding to its strength (Wolf & Latané, 1981).

Social Identity Theory

Informational and normative processes are fundamental to social influence, whether the influence comes from a majority or a minority, and whatever the basis of the influencer's power. Both processes may be affected by the shortcuts in processing known as heuristics. Recent research has shown that another important element in social influence is the social category to which people feel they belong. Identifying with a social group leads people to be willing to accept their views (or the views they are imagined to hold). Abrams and Hogg (1990) have used Social Identity Theory (Turner, 1985) to explain conformity. A person will change behavior to fit in with the social category which contributes to his or her sense of identity. People have been shown to change their behavior in *anticipation* of joining the group. Here, the change cannot have been due to pressure from group members. People like to act in a way which fits their own self-categorization—the social identity they hold. Behavior should not, according to this view, be regarded as various isolated acts. Social identity theory underlines the significance of the social context of behavior. The way we act may reflect who we believe ourselves to be.

SUMMARY

Majority influence has been studied for many years, showing that change in behavior can be produced as a result of perceived group pressure, especially where there is ambiguity and where responses are public. These variables reflect different types of influence—informational and normative—respectively changing beliefs via internalization, and changing public behavior as a result of compliance or identification.

Many studies look at simple behavioral compliance, such as foot-in-the-door (FITD) or door-in-the-face techniques. The effectiveness of these techniques may depend on their implications for the subjects' self-perceptions, although FITD may also be mediated by the subjects' discovery that compliance is more pleasant and less threatening than they had feared. Obedience may arise through similar processes, although it also depends on the authority of the influencer.

People may sometimes respond with a compliance "script," complying automatically and without processing information. In other circumstances, an influence attempt may be met with reactance and resisted. Sex differences in being influenced may reflect perceived status differences, but it seems that males and females exert influence differently and may interpret an influence attempt differently.

Deviants in groups are often subject to group pressure, but they themselves may become sources of influence for the group. This is most likely to be the result of their behavioral style. Minority influence may lead to conversion rather than compliance. Majority influence may sometimes be internalized, but it may lead to a change in behavior only. Whether majority and minority influence are the result of the same process is currently a matter of dispute. Recent work on attitude change may inform this debate.

PART III

Group Structure

CHAPTER 5

Roles and Relationships

A. Paul Hare

As you, the reader, go through the material in this chapter, you may wish to have some actual group in mind so that you can test the generalizations presented against your own experience. If you find that the ideas about informal roles, hierarchies, functional group size, and intimate relations are all familiar to you, then you can be assured that you already have a firm grasp of the implications of these phenomena for interaction in small groups. If you discover a new idea, you could see if it makes you any more effective as a leader or member in your next group activity.

If no particular group comes to mind that you would like to use as an example, you could recall the events in William Golding's *Lord of the Flies* (1959). The schoolboys who find themselves on a deserted island after a plane crash have a lot in common with many informal groups of students or others. For the boys on the island, the interaction develops without a given formal structure in their case since there are no adults to provide the formal organization. They also have a rather general task—survival until help comes—but not specific ways of reaching the goal. Some of their previous roles, such as members of the choir, provide a basis for the new role organization and alignment, including the capes and caps with badges as reminders of their former relationships. Other formal roles are developed, as the idea of possessing the conch shell when a person wants to speak. Some seem to be "natural" leaders (Ralph), or supply resources (glasses by

This chapter is based partly on A. P. Hare (1994), "Roles and relationships," in A. P. Hare, H. H. Blumberg, M. F. Davies, & M. V. Kent, *Small group research: A handbook* (Norwood, NJ: Ablex, pp. 141–154). Reprinted with permission from Ablex Publishing Corporation.

Piggy), or have special insight into the "meaning of all this" (Simon). However, as it often happens, the bearer of "truth" is done in for his pains.
Stages in group development can be identified, including an abortive attempt to light a signal fire, during which they burn down one side of a
mountain and lose one of the boys, because they were not yet organized
for the task.

If you are not familiar with Golding's book, you might imagine an occasion when you are asked to join two other students for a group project.
Suppose that the instructor does not assign any formal roles to the group
members. How will you decide who will be the leader, if there is to be
one? Will it be on the basis of age, gender, knowledge of the topic, skill in
using a word processor, or other characteristics that the individuals bring
to the group? Or will you let roles develop informally as you work together
and discover who tends to take the initiative or have the best ideas for the
task, who thinks to bring coffee or soft drinks and cakes for the group
meetings, or who has access to libraries or other sources of information
that you will need. Whatever the distribution of resources, is the person in
the weaker power position excluded by the other two, or does this person
form a coalition with someone with higher power and thus exert more
control than the resources would warrant?

However, if you spend too much time becoming aware of all the formal
and informal relationships in your group, you may never get on with the
project. Also, the material in all the other chapters in this text is relevant
for your purpose. Even then, there is more to social interaction than we
have been able to make explicit in this text. Even if we had told you everything you needed to know—but possibly had been afraid to ask—the task
of giving appropriate weight to each of the variables is left to you. So,
enough introduction, let us return to a consideration of roles and relationships in small groups.

ROLES

The concept of role, as a set of rights and duties and behaviors that are
associated with a position (status) in a social group, is important whether
the group under consideration is small or large, or even constitutes a whole
society. For this reason, much is written about roles in organizations or
societies that is also applicable to small groups. Indeed, to the extent that
a small group represents a "microcosm" of a society, all of the roles that
have been identified in small groups have their counterparts in larger social
systems. Moreover, the status that a person has in a larger system often
carries over into a small group, even though it may not be especially relevant for the functioning of that group.

Thus it is difficult to draw the line between the social-psychological literature that pertains to larger organizations and that which is especially relevant for the small group. For example, Thornton and Nardi (1975) describe four stages in the acquisition of a role (anticipatory, formal, informal, and personal) that would apply at any level of society. Similarly, Sieber's (1974) observation that the benefits to a person from accumulating a number of roles far outweighs any stress to which ensuing conflicts in roles might give rise, could provide a suitable point to begin the analysis of role conflict in small groups. Adato's (1975) description of "leave-taking," that terminates the sense of occasioned presence and being together, but does not necessarily terminate focused interaction, would be useful in the analysis of the termination of a group activity. Gudykunst's (1983) review of the relationship between "host" and "stranger," with primary reference to intercultural contexts, could be applied to the introduction of the newcomer in a group.

Another difficulty in defining roles in small groups is that for some research the term "role" is used to refer to well-recognized formal positions in a group, such as chairperson, secretary, or member; and for some authors, "role" refers to informal positions such as the joker or the scapegoat; whereas for others, "role" refers to the extent to which a relationship is "intimate" or not, or to a type of behavior that predominates, as when someone is identified as a "silent member" or a "nonconformist." Formal roles, such as that of "chairperson," seldom change in the course of a group meeting. Informal roles, such as "joker" or "scapegoat," may change several times. Dramaturgical roles, such as director, protagonist, auxiliary, or audience member, are the most transitory and likely to shift as a new image or theme becomes the focus of discussion or action, or the group moves to a new phase in problem solving or development.

Individuals vary in their ability to play a given role. The expectations for a role are most easily met by the individual whose personality fits the role. In general, the dimensions used to describe roles are the same as those used to describe interaction and personality. The first person to occupy a new position in a group has the opportunity to create a role that fits his or her personality. If the first person's personality traits are somewhat unique, the group may have difficulty filling the role again after the first person leaves the group.

Persons have the ability to play multiple roles, usually with different sets of others or with the same set at different times; but occasionally roles conflict, collide, or are confused by ambiguous expectations from different sets of others (i.e., superiors, peers, and subordinates). However, clarity of role expectations is an important aspect of role. After interviewing members of various kinds of successful teams, Larson and La Fasto (1989, p. 53) reported that for tactical teams, such as a cardiac surgical team, there must be high task clarity and unambiguous role definition.

DEVELOPMENT OF INFORMAL STRUCTURE

With the exception of very simple tasks, such as taking part in one side of a "tug of war" in which two teams pull on opposite ends of a rope, some role differentiation is necessary to take full advantage of the productive capabilities of a group. If no formal structure is provided, then an informal structure or set of role relationships will develop. Even when there is a formal structure, there is likely also to be an informal structure. The informal structure may fill in gaps in the formal structure to provide functions necessary for the task, or it may be in opposition to the formal structure to provide some relief from the task or to provide alternative modes of achievement.

The formal structure of roles usually represents the third phase in a four-phase model of group development. In the first phase, a group must agree on the overall definition of the situation and the nature of the task at hand; in the second phase, it must secure or develop the resources necessary for the task; in the third phase, it must develop an appropriate set of roles and level of morale; and in the fourth phase, the group must coordinate the resources and the roles in specific goal-related activity. However, in laboratory groups or therapy-like groups that are the subject of most of the research on group development, the nature of the task, the resources, and the formal roles are all designated by the experimenter or the group leader. All that is left is to develop the informal roles to supplement the formal roles. Thus most of the theories of group development actually describe the informal activity in the fourth overall phase of group development.

FLUCTUATIONS IN ORGANIZATION

The organization of a group may vary over time for at least two reasons. One, to be discussed below, is that it may take several periods of conflict before an informal "pecking order" can be established that is appropriate for the task of the group. The other reason is that the activities required in each phase of the development of a group may call for a different constellation of roles. Members who move in and out of a group from newcomer to full member, to ex-member, provide one source of fluctuation (Moreland & Levine, 1982).

Phases

Farrell, Heinemann, and Schmitt (1986) provide an example of the change in salience of roles with phases of group development in their study of interdisciplinary health care teams. They identify four phases in group development following the formulation of Tuckman (1965), and note the roles that are prominent during each phase.

Phase One: Testing and Dependency. In this initial phase of team development, members are uncertain about what is to be gained by membership in the group, and they are preoccupied with obtaining orientation and guidance. The salient informal roles are those of the centralized leader and his or her helpers. The leader may be a *tyrant* who runs the team in a highly structured manner. Or the leader may be a *superman* or *wonderwoman* who sets a pace of work output and competence that the members try to emulate. A leader may play *party host* or *hostess*—cracking jokes, bringing refreshments, and attending to each member's needs. Or the leader may be a *reluctant candidate*, one who tries to escape responsibility for team decisions, but who is repeatedly coaxed into making decisions for the dependent group. The *helper* is a member who interprets and defends the leader's behavior and makes concerted efforts to please him or her. If the effectiveness of the team drops and tension mounts, one member may be isolated as a *scapegoat*. The dependency needs of this member may be exaggerated, or this member's actions may be interpreted in a distorted way as to make him or her appear incompetent.

Phase Two: Conflict. The second phase of the group is characterized by polarization and conflict. A new set of roles is likely to emerge to deal with tension. Members who are anxious about expressing their discontent may encourage one member, the *hatchetman*, to be the spokesperson for shared anger. A second likely role is the *nice guy* or *social-emotional leader*. This member shows warmth and understanding to persons on all sides of the controversy. A third role is the *clown*, a well-liked member who is expected to play a humorous or joking role in team meetings. The *scapegoat* may reappear as the object of attack by the *hatchetman*.

Phase Three: Cohesion and Consensus. The conflict phase is often followed by one of heightened solidarity. Members develop increasing trust in each other, increasing confidence in their ability to master work demands, and increasing courage to speak out about their dissatisfactions. The salient roles at this stage are enacted by a *coalition of colleagues*, that is, members who have come to respect each other's competence and who play a central part in articulating team values and norms.

Phase Four: Functional Role Relatedness. At this phase, members have successfully negotiated their own culture and structure, and are able to cooperate using some appropriate division of labor. The *coalition of colleagues* is still salient during this phase, and the *clown* may still play a part. If the roles of *hatchetman*, *scapegoat*, or *nice guy* reappear, the team may quickly recognize the dynamics and call a halt to them. The *hatchetman* will be asked to let dissatisfied members speak for themselves. Tensions displaced on the *scapegoat* will be traced to their original source. Tensions that might have been absorbed by the *nice guy* will be confronted in administrative meetings.

Since groups which are well organized are usually the most productive, any movement of members from one position to another within the role structure, or any discrepancies in the criteria for establishing status in the group, such as age and pay, result in more activity in the social-emotional area in an attempt to reestablish the structure or to resolve the differences. This can result in a temporary decrease in productivity until the problems have been solved.

POWER AND PERFORMANCE

Two bases of status in a group that have received considerable attention are power and performance. Persons who have the power to give rewards and punishments have high status and so do those who perform well on the task. The use of reward power by a group leader increases group productivity, whereas the use of coercive power decreases productivity. Further, the extended use of coercive power is taken as an indication of weakness of the leader. Relative to males, females with high power in a laboratory simulation made fewer influence attempts, used a more limited range of influence strategies, and used fewer reward strategies. Persons who are on their own "turf" have a power advantage over outsiders.

A test of the relationship between power imbalance and power use was performed by Molm (1985) using pairs of university students as subjects who took part in the experiment to earn money in a series of exchanges with their partners. Nine different combinations of dependent relationship were tested. If the two persons were unequally dependent on one another, the less dependent person had a power advantage. A power imbalance was predicted to lead to asymmetrical exchange, with the more dependent person giving more than he or she receives. This occurs when the less dependent persons use their power advantage—giving or withholding rewards contingent on the others' behavior—to shift the ratio of exchange more in their favor. Previous studies had assumed that the greater the asymmetry in the exchange, the greater would be the power use. However, Molm's study indicated that power imbalance is not a unitary variable, and that the dependencies of the weaker and stronger persons in the relationship can have very different effects on power use. Molm found that the dependence of the weaker person had a strong and predominantly linear effect on power use, whereas the dependence of the stronger person had a weak and curvilinear effect. In addition, the relations were causally mediated by the reinforcement contingencies that the powerful person established to control the other's behavior. These contingencies mediated the effects of the stronger person's dependence, but not the effects of the weaker person's dependence.

Persons who are judged to have low status in a paired relationship because of poor performance will receive less than an equal share of the payoff, especially if they are perceived as investing less effort. However, partners who are perceived to have lower ability than the subject may be judged to be more cooperative, friendly, and trustworthy, especially when they enhance the subject's own estimate of ability. Persons with low power look at a partner more when listening than when speaking. Power may also "command obedience," but even in modern military settings there is also an obligation to disobey illegal or inhuman orders.

DIFFERENTIATION IN HIERARCHIES

A striking feature of the initially leaderless groups of university students that were observed in small groups laboratories in the 1950s was that they regularly developed a status hierarchy within the first few minutes of interaction. Berger explained the inequality of status as the result of "performance expectation states." These expectations are ideas about the relative task ability of each member that develop during the initial phases of interaction, since other group members will want to pay attention to and reward others who have high ability (Webster & Driskell, 1983, pp. 57–58). When it is apparent that group members have a different status in other groups, based on age, sex, ethnic group, or other variables, then there may be "status inconsistencies" that will affect group performance.

Berger, Rosenholtz, and Zelditch (1980) define a *status organizing process* as any process in which evaluation of, and beliefs about, the characteristics of actors become the basis of observable inequalities in face-to-face social interaction. A key concept in this theory is the *status characteristic*— any characteristic, such as age, sex, or ethnicity, of actors around which evaluations and beliefs about status are organized. As noted above, the phenomenon with which this theory is concerned is often observed in the study of problem-solving groups whose members differ in status characteristics that are significant in the larger society. These groups do not create a new social organization, but maintain the external status differences inside the group. These status characteristics, plus judgments about future performance that arise from the task-related interaction of group members, give rise to "expectation states" concerning the relative value of the contributions of the members.

PATTERNS OF ROLE DIFFERENTIATION

Probably the most common set of roles reported in the small group literature is the division of leadership functions between a "task" leader, with a primary concern for group productivity, and a "social-emotional" leader, with a concern for group morale. In many groups, men, during the years that these studies were conducted, were more likely to be the task leaders and women the social leaders, and this is the result of status differences. In groups in the United States, men were expected to be more competent than women, and therefore competitive or dominating behavior was "legitimate" for men but not for women. (See Chapter 6 for a discussion of leaders' roles.)

A temporary group role is that of a "newcomer." As a test of the influence on a person's behavior when the person is a newcomer in a group, Moreland (1985) conducted a laboratory experiment with 20 groups of university students. Each group contained five unacquainted subjects of the same sex who met once a week to discuss topical issues. Within each group, two randomly selected subjects were told that they were "newcomers" entering a group of "oldtimers." The three remaining control subjects received no such information and instead believed (correctly) that everyone was new to the group. The experimental subjects who thought they were newcomers exhibited strong ingroup-outgroup (new-old) biases in that they behaved more favorably toward each other than toward the control subjects. However, by the third week, the differences between the two sets of subjects had disappeared since the "newcomers" were fully assimilated in their groups.

Whatever the pattern of role differentiation in a group, whether informal or formal, persons are likely to experience difficulty in performing a role if the expectations for the role are ambiguous, or if the expectations are in conflict with another role that they are also playing.

GROUP SIZE

Most "natural groups" (i.e., casual work or play groups) consist of only two or three members. However, natural groups of children and adolescents are usually larger than those of adults, and larger for adult women compared with adult men. In free-forming groups, as in a conversation lounge, individuals are more likely to leave a group as group size increases. As group size increases, each individual has to relate to a larger and larger number of individuals and potential subgroups. Considering only "symmetrical" relationships, where persons or subgroups respond in the same way to each other, the number of potential relationships between individuals, between subgroups, and between individuals and subgroups increases exponentially. For a group of two, there is one potential symmetrical relationship, for a group of three, there are six relationships, and for a group of seven there are 966 potential relationships.

The optimum group size for many group discussion tasks is five members. In smaller groups, individuals are forced to be too prominent; and in larger groups, there are fewer opportunities to speak and more control is required. In a group of five, strict deadlocks can be avoided (because of the odd number of members) and members can shift roles easily. To select the appropriate-sized group for a given problem, Thelen (1949) has suggested the "principle of least group size." The group should be just large enough to include individuals with all the relevant backgrounds and skills for the problem's solution. For example, in the use of "Synectics," a form of creative problem-solving developed primarily for business applications, Gordon (1961, pp. 72–73) finds that five persons representing a cross section of a business firm are enough to provide all the necessary skills and points of view.

Once a group exceeds size three, there are no new sociometric or cognitive properties to consider. There may also be no gain in the reliability of the group decision process. The effects of having a large number of people in the same space, who are not necessarily members of the same group, are described in Chapter 1 on the physical situation.

A number of studies report changes in individual behavior or group activity that are correlated with increasing group size. As size increases, individuals become less self-conscious, there is less inter-member interaction and less satisfaction, members use less effort with lower performance, with less cooperation, and only a few members may actually take part in decision making (especially for types of problems for which the group is given credit for solving a problem if at least one member can solve it), and there will be more subgroups and cliques. Despite the fact that the average contribution per member may be less in larger brainstorming groups, the larger group may still produce more ideas. Also, in larger groups, members are more likely to use a "truth-supported wins" process of making decisions, in which two correct group members are necessary and sufficient for a correct group response. (See also, Chapter 8 on group decision-making.)

The number of members in a group compared to the number needed for the task has been referred to as "manning." Tasks may be "undermanned" or "overmanned." Having more members than necessary is found to produce more variable feelings of involvement (Wicker, Kirmeyer, Hanson, & Alexander, 1976). In a situation where there are less than the required number of persons, members work harder and are more likely to accept new members (Cini, Moreland, & Levine, 1993). Overmanned groups are more likely to reject a deviant member. In a simple task that requires a low level of creativity (rope pulling, for example), individual performance declines significantly with the addition of one or two co-workers (Ingham, Levinger, Graves, & Peckham, 1974). For simple tasks or tasks in which the individual's contribution is not clearly recognized, members are inclined to decrease their effort and engage in "social loafing" as more members are added to a group (Latané, Williams, & Harkins, 1979).

An example of research related to "manning" is the study by Bray, Kerr, and Atkin (1978). They designed an experiment to examine the influence of group size, task difficulty, and sex of members on the relationship between actual productivity and potential productivity, and also to test the predictive accuracy of "hierarchical" and "equalitarian latency" models of performance. University students worked on three intellectual problems of varying difficulty, either as individuals or as members of same-sex groups of two, three, six, and ten members. The easy problem was presented as follows:

As a prospector you have been very successful. You must now discharge a small debt by paying *exactly* 27 ounces of gold dust (no more, no less) to a friend. You have three containers which hold exactly 9 ounces, 42 ounces, and 6 ounces, respectively. How would you remove the *exact* amount from the safe, using only these containers? You must use all three containers. (Answer: Fill the 42-ounce container; from it fill the 9- and 6-ounce containers, leaving 27 ounces.)

The medium problem and difficult problem were similar, but required more filling and emptying of different sized containers. The actual performance of the individuals and groups was assessed using indexes of the proportion of solvers and the time to solution. Potential performance scores were generated from the theoretical models for the same indexes. Group performance on both indexes generally fell below potential as size and difficulty of problem increased. The sex of the group members generally made no difference. The concept of "functional size" was advanced to explain the observed pattern of group performance. As group size was increased, the number of nonparticipants also increased, resulting in a functional group that was smaller than the actual size. The groups solved the problems at the rate of the fastest member of the functional group.

Of special interest in the United States has been the comparison of six-person and twelve-person juries, since there was an interest on the part of State legislatures to reduce jury size. In one study, jury size had no effect on conviction when apparent guilt of the defendant was low. But when apparent guilt was high the six-person juries were more likely to convict (Valenti & Downing, 1975), perhaps because the probability of a dissenter being present was reduced. (See discussion of juries in Chapter 8.)

The contrasts between small groups and larger groups are similar to those between groups led by democratic leaders and those led by authoritarian leaders, groups with decentralized communication networks and those with centralized communication networks, and groups whose members are cooperating and those whose members are competing. For large groups, those with authoritarian leadership, those with centralized communication networks, and those whose members are competing, one finds an increase in productivity coupled with low satisfaction for the average member. Thus the effects of increasing the size of a group may well be countered by the influence of some other variable such as leadership, communication network, or the requirements of the task.

DYAD

Early research on the dyad (two-person group) and the triad (three people) indicated that each type of group had special characteristics. Interaction in the dyad is characterized by a delicate balance of power and more tension between members. Over time, one member of the pair becomes more active. Many studies refer to the dyad in the title of the research, and indeed refer to the interaction between two persons. However, no comparison is made to larger groups to show that the behavior observed is especially related to the fact that only two persons are present. Since, in groups of any size, individuals primarily relate to one person at a time, all of the findings summarized under the category of "dyadic interaction" apply equally well to interaction between persons in larger groups.

The performance of dyads is better if the members like each other and have the same intellectual background. Competitive pairs have different interaction patterns than cooperative pairs; and relative power is important, especially in a competitive situation, and is related to learning ability in children. When pairs do tasks involving analogies and crossword puzzles, a division of labor is efficient, but sharing labor is more effective.

INTIMATE RELATIONSHIPS

The study of intimate relationships comes closer to the earlier research on the dyad since one of the special characteristics of a pair is the possibility of intimacy. However, from a broader perspective, the research on intimate relations is similar to research on friendship, since friendships may include only pairs, but they may also involve larger sets of persons who meet face to face or in a network. Thus the findings concerning intimate relationships are essentially the same as those on friendship.

Levinger (1980) provides some models of close relations in which he addresses two questions: (1) How does one distinguish among relationships differing in closeness at any single point in time? (2) How do relationships change over either a short or long time span? The first question suggested looking inside the Person-Other "intersection." Here he looked at three logically distinct levels of relatedness.

1. P has a unilateral awareness of O without any implication of reciprocity; examples include phenomena such as impression formation or interpersonal evaluation, where one person judges another without the second persons's awareness.

2. Bilateral surface contact where there is some P-O interaction, but it is confined to casual role-related matters; examples include initial interaction between strangers, and also repeated interactions among acquaintances or co-workers who limit their behavior to culturally prescribed roles.

3. Going beyond culturally prescribed roles; this refers to gradations in P-O mutuality, where interaction becomes increasingly personal and unique and interdependence deepens.

The relationships of deep mutuality are marked by intimate disclosure, knowledge of each other's personal feelings, joint development of pair norms, and mutual responsibility for one another's outcome, with strong mutual attraction.

Levinger's second question led to a consideration of short-term and long-term processes. Regarding long-term pair processes, he noted a five-phase sequence that extended from (1) initial attraction to (2) building a relationship, (3) continuation, (4) deterioration, and (5) ending. He has written a model in the form of a computer program, called "Relate," that has been used to simulate a variety of interpersonal encounters, including the occurrence of "altruism" in mixed-motive situations, the analysis of interpersonal disclosure, and the hypothetical development of a romantic relationship between two imaginary young people.

Kelley et al. (1983) also provide a framework for the analysis of close relationships and extensive reviews of related literature. They focus primarily on heterosexual couples. In their view, any social relationship can be seen as a pattern of interdependence: the ways which two people influence each other's thoughts, feelings, and actions. A relationship, whether it is cordial or conflict ridden, is "close" to the extent that people have a strong, frequent, and continuing effect on one another. Events in the relationship are multiply determined by several sets of relatively stable causal conditions: those that reside in individuals, in the fit between the two individuals, in the physical environment, and in the social environment. The causal links are causal loops: causal conditions affect patterns of interaction, and these patterns can modify the causal conditions. As causal conditions change, relationships themselves develop and change.

Relationships between persons are found to be closer if they have the same birth order, similar status, similar values and interests, and if each is close to the "ideal self" of the other. In addition, if the pair are complementary with regard to the affiliation dimension of interaction, that is, if both are friendly or both are unfriendly, then there will be a correspondence in the relationship. However, complementarity on the control dimension may have different results depending upon the situation. On some occasions, dominant persons prefer to have submissive persons to follow them and vice versa. On other occasions, dominant persons may seek the stimulation of others who are equally active, and submissive persons prefer the company of others who are equally unassertive. If persons are asked to associate with others who are unlikable and obnoxious, they may learn to live with them.

In situations where the social identity of a person is highlighted, for example, when there is intragroup conflict, persons who most strongly identify with a group will choose others according to the extent that the others personify the ideal group image and not simply on the basis of interpersonal attraction (Hogg, Cooper-Shaw, & Holzworth, 1993).

If there is a positive relationship, the members will make more equal claims on resources. However, if their claims on resources are incompatible, there will be conflict. Over time, positive relationships become more rewarding and less costly. Relationships are terminated when alternative sources of satisfaction are less costly. There may be an ebb and flow of competition, as the members are more likely to express both positive and negative feelings and have physical contact.

Intimacy increases over time, as does satisfaction. If the partner is disagreeable, fewer and less intimate topics will be discussed. If the intimate pair are of opposite sex, each member may use "secret tests" to discover what other relationships the partner has. In military settings, superiors appear to be free to approach subordinates at distances that indicate intimacy, while subordinates are not at liberty to do so.

An example of research in this area is the study by Davis (1976). Using a method associated with Jourard (1971), he conducted an acquaintance exercise to investigate the process thorough which members of a dyad negotiate the level of intimacy of their exchanges. Pairs of university students of the same sex were asked to take turns disclosing information from an intimacy-scaled list of topics. The main results were that intimacy increased as the encounters progressed, and that the matching of levels of intimacy was achieved, not as a result of mutual reciprocity, but through a process of role differentiation whereby one partner assumed the major responsibility for prescribing levels of intimacy and the other reciprocated.

A second example is the research of Yoder (1981) who introduced a laboratory procedure for developing a positive relationship between strangers for the purpose of examining the effects of a cost, in the form of a disagreement, on the continuation of that relationship. Yoder hypothesized that after a disagreement subjects will select fewer and less intimate topics to discuss with their partner, and speak for a shorter duration than subjects whose partners are in agreement. As a test, 60 female undergraduates and a female confederate exchanged information about themselves over eight trials that became increasingly more intimate. The confederate then disagreed with the subject on some issue. The subjects were again asked to select topics to discuss with the confederate. Subjects who had experienced disagreement selected fewer topics.

TRIAD

The power of a majority over a minority is especially marked in groups of size three. In this size, any minority must be that of a single person, who is thus left isolated without the support of any other group member, at least with respect to the immediate discussion.

On the other hand, the three-person situation is one in which an individual has the opportunity to control through the techniques of "divide and conquer." If the power distribution in the group is unequal, these observations may not hold, since the most powerful person may prevail, or the weakest person may form a coalition with the strongest.

The characteristic of a triad that is most often recorded is the division of two against one. In this respect, the research on triads is similar (1) to that on coalitions in general (see Chapter 10); (2) to research reporting relationships between person (P), other (O), and "X," where X is an object and not a person; and (3) to other examples of balance in triadic relations.

As with the research with "dyad" in the title, so the findings from research labelled "triad" are not necessarily limited to a situation in which only three people are present. For example, when a subject is interacting with both a male and a female in a three-person group, the gender of the other person is not found to be related to being gazed at. Similar negative results could undoubtedly be obtained in larger groups.

TASK AND STRESS

Members of a group that is successful will be more satisfied. Individual members who are successful are more likely to think that others will be. However, if a team is unsuccessful, the members are more likely to attribute the outcome to external causes—a finding that would be expected from attribution theory that predicts that favorable outcomes are more likely to be attributed to the self.

In a simulated military conflict, high information loads for group members were found to lead to tension (O'Connell, Cummings, & Huber, 1976). However, with husbands and wives, compatibility was not found to be strongly related to stress management (Burke, Firth, & McGrattan, 1974).

Those who wish to avoid stressful situations will be pleased to learn that affiliative smiling takes place in situations that involve greetings and departures, while laughter takes place in a recreational context. It may not be a surprise to learn that drinking a little alcohol while having a discussion in an experimental laboratory with a member of the opposite sex increases elation, giddiness, and happiness.

SUMMARY

As a formal definition, a role is a set of rights and duties associated with a position in a social group. However, the term role is used not only to refer to formal positions in a group, such as chairperson, secretary, or member, but also to informal positions, such as joker or scapegoat, or to identify a person by a predominant type of behavior, such as silent member or nonconformist. In addition, there are transitory dramaturgical roles, such as protagonist or audience member. Task specialization in roles increases interdependence of group members, while actor specialization creates isolation. Research on roles in larger groups concerning role conflict, leave taking, or other phenomena can also be applied to the small group.

In addition to the formal structure of a small group, an informal set of relationships usually develops to deal with aspects of group function that are not met by the formal structure. The organization of a group will vary over time, either because the appropriate structure is slow to develop or because different sets of role relationships are necessary at different phases of group growth. Persons who have the power to give rewards and punishments, and those who perform well on the task, are given high status in a group. Age, sex, and ethnicity are also taken by group members as indications of presumed task ability. These attributes lead to expectations, early in a group's life, concerning the potential contribution of a group member and relative status.

The most common set of roles in a group is a division of the leadership functions between a "task leader," with a primary concern for group productivity, and a "social-emotional leader," with a concern for intermember relations. Men have been more likely to take the task role, and women the social-emotional role.

The optimum size for many discussion groups is five members since in smaller groups individuals may feel too prominent, and in larger groups there may be fewer opportunities to speak and more control may be required. As groups increase in size, members may become less self-conscious, but they may also use less effort, with the result of lower performance.

Research on intimate relations is similar to early research on the dyad and on friendship. Relationships between intimate pairs include intimate disclosure, knowledge of each other's personal feelings, joint development of pair norms, mutual responsibility for one another's outcome, and strong mutual attraction. Relationships are generally closer if the persons have similar social characteristics and compatible personality traits.

In a triad, the characteristic pattern of division is two against one. For groups of any size, success in the task with minimal stress produces more satisfied members.

CHAPTER 6

Leadership

M. Valerie Kent

The actions and qualities of leaders have been noted since human historical records began, whether in poem or song, drama or literature. It is perhaps not surprising that, when social psychology developed as an intellectual discipline early this century, research about leadership focused on discovering the distinguishing characteristics of leaders. The outbreak of World War I created a need to identify large numbers of potential officers. Psychologists at the time, having recently devised psychometric tests, naturally used these to help in officer selection. They accepted the seemingly common-sense view that leaders were different kinds of people from followers.

THE TRAIT APPROACH

Methodology, Issues, and Evidence

Researchers studied leaders in established groups and also leaders who emerged in groups created in the laboratory by inviting previously unacquainted individuals to discuss or work together. Hundreds of studies were done, using a wide range of personality or individual difference measures. In the early research, women were generally not included—being female seemed to be regarded as a disqualifying individual difference!

It was clear in the 1940s that there was no obvious pattern of leadership qualities (Stogdill, 1948). Mann (1959) reviewed 125 studies and concluded that leaders tended to be somewhat more dominant, extraverted, intelligent, and well-adjusted, and less conservative. However, correlations were weak, and different studies showed different characteristics to be important. No one trait or set of traits appeared to be overly important.

More recently, meta-analyses of earlier studies have pointed to some consistent findings. Lord, de Vader, and Alliger (1986) looked at 27 studies and found intelligence, dominance, and stereotypical masculine characteristics (e.g., decisive, unemotional, aggressive) to be significantly related to leadership emergence.

The idea that a characteristic or set of characteristics is related to being a leader needs to be considered more fully. It implies some or all of the following:

—the trait causes leadership

—this applies generally across situations, culture, and history

—leadership qualities are inborn and cannot be learned

—leaders are different from followers.

This chapter will return to these issues of cause, generality, innateness, and distinctiveness at various points.

Even if the trait approach had been successful, other possible explanations are available in terms of the stereotypes or expectations that people have of what a leader is like. It might be that only people who fit the stereotype are appointed as leaders, or are accepted by followers, or even feel they should attempt leadership in the first place.

Lord, de Vader, and Alliger (1986) found that the success of a leader depends on achieving a match between the leaders' and followers' implicit personality theories about what makes an ideal leader. Lord and Maher (1990) have also argued that followers check the match of their implicit theories about leaders' attributes against their perceptions of a leader.

Perhaps, in seeking the qualities of leaders for so long, psychologists themselves were exhibiting the fundamental attribution bias. That is, they were seeking to explain events in terms of a leader's internal qualities rather than looking to other elements such as the situation of the group, the task, or the group members and their interactions with each other and with the leader.

In trying to identify what made a "Great Man," psychologists were looking for internal attributes rather than actual behavior. Great Women were not considered—where they existed, they were perhaps regarded by themselves and others as honorary men! Prime Minister Margaret Thatcher was sometimes called "the best man in the Cabinet," used ambiguously as both admiration and abuse. Queen Elizabeth I of England said on the eve of battle, "I know I have the body of a weak and feeble woman, but I have the heart and stomach of a king."

Some confusion exists in this area because of the difference between our information about historical figures and the data from research studies of small groups, which tend to favor democratic working on limited tasks.

Winter (1987) looked at the match between motive profiles of American presidents and their contemporary society, by looking at the content of their inaugural addresses and at other contemporary written sources. He found that presidents who received a high percentage of the vote or who ran for re-election tended to have motive profiles which matched those of the population. However, when considering how presidents were evaluated by historians, Winter noted that highly rated presidents such as Washington, Lincoln, Truman and Kennedy were discrepant from their wider society. This issue of whether leaders influence or reflect their followers will be developed throughout this chapter.

Generality

Most research did not really address the "great man/person" issue directly. Where it has done so, by looking for people who are in a series of different groups and emerge as leader often, two points became evident. First, it has long been suggested that the type of task may affect who becomes a leader. Carter and Nixon (1949) showed that different people would emerge as leaders for mechanical, clerical, and problem-solving tasks. Second, there is some recent evidence to suggest that personality may indeed play a part in leadership emergence across situations. What has changed is that this is now seen in relation to the demands on the group and the needs of the followers. Kenny and Zaccaro (1983) suggested that leaders were those able to perceive the group's needs and goals, and were able then to modify their approach. Also, recent work on individual differences looks at very different variables from the research of 30 and more years ago. In a round-robin (rotation) study where groups had to deal with four tasks (each with very different demands), Zaccaro, Foti, and Kenny (1991) wanted to see if the same people would emerge as leaders regardless of the task and the group. Another possibility was that different types of task would tend to produce different leaders. Their findings provide some evidence that personality may be related to leadership. In this case, subjects were assessed on a self-monitoring scale. Those who were consistently leaders in different tasks scored high on self-monitoring, which measures in part a tendency to attend and adjust to the immediate situation. Here, the trait associated with leadership generality appears to be flexibility.

Similarly, Leary, Robertson, Barnes, and Miller (1986) found that potential leaders varied their self-presentations to the group according to the image of effective leadership which they believed the group held.

It might be thought that intelligence would always be an advantage in leadership. Early work with groups of children showed that leaders were often rejected if their intelligence was more than two standard deviations above the norm (Hollingworth, 1942). She suggested that these leaders were perceived to be too different. A leader with high intelligence but a nondirective style may overwhelm a group with ideas, or may be regarded as not giving enough guidance (Fiedler, 1987). Fiedler also found that intelligence does enhance leader effectiveness where the leader is directive, the group is supportive, and the group environment is free of stress.

DEFINITIONS

It is difficult to study a concept which is not clearly defined. However, the very definition of leadership occupies an entire chapter of Bass's recent handbook (1990). It is followed by a chapter on typologies and taxonomies of leadership. A much briefer discussion is possible here.

A leader has been seen as the person who most helps the group to achieve its goals or objectives. The leader may also set those goals, however. In taking the group to its goal, the group must also be kept intact and motivated. The work of Bales on informal discussion groups showed that, over time, two different types of leader behavior may emerge. One concentrates on the task—coming up with ideas, talking a lot, and being seen by the others as the leader. The other, whom Bales called the socio-emotional leader, while also contributing to the task, was the person who kept the group together, dealing with or deflecting tension (Bales & Slater, 1955). This was early evidence of what have become clearly identified as the two main aspects of leadership: that the leader should direct the group to achieve its goals and also maintain the members in harmony with one another.

We now face three of the major issues in this research area.

First, the idea that the focus should be on the leadership process rather than on the qualities of leaders: how do groups get things done and also survive?

Second, there are two major factors: concern for the task, and concern for the group members. Are they incompatible? Can the same person do either, according to the circumstances of the group? Are the qualities needed for task leadership unlikely to exist in the socio-emotional leader? Bales found the two roles to separate out only over time, when the task was putting strain on the group, which suggests that the group members began to act differently according to the demands of the situation. This distinction between these two roles continues to be seen as the most appropriate when the leadership function splits (Latham, 1987).

Third, when people behave in a more task-oriented manner, or else in a way which shows more concern for group members, are these differences reflections of underlying personality? Might the differences in behavior be due to learning? If the behavior can be learned, does this have the same result for the group as "natural" task or social-emotional leadership?

Lippitt and White (1943) conducted what is now regarded as a classic study. The same individuals acted as leaders in different boys' groups, adopting a different style in different groups. In some, they were authoritarian, controlling what went on in carrying out the group task (mask-making). In others, they were democratic, generating an open communication style. A third style, laissez faire, just let the group get on with it. The democratic style led to the best masks and the best intragroup relations. The authoritarian-led groups were more hostile, scapegoating, and unlikely to carry on without supervision. They produced the most masks but these were judged to be of poorer quality. Thus, the leader's style was seen as important rather than personality. Later research, to be discussed below, suggests that this type of open-ended unstructured task is generally likely to be done better under democratic leadership, which includes consideration for the followers.

Consequences of Leader Behavior/Criteria for Measurement

Most early research focused on the differences between leaders and followers. Whether in the real world of organizations, politics, or great historical figures, the emphasis was on what made these people different. Equally, in laboratory studies of small informal task or discussion groups, the focus was on who was influential or rated as leader.

Another kind of difference has also been examined, to a lesser extent, although it is perhaps more important. This is: what is the difference between an effective leader and an ineffective leader? In these terms, an effective leader would help the group to achieve its primary goal and, if the group is to endure, to maintain the morale and commitment of its members. Effectiveness is very important, and Hogan, Curphy, and Hogan (1994) discuss applications of leadership effectiveness research in organizations and other "real world" settings.

It is worth asking just who says the behavior is effective, especially when looking at leaders in organizations, in politics, or in history. History may be written from the perspective of the winners, and success may be defined in short-term or inappropriate ways. As already noted, a popular president may appear effective at the time, but those seen as effective by historians, in terms of their long-term influence, were less in tune with their contemporaries (Winter, 1987).

The Basis of Power

Leaders do not all have the same basis for power. In the laboratory, groups of strangers are brought together. There is no initial role differentiation; the point is to see how that happens. The group process is stripped bare of history, of prior relationships, and of any external power base. In the world outside, leadership may be underpinned by many different types of power. French and Raven (1959) outlined the following: coercive (power to reward or punish), referent, expert, and legitimate. In legitimate power, the leader has gained that status as the result of an accepted procedure, for example, election by majority, electoral college, heredity, rotation, or seniority.

Leaders who are seen by their group to have usurped power have less support from their groups than when power is seen to be legitimate (Wilke, de Boer, & Liebrand, 1986). Other researchers have compared different ways of achieving power legitimately, usually by manipulating the laboratory group situation so that some groups believe that the person who is announced to be leader has been elected to that position, while others are told that the leader has been appointed by the experimenter. In a similar manner, Hollander and Julian (1970) led group leaders to believe that they had been either elected or appointed. Those who believed that they had been chosen by the group were more likely to suggest solutions to the problem task that were different from the ideas of the other members. They also believed they were more competent at the task. This is important, as it indicates that the source of the leader's power affects the leader's own behavior and beliefs, not merely those of the followers.

However, in a parallel fashion, followers also believe that elected leaders are more competent than leaders appointed by the experimenter, according to a study of discussion groups of university students by Ben-Yoav, Hollander, and Carnevale (1983). They were also perceived as more interested in the task and more responsive to followers.

Hinkin and Schriesheim (1989) measured (1) satisfaction with supervision and (2) the five bases of social power experienced by a range of people, including employees at a psychiatric hospital and part-time MBA students. Across the combined samples, the use of expert and referent power was significantly related to satisfaction. There was a weaker relation between satisfaction and reward or legitimate power. As might have been expected, coercive power led to negative responses. In the real world, it may in practice be difficult to separate several types of power which may co-exist (Podsakoff & Schriesheim, 1985).

Leadership as a Process of Influence

Many have defined leadership as a process of influence. Homans (1961), far from seeing leaders and followers as distinct, argued that the process was a transaction; that everyone influenced everyone else to some extent, and the person with the most influence is the one seen as the leader.

A crucial aspect of this view is that followers are important. Sanford (1950) argued almost 50 years ago that followers were arguably the crucial component in leadership: "Not only is it the follower who accepts or rejects leadership, but it is the follower who *perceives* both the leader and the situation and reacts in terms of what he perceives (p. 4)."

Similarly, Merei (1949), in a study of nursery school children, found that a newly introduced "dominant personality" older child did not just take over a group of "submissive personality" children. First, they fitted in with the group's already established practice, perhaps telling them to do what they would have done anyway. Another strategy was to claim that all the toys belonged to them, but then go on to say that the others were allowed to continue playing with them. Only gradually did they impose changes.

Idiosyncrasy Credit

Hollander's view of leadership also focuses on influence. He pointed out that, since leaders introduce new ideas, any theory must explain how leaders are able to influence others from what may be seen by the group as a deviant position. He argued from a social exchange viewpoint. Group members incur costs and receive rewards in interaction; people will seek to maximize their outcomes. In this view, being influenced by others is a cost, being influential is rewarding. The leader is the person who has most "credit" from conforming to group needs and demands, and hence can "spend" from this "account" on innovation which is costly (Hollander, 1958). In the refinement of this view over 30 years, this conceptualization has been developed, fitting very well with the increasing emphasis being placed on followers' perceptions of leaders—their implicit theories of leadership (Hollander, 1992). The leader is also seen as having latitude to bring about change as a function of "followers' perceptions of the leader's competence and signs of loyalty that engender trust. This credit-building process, and its consequences, resonate with modern-day attributional concepts" (Hollander, 1992, p. 72).

This view differs radically from that of the influential deviate, the persuasive minority (see Chapter 4). In that view, minorities (here, leaders) are influential because of their behavioral style (Moscovici & Paicheler, 1983). Their very distinctiveness and their consistency, while being fair in other respects, impresses followers and gives rise to "conversion," based on a belief that this person is an expert who really understands how things work. Thus we can see that minority influence is based on expert power.

It may be, however, that while influential, minorities are not seen as leaders of the group unless they also have legitimate power. Moscovici's idea may really be a subset of Hollander's, emphasizing the perceived competence element and disregarding the effect of perceived group loyalty. These two views are also discussed in Chapter 4.

SITUATIONAL VARIABLES

Researchers, unable to pin down any clear individual characteristics which were uniquely associated with leaders, also looked at what aspects of the situation might determine leadership. The argument here was that leaders arise to suit the zeitgeist—the spirit of the time. Here, the circumstances could be said to create the leader rather than the other way around.

The situation is generally defined very broadly, and research covers a range of issues, some of which are discussed more fully in other chapters.

Communication Networks

There is a long history of studying small groups whose pattern of internal communication is controlled by the researcher (Shaw, 1981). As an overall conclusion, groups with a clearly central person are more productive, detect fewer errors, and have lowest overall morale. More decentralized networks have higher morale and are better able to deal with complex problems than centralized networks (see also Chapter 7). It is worth remembering that in the real world, people may actively seek the central position in a group. Research suggests that these people are more likely to score highly on tests of internal control, and to have had other leadership experience (Hiers & Heckel, 1977).

Other important situational factors include:

—*type of power* available to the leader

—*reasons for group membership*: cohesiveness and sense of social identity (Hogg, 1992)

—*group composition*: what kinds of people, including whether single- or mixed-sex groups

—*type of task*: simple, complex, open-ended

—*urgency of task*.

Leading in a Crisis

When leaders are under threat from within the group, they may, in order to maintain their position, emphasize the threat posed by external groups in order to survive. This is familiar in political leadership, and has been demonstrated in research by Rabbie and Bekkers (1978). Using a union-management simulation, they found that leaders who could easily be deposed by the group were more likely to choose a competitive strategy in bargaining with the other side.

Faced with crisis, groups seek influence from a leader, especially an elected leader. Failure to resolve the problem leads to discontent and the leader's removal if this is within the group's power (Hollander, Fallon, & Edwards, 1977).

Followers and Leaders

Neither trait nor situational approaches took account of the follower as an active element in group dynamics. The approach is still a simple kind of determinism, with factors in the situation now regarded as crucial. One has to consider why people are in the group and what the consequences are for them if the group fails in its task or if they wish to leave the group. Social exchange is important, as is a sense of equity. Followers will reduce their endorsement of a leader who is perceived to act unfairly (Hollander & Julian, 1970).

Arguably, followers are the crucial element in leadership. Although Sanford pointed this out many years ago, research still tends to ignore the role of the follower in the leadership process. Followers prefer democratic leadership on the whole (Heilman, Hornstein, Cage, & Herschlag, 1984), and those who are high on internal rather than external control prefer participatory leadership and are less likely to accept the leader's demands (Rucker & King, 1985). However, more direction from the leader will be followed by those who are less competent at the task (Price & Garland, 1981a, 1981b), or if there is a crisis.

Followers will react not only to the leader's behavior, but also to the perceived authority and legitimacy of the leader. Followers' reactions will also be affected by why they became part of the group in the first place, and the continuing level of cohesiveness of the group (Hogg, 1992).

A person's membership of a work group or organization has at least some different elements from being in a group of friends or belonging to a particular nation. Similarly, the leader in such groups may have very different power bases. Much social psychology research has looked at the emergent leader from a group of randomly selected individuals with no prior acquaintance. Arguably the person who emerges will be the person who is perceived by followers to help the group gain the best outcomes at either the lowest cost to the group, or at least the most equitable outcome for members. In the main, this kind of research will tend to favor democratic leadership styles.

Participation Rates

It has been widely observed that the person who is seen to be the leader is also the person who talks the most—little place here for the strong, silent type beloved of the movies (Lord & Alliger, 1985; Stein & Heller, 1983). In the early work of Bales, talking the most was one index found to relate strongly to task leadership. Some studies have manipulated who talked most, and found that even when participation rates are increased or decreased artificially according to the researcher's schedule, followers would rate the person who talked most as the leader. In a problem-solving group, a key suggestion was less likely to be accepted from a low participant than if it came from a high participant (Riecken, 1958).

There seem to be five possible explanations, as follows.

1. The person who talks most may be reducing the ambiguity of the situation for the others, clarifying the situation, and reducing embarrassment.

2. The high participant (HP) may be allowed to talk most because of pluralistic ignorance—all the others may doubt the validity of the ideas but not like to say so: this is most likely to affect short-term laboratory groups although, at the other extreme, it may be manifested as Groupthink (Janis, 1982), where each person is kept unaware of the dissent of others and is too afraid to disagree with the dominant participant (see also, Chapter 9).

3. The behavioral style of the person who talks a lot may lead to an attribution of competence. Group members may be subject to a minority influence effect, genuinely believing that high participation is a reflection of competence.

4. The high participant may talk most because he or she knows a lot.

5. The others are participating less because they believe that the high participant is right and so allow him or her to speak. This may occur in long-term groups rather than in the laboratory, although in the laboratory, when people have been introduced to a group as expert, they are more influential.

Thus, even though there is a consistent finding that leaders have high participation rates, the reasons for this may differ. Leaders are not simply talkative, although it is reasonable to assume that they do not find that the costs of talking outweigh the benefits. In the transactional, mutual influence view, even a very shy person might talk a lot on a subject where the group's survival might depend on his or her own expertise. A group might attend to a person with a severe speech impediment, who might normally gain little attention, if that person were the only one who knew how to escape from a burning building. Participation rate may be an indicator of who is leading a group, but it does not explain why they are doing so.

CONTINGENCY APPROACHES

Dissatisfaction with the simplistic solutions which had been sought but not found in trait or situational approaches led to more complex theorizing. The suggestion was that leadership is the result of the interaction of both individual and situational factors. Whether or not particular people became leaders would be contingent upon the way their own qualities fitted the situational demands. A similar view was taken for the effectiveness of leadership: effective leadership was contingent upon both personal qualities and situational variables. Is there a most effective style for leaders, or is the effectiveness of the style dependent on the situation (Blake & Mouton, 1982)?

The Ohio State studies of leadership identified two main factors of leadership behavior: initiation of structure and consideration (Stogdill, 1974). To measure these, the Leader Behavior Description Questionnaire (LBDQ) was developed. It is a 150-item rating scale to be completed by followers. The two factors are similar to the ideas of task and socio-emotional leadership. In Stogdill's model, a person has a score on each factor; they are not polar opposites, and a person may score highly on both. Indeed, Stogdill thought such a profile would be associated with the best leaders. Sorrentino and Field (1986) found that leaders who were elected after five weeks of testing in problem-solving groups had scored highly throughout on both consideration and initiation of structure. People who score highly on consideration will do well in different situations from high scorers on initiating structure.

A further significant point in this approach is that the individual difference factors are described in terms of leader behavior, as seen by group members. Thus, the idea that it is inherent personality is not assumed. A leader may have learned to behave in this way.

Equally, however, followers' questionnaire scores may not reflect actual leader behavior. They may even say more about followers' theories about what constitutes a good leader than what a leader does. In having a two-factor model, Stogdill's work may sit well with recent suggestions that good leaders are flexible and can modify their behavior according to situational demands.

The more widely researched contingency model is that of Fiedler (1978), which has tended to dominate the leadership literature for the past three decades. Like Stogdill, Fiedler has also developed his own measure to assess the individual difference variable in the leadership process. Neither researcher uses the traditional personality measures which were part of earlier studies of leadership.

Fiedler's measure is based on the leader's perceptions of the person he or she has least liked to work with—the Least Preferred Co-worker (LPC). Using a leader's responses to a standardized set of bipolar adjectives (e.g., friendly-unfriendly) on a seven-point rating scale, an overall LPC score is calculated. If the LPC score is high—that is, the leader rates even the least-preferred co-worker rather highly—the leader is said to have a relatively permissive, relationship-oriented approach. If the score is low, the leader is said to prefer to be controlling and task-oriented.

The LPC is the "individual difference" or trait aspect of Fiedler's model. The situational element is conceptualized in terms of the actual level of situational control of the leader. Situational control has three dimensions, in the following descending order of importance.

1. The quality of leader-member relations. With good relations, situational control is greater.

Table 6.1
The Relationship between Situational Control and Effectiveness of Leadership
Style: A Simplified Table Based on Fiedler's Contingency Model of Leadership

Level of situational control	Effective leadership style
High: Good relations; structured task; high position power	Controlling (Low LPC)
Intermediate: Good relations and unstructured task OR poor relations and structured task	Permissive (High LPC)
Low: Bad relations; unstructured task; low position power	Controlling (Low LPC)

2. The nature of the task. Structured tasks allow more situational control than unstructured tasks.

3. Position power. The more power the leader has to fall back on if necessary, the greater the situational control.

Each of these variables is, like LPC, seen as dichotomous. In a situation with highest control, all three will be high. Where relations are bad, the task is unstructured, and position power is weak, situational control is lowest. There are eight possible combinations, and Fiedler refers to each category as an octant. A simplified version of the model is shown in Table 6.1.

The criterion variable for Fiedler's model is whether or not the leader is effective in the situation. The contingency model finds that where the leader has high situational control—that is, the group atmosphere is good, the task is structured, and the leader has an externally supported power base—then task-oriented leadership is more effective. Equally, task orientation is the effective style when situational control is weak—poor group atmosphere, unstructured task, and little position power. It is in areas of intermediate situational control that the high LPC, relationship-oriented leader is the more effective. Where the atmosphere is good and the task open-ended, the high LPC leader is better. This probably typifies many laboratory experiments on group discussions, as well as the Lippitt and White study of boys making masks.

However, there is another sort of intermediate control, where the relationships are not good, but the task is structured and its demands clear-cut. Here, again, a style which considers people rather than emphasizing the task works better. The group maintenance function is more important than task completion, since the latter can more or less look after itself. Again, this probably is the case for most laboratory task groups, where relationships have not been built up but the experimenter is imposing task demands. Overall, laboratory experiments would tend to fall in the area of intermediate control and thus favor relationship-oriented leaders.

Hundreds of studies have been carried out to examine the effects of the interaction of LPC and the eight types of situational control. The dependent measure is the effectiveness of leadership, assessed by how well the group achieves its primary goals. Fiedler's early work looked at a wide range of real-life male groups—in industry and in the Belgian Navy, for example— and was certainly not confined to the laboratory. Subsequently, informal groups with emergent leaders and groups which included female leaders were also studied (Schneier & Goktepe, 1983).

On the whole, individual studies and also meta-analyses of the studies have offered support for his model (Peters, Hartke, & Pohlmann, 1985; Strube & Garcia, 1981). Some have suggested that the model works better if the situational control variables are ranked in a different order, with power more important than task structure (Singh, Bohra, & Dalal, 1979). There has also been some questioning of the test-retest reliability of the LPC measure (Rice, 1978).

The approaches of both Stogdill and Fiedler suggest the importance of a group member/maintenance variable and a task/control variable, as Bales had found and as Hollander's theory also implies. Fiedler, however, sees these concepts as being at opposite ends of a unidimensional scale, whereas in Stogdill's model they are independent factors. There are other differences between these two contingency approaches. The LPC assesses the leader's perceptions, whereas Stogdill looks at group members' perceptions of the leader's behavior. Furthermore, the LPC score is usually seen as reflecting an underlying unchanging tendency, rather than as a style which can be learned and used according to circumstances.

A useful aspect of Fiedler's model is its capacity to predict changes in effectiveness when a leader's actions affect situational control. The leader may turn a confused and unstructured task into one which is clear and structured. Group relations may be changed from bad to good, or vice versa. The prediction, confirmed by many studies, is that the leader will then not continue to be effective because the style which was appropriate for a certain level of situational control will no longer be what is required. In Fiedler's terms, the level of situational control and the leader's LPC score no longer "match." A logical extension of this point is that some training schemes for leaders may actually make them less effective, if a single style of "good leadership" is taught without any regard to the leader's preferred style. This was confirmed in a study of ROTC cadets (Chemers, Rice, Sundstrom, & Butler, 1975).

Leader Match Training

Fiedler assumes that training for leadership should involve three elements (Fiedler & Mahar, 1979). People should learn:

—to recognize their preferred leadership style (either task-oriented or relationship-oriented)

—to understand the favorableness of the situation

—to work out how to find a better match between the two.

This largely means teaching people to recognize and modify their situational control. He does not feel that training should be aimed at modifying the individual difference variable as reflected by the LPC score, because this is much more difficult to change.

His six- to eight-hour training program teaches people how to change situational control. They may, for example, change the group atmosphere, by being more or less approachable or friendly. A person might also make the task more or less structured, again to suit their preferred level of permissiveness or control.

Other researchers have predicted that where the leader's LPC does not match the prevailing situation, the leader will suffer stress. For example, a study of university administrators measured their LPC scores and their perceptions of their situational control. Those who were, in Fiedler's terms, in an inappropriate job had higher stress scores and also reported more physical ill health than those who were well matched to their work (Chemers, Hays, Rhodewalt, & Wysocki, 1985).

Rice and Kastenbaum (1983) have suggested that Leader Match Training works because leaders are sensitized to relevant aspects of their situation, and learn that it is possible to change it. This idea would serve to support the emerging notion that if there is a general quality of effective leaders, it is likely to be found in their ability to be flexible and adaptable when necessary.

GENDER

For many years, studies of leadership tended to be of all-male groups, but later studies included mixed but still randomly selected groups. This led to the impression that females were not likely to be leaders, since in mixed groups males tended to emerge as the leader. There may be several reasons for this. As Hollander and Yoder (1980) pointed out, males were more likely to have group experience, so were more likely to engage in leadership behaviors. Females, aware of their relative lack of group experience, may accept their influence attempts. This may be heightened where the group task appears to favor male skills. Where female skills are engaged, females may be accepted. Making a comparison between females who had achieved leadership positions and male leaders showed that there were few differences (Hollander, 1985).

The following questions must be addressed.

—Do males and females behave similarly in groups?

—How are the behavior of males and females perceived and evaluated by other group members?

—How are the successes and failures of male and female leaders perceived?

—Are the group maintenance and task orientation elements synonymous with femaleness and maleness respectively?

—What, so far, are the overall conclusions about women and leadership?

Eagly and her colleagues have carried out meta-analyses on women and leadership, looking at leader emergence, style, and effectiveness. Eagly and Johnson (1990) found that women tended to lead more democratically than men, which fits the stereotypes about women's concern for feeling and their interpersonal skills. On the other hand, men and women in organizations were equally likely to be task-oriented or relationship-oriented. This may reflect selection policies in terms of the job that needs to be done.

Eagly, Makhijani, and Klonsky (1992) analyzed data from 60 studies and found that the evaluation of women as leaders was only slightly less positive than the evaluations of men. Interestingly, negative evaluations were more likely to arise where the women adopted a stereotypically masculine style.

An experiment by Ridgeway (1982) used male and female accomplices who offered the same suggestions to the groups of subjects in which they were placed, but used different styles. She found that their interventions in mixed-sex groups were effective if oriented to the task and made by a male accomplice, or oriented to relationships and made by a female accomplice. The anti-stereotype interventions were rejected. Similarly, Butler and Geis (1990) found that when male accomplices acted in a cordial but assertive manner in mixed-sex groups of students, their interventions were favorably received, with few negative responses. Group members reacted more negatively and with fewer positive responses to female accomplices acting in the same way. Butler and Geis suggest that the devaluation of female leadership is not merely the result of individual bias but is also supported by social mechanisms in the group.

Perhaps females have learned to manipulate these stereotypical expectations successfully. Forsyth, Schlenker, Leary, and McCown (1985) found that leaders' self-presentations were mainly a result of their own sex-role stereotypes rather than factors in the situation. Males stressed their task and social influence skills, while females pointed to their abilities on interpersonal and socio-emotional dimensions.

Other differences have been found in relation to gender. These are not necessarily inevitable, but may reflect current social values. For example, Nemeth, Endicott, and Wachtler (1976) studied the contributions of members of simulated juries to the deliberations and to the ultimate decisions.

They found that differences in behavior were not noticeable, nor were females in fact less influential. However, the inputs made by women were evaluated less favorably than those of men, in the eyes of both male and female jurors.

In terms of group success or failure, Rice, Bender, and Vitters (1980) studied experimental groups confronted with a task, and found that where the group was led by a female and succeeded, success was attributed to the group. For a male leader, it was attributed to the male's leadership qualities. Conversely, failure was blamed on the female leader but attributed to circumstance by the followers of a male leader.

GROUP DYNAMICS AND LEADERSHIP

Some of the studies cited in the preceding section looked at the behavior of male and female leaders and how it is seen by group members. Johnson (1992) has argued that much more such work on group dynamics is needed if we are to understand the ways in which gender affects leadership. Stogdill and Fiedler, although they have both made a great contribution to an understanding of leadership, have also both been criticized (as have other researchers) for neglecting to study the dynamics of group interaction. Despite all the early efforts to emphasize the role and power of followers, this is not really reflected in the research.

People in interaction can be studied using the twelve-category system developed by Bales (1950) for coding observations of the interactions of group members. This system, called Interaction Process Analysis, is described more fully in Chapter 7. Each group member can be included, not just the leaders. The procedure has been used to look at the interaction of men and women in groups, such as the work on juries by Nemeth, Endicott, and Wachtler (1976).

Bales has, more recently, developed a three-factor model for assessing interaction, called "SYMLOG," which is discussed in detail in Chapters 2 and 7. The three dimensions are:

—*Upward-Downward* (dominant versus submissive),

—*Positive-Negative* (friendly versus unfriendly), and

—*Forward-Backward* (accepting versus opposing the task orientation of established authority).

These three factors are seen by Bales and his colleagues to encapsulate all the elements of research on group dynamics and leadership which have arisen during the half century since Bales began work in this area (Bales & Cohen, 1979; Hare, 1989).

In an unpublished paper, Bales (1987) has argued that these three factors are in fact very similar to those described in Fiedler's model as the dimensions of situational favorableness. A questionnaire has been developed which can be answered by every group member about themselves, other members, the leader, or their ideal group member or leader. Norms are being developed for various kinds of groups so that people can, for example, see how their profile matches the ideal. The SYMLOG training program suggests ways in which group members can move their position in a three-dimensional space in a manner which will help the functioning of the group. The assumption here is certainly that people can learn to behave differently in the light of feedback both from their group and from the expertise of trainers. Also, they can move on any one or more of the three dimensions: these factors, like Stogdill's, are not mutually exclusive. If, as Bales suggests, they actually map onto Fiedler's dimensions of situational favorableness, rather than relating to individual difference variables, then it would appear that at the end of the twentieth century some common tentative conclusions about leadership are forming, even though many issues must continue to be debated.

SUMMARY

Research on leadership has moved from a search for the characteristics which differentiate between leaders and followers. Situational factors have been identified which may have important effects on who becomes a leader or how effective their leadership attempts may be.

Both task-related and relationship-oriented elements of leadership are important, and they may be undertaken by different people in some circumstances. The debate as to whether these elements are rooted in personality or simply learned behavior is not finally resolved.

Individual difference variables in leadership have not been entirely rejected but have been refined. In addition to Stogdill's concepts of Initiating Structure and Consideration, and Fiedler's Least Preferred Co-worker score, other individual differences have emerged as important. Most interesting here are the findings that people who consistently emerge as leaders are highly flexible and adaptable.

Groups which are large, centralized, competitive, or authoritarian tend to be productive in the short-term but have low morale and poor interpersonal relations. Small groups, those with a decentralized communication system, those which are cooperative and democratic have higher morale, better interpersonal relations, and better output in the long run.

People's implicit leadership theories are also receiving attention, and these may help to explain some gender and personality effects. Followers are still a neglected topic of study, and there is a need for more work on the internal dynamics of groups.

PART IV

Group Process

CHAPTER 7

Social Interaction

Martin F. Davies

At a very basic level, social interaction can be categorized in terms of its form and content. The *form* of the interaction can be described in terms of: *communication modality*—verbal (the spoken message) or nonverbal (gestures, eye contact, facial expression, etc.); *participation rate*—the amount of communication by each group member; and *communication network*—who is communicating to whom. The *content* of interactions is more difficult to identify, and there are a number of different schemes for analyzing social interaction. One common distinction, however, is between *task activity* (directed toward achieving the group's goal) and *socio-emotional activity* (directed toward the resolution of personal, interpersonal, or group problems).

THE FORM OF SOCIAL INTERACTION

Communication Modality

Clearly, a great deal of interaction in groups consists of people talking to each other (verbal behavior). Until the 1960s, most research on social interaction was concerned with verbal communications and the content of such communications. Since the 1960s, a great deal of research has been carried out on nonverbal communication. Nonverbal behavior is especially

This chapter is based partly on M. F. Davies (1994), "Social interaction," in A. P. Hare, H. H. Blumberg, M. F. Davies, & M. V. Kent, *Small group research: A handbook* (Norwood, NJ: Ablex, pp. 169–193). Reprinted with permission from Ablex Publishing Corporation.

Table 7.1
Dimensions of Verbal Behavior, Nonverbal Behavior, and Group Behavior

VERBAL BEHAVIOR (Osgood, et al., 1957)	NONVERBAL BEHAVIOR (Mehrabian, 1969)	GROUP BEHAVIOR (Bales & Cohen, 1979)
(1) EVALUATION e.g. Good-Bad Pleasant-Unpleasant	(1) IMMEDIACY e.g. Forward lean Direct orientation	(1) POSITIVE-NEGATIVE e.g. Friendly-Unfriendly
(2) POTENCY e.g. Strong-Weak Heavy-Light	(2) RELAXATION e.g. Sideways lean Relaxed posture	(2) UPWARD-DOWNWARD e.g. Dominant-Submissive
(3) ACTIVITY e.g. Active-Passive Fast-Slow	(3) ACTIVITY e.g. Gesticulating Speech rate	(3) FORWARD-BACKWARD e.g. Task oriented-Expressive Conforming-Nonconforming

interesting because it is less consciously controlled and it may contradict verbal behavior. The nonverbal message may, in some circumstances, be more important in conveying information than the spoken message. Mehrabian and Weiner (1967), for example, argue that the face is trusted the most, tone of voice trusted next, and the spoken words are trusted the least.

In general, there appear to be three dimensions underlying all forms of communication. Analysis of the "meaning of meaning" (Osgood, Suci, & Tannenbaum, 1957) indicates that verbal communications can be defined in terms of *evaluation, potency* (or control), and *activity* dimensions. Similarly, analysis of nonverbal behavior (Mehrabian, 1969) suggests three dimensions: *immediacy* (liking/disliking), *activity* (responsiveness/unresponsiveness), and *relaxation* (indicating status differences). These dimensions of verbal and nonverbal behavior can be mapped onto the three SYMLOG dimensions of group behavior (outlined in Chapter 2) as shown in Table 7.1. Note that the nonverbal dimension of *relaxation* does not seem to correspond with the verbal dimension of *potency* or with the SYMLOG dimension *upward-downward*. This is because Mehrabian was concerned with status in an *existing* hierarchy. When people are trying to *establish* dominance, the nonverbal patterns are different. Upward, dominant nonverbal behavior is shown by greater eye contact when speaking, a direct and erect posture, and a loud voice. Positive, friendly behavior is conveyed by frequent looking at the other person, an open and relaxed posture, a close interpersonal distance, more touching, and a warm tone of voice; but perhaps the most important indicator of friendliness is facial expression—particularly smiling. Forward, task-oriented behavior is indicated by more gazing and a direct but relaxed posture.

Nonverbal behavior serves five main functions (Patterson, 1982): (1) *providing information* about feelings and attitudes, for example, communicating liking or status; (2) *regulating interactions* such as indicating when someone is going to start or stop speaking; (3) *expressing intimacy*, for example, by touching or gazing intently; (4) *exercising control*, for example, establishing dominance by eye contact or posture; (5) *facilitating goal attainment* when working together, for example, by pointing.

Different parts of the body act as different channels of communication. The main channels are gaze and eye contact, facial expression, posture, gestures, touch, spatial behavior (for research on interpersonal distance, see Chapter 1), and tone of voice. Communication via a number of channels may combine to give a particularly clear meaning.

Gaze and Eye Contact. The eyes are perhaps the most important channel for nonverbal interpersonal communication. In two-person interactions, people gaze at each other for about 61% of the time, although only 31% of the time involves mutual eye contact (Argyle & Ingham, 1972). There are a number of distinctions to be made here. First, the term "gaze" is used when only one person is looking at another person; the term "eye contact" is used when both people are gazing at each other at the same time. Second, there is the distinction between a "look" and a "stare." A "look" involves a dynamic eye presentation, whereas a "stare" involves a more static eye presentation. A stare may be taken as a cue to approach or avoidance depending on the context. For example, Ellsworth, Carlsmith, and Henson (1972) found that drivers waiting at an intersection moved on more quickly when they were stared at by a pedestrian standing at the intersection.

As with nonverbal behavior in general, research on gaze and eye contact concludes that gaze can be an indicator of dominance, interest, and can serve as a regulator of interaction by indicating that it is time for someone to start or stop speaking (Kleinke, 1986). An obvious exception is that persons without sight need to rely on other cues (Rutter & Stephenson, 1979).

A dominant person tends to look more at another person while speaking; a less dominant person tends to look more while listening. This *visual dominance* can result from personality traits, expertise with the task, or social status. Women engage in more eye contact than men, but they are less likely to stare and tend to avoid the gaze of others (Duncan, 1969). Henley (1977) suggests that this pattern of looking reflects the lower status accorded to women than to men.

Eye contact together with other nonverbal indicators of closeness, such as physical proximity or smiling, results in more positive evaluations and increased intimacy. Thus, people look more frequently but do not stare at others whom they like (Exline & Winters, 1965), and amount of gazing at the other person is an indicator of the intimacy level of the encounter (Rubin, 1970).

As well as a signal for starting conversations, looking regulates the subsequent interaction. A listener will look at the speaker in order to "take the floor," and a speaker will look at a listener when s/he is about to stop talking. However, successfully taking or yielding the floor requires a subtle combination of head nods, direction of looking, and speech pauses (Duncan, Brunner, & Fiske, 1979).

Facial Expression. Facial expressions that represent the various combinations of dominant, positive, and forward behavior, and their opposites, can be identified. Generally, only six emotions can be reliably identified from *posed* facial expressions—happiness, surprise, fear, anger, sadness, and disgust (Ekman, 1982). *Spontaneous* facial expressions, however, are not as easily identified (Wagner, MacDonald, & Manstead, 1986).

Happiness is the most accurately identified emotion, and smiling is one of the most clear-cut facial expressions, as well as being one of the most widely researched. In addition to expressing happiness, smiling conveys friendliness and is a potent reinforcer of another person's actions, especially talking. The social nature of smiling was confirmed by Kraut and Johnston (1979), who reported a series of observations in everyday settings as shown in Figure 7.1. In a bowling alley, bowlers smiled more when looking at their companions, but not necessarily after scoring a spare or a strike. At hockey games, fans showed more smiling both when they were socially involved, and following outcomes favorable to their team. Pedestrians were much more likely to smile when interacting with others, but only slightly more likely to smile in good weather than in bad weather.

Lockard, Fahrenbruch, Smith, and Morgan (1977) observed the smiling and laughter of pairs of adults in social situations that included goal-oriented interactions, work breaks, chance encounters, and leisure episodes. They concluded that their data support the hypothesis that the human smile has its origin in the silent bared-teeth submissive grimace of primates, and that the facial expression accompanying laughter evolved from the relaxed open-mouth display of play. Affiliative smiling occurred in greeting and departure interactions, whereas frank laughter was almost exclusively seen in a recreational context.

Posture, Gesture, and Touch. As with facial expression, posture, gesture, and touch, alone or together, can be used to communicate all combinations of dominant, positive, and forward behavior. For example, Bond and Shiraishi (1974) conducted a study in Japan in which student volunteers were interviewed by confederates who leaned forward 20 degrees in half of the interviews and leaned backward 20 degrees in the other half. The forward-leaning interviewers appeared more polite and more flexible (not in the literal sense!) than the backward-leaners. Posture can also convey status relationships. A higher-status person adopts a more open and relaxed posture, whereas a lower-status person will adopt a more closed and rigid posture.

Figure 7.1
The Social Nature of Smiling

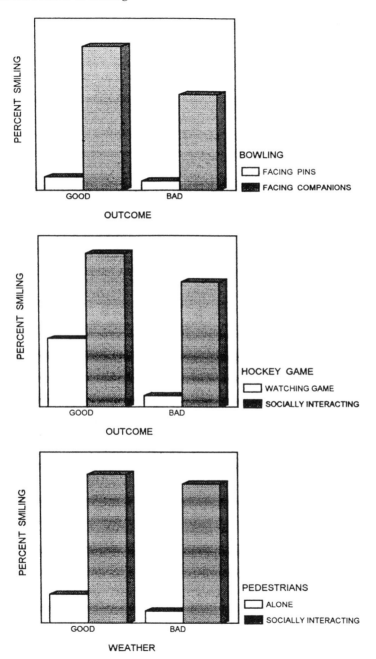

Observing pairs of college students, Bull and Brown (1977) were interested in postural changes associated with the introduction of new information into a conversation. They observed that postural shifts involving at least half of the body indicated a shift in the talking point, whereas smaller movements were associated with the specific type of speech they preceded (e.g., question, answer). Persons who assume the same posture and "mirror" each other in a social setting are generally more involved in the interaction and like one another more (LaFrance, 1979).

Gestures can be "illustrators" (complementing what is being said), "emblems" (substituting for speech, such as the thumbs-up signal), or "batons" (emphasizing points while speaking). McNeill (1985) suggests that speech and gestures are part of the same language system, such that gestures are manifestations of inner speech just as overt speech is the usual external manifestation. Gestures are also used by listeners as "back-channel" responses (telling the speaker that they are still listening—especially nodding and shaking the head) and as regulators of conversation, such as turning the head away before replying to a question, or raising a hand to claim the floor. Originally, Condon and Ogston (1966) suggested that there is a very fine degree of *interactional synchrony* for body movements during conversation. This "gestural dance" between speaker and listener was found to be closely linked to speech. However, a reappraisal of the phenomenon by McDowall (1978) suggested that the original results could have been due to chance, and McDowall was unable to find significant degrees of synchrony in either strangers or friends.

Although the member of a pair who initiates touching is generally more dominant or of higher status, and touch may be important in securing compliance to a request, most of the research on touch deals with it in reference to the positive-negative dimension of behavior. A person's sex is an especially important variable in reactions to touch (Henley, 1977). Women like being touched more than men, but touch from an opposite-sex stranger is considered unpleasant by women, whereas men find touch from a same-sex stranger unpleasant (Stier & Hall, 1984). In a medical setting, Whitcher and Fisher (1979) found that female patients benefited therapeutically from increased touching by nurses, whereas male patients were affected adversely. A sex-role explanation was proposed for these findings: females are socialized to be comfortable with dependency and thus experience nurse-patient touch as a sign of caring and warmth, whereas males are socialized to be uncomfortable with dependency and experience nurse-patient touch as inferiority and submission.

Paralanguage. Vocal sounds and speech modifiers, which are nonverbal but which convey meaning, are not language as such but paralanguage. Paralanguage indicators such as speaking order and talking time are associated with dominance (Lamb, 1981). In order to avoid interruption, a speaker will often fill pauses in conversations with "er," "um," or other sounds (Beattie, 1977). Another type of pause is the "awkward silence" that often occurs after there has been a minimal response to some statement and is followed by a series of questions and answers (McLaughlin & Cody, 1982).

Tone of voice is an indication of emotion and may be more revealing than facial expressions which are more controllable and closer to one's awareness than vocal cues. In an experiment in which undergraduate listeners attempted to identify the emotions from content-filtered recordings, sadness was more accurately identified than anger, happiness, or surprise (Apple & Hecht, 1982). Scherer (1986) analyzed the acoustic-phonetic correlates of physiological responses associated with different emotional states and identified three major *voice types* (wide-narrow, lax-tense, and full-thin). Specific emotional states are associated with particular voice-type patterns; for example, wide, lax, and slightly full for happiness; narrow, lax, and thin for sadness.

Participation Rate

One of the most consistent findings in research on social interaction is that some people talk more than others. The person in a group who talks the most also receives the most communications from others, and this person also addresses more communications to the group as a whole than to specific individuals.

A variety of factors affect an individual's participation rate. As the size of the group increases, the contribution of most group members decreases, while a few members dominate discussions; this divergence is most marked between the leader and the rest, as shown in Figure 7.2 (Bales, Strodtbeck, Mills, & Roseborough, 1951). The rate of interaction for any given member is inversely related to the rates of other members: if other people are not talking much, then you will talk more than if others are talking a lot (Borgatta & Bales, 1953).

A frequent finding is that the person who participates the most in a group is likely to become the leader (Stein, 1975). Sorrentino and Boutillier (1975) had a designated group member systematically vary quality and quantity of participation. Although quality of verbal participation influenced perceptions of influence and contribution to the group's goal, only quantity of participation influenced perceptions of leadership. Similarly, status is related to participation rates in groups. More communications are both sent and received by high-status members, and the content of such communications tends to be more positive than for low-status members. In one experiment, low-status members sent more communications to high-status persons even when the high-status persons were not initiating most of the activity (Kelley, 1951). The physical situation of the group can affect participation rates (see Chapter 1) so that a person who occupies a prominent

Figure 7.2
Participation Rates as a Function of Group Size

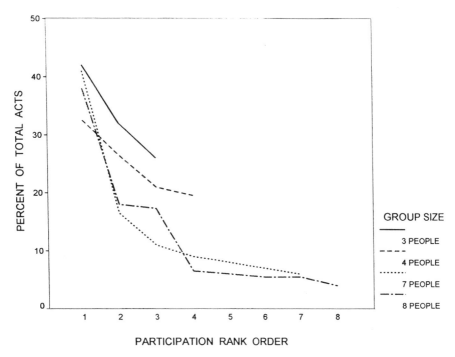

PARTICIPATION RANK ORDER

Source: Bales, R. F., Strodtbeck, F. L., Mills, T. M., & Roseborough, M. E. (1951). Channels of communication in small groups. *American Sociological Review, 16,* 461–468.

location in the group—such as at the head of the table—participates most and is likely to be perceived as a leader (Strodtbeck & Hook, 1961). Personality variables and social characteristics also affect a person's participation rate (see Chapter 2). Thus, dominant and assertive individuals participate more than submissive and unassertive individuals, and males participate more than females.

Communication Networks

Early in the life of a small group, an informal hierarchy tends to form based on participation rates, with one or a few members sending and receiving a majority of communications. In organizations, formal structures are usually established to regulate communications among members. If a group is to operate effectively, its members must be able to communicate easily and efficiently. This was recognized early on in research on groups and organizations. Researchers were particularly concerned to find out what sorts of communication networks produce the most efficient working groups, and it was assumed that some form of hierarchical and centralized network was the most efficient. A number of investigations were carried out into the effects of different communication networks by imposing constraints on who could communicate with whom in a group (see Shaw, 1964). A number of such networks are shown in Figure 7.3. The circles indicate members or positions in the group, and the lines represent channels of communications between positions (which can be one-way or two-way). Typically, the group has to work at a task which requires working together and exchanging information to solve the task.

Leavitt (1951) found that a centralized network such as the "wheel" or the "Y-shape" was the most efficient for solving problems, whereas the "circle" was least efficient in terms of time to solution, number of errors, and number of communications. However, an important qualifier of these findings is task complexity. Leavitt used a simple task that only required one member of the group to collect all the relevant information to solve the problem. Each member was given a card which bore five symbols, but only one of the symbols appeared on everyone's card, and the task was to discover what the common symbol was. When the task was more complex, involving problem-solving, analysis, and integration (such as human-relations dilemmas or math problems), a decentralized network such as the "circle" was found to be more efficient in terms of speed and errors (Shaw, 1954). This runs counter to the early assumptions of organizational psychologists that a hierarchical structure is more efficient. One explanation for differences in the efficiency of communication networks as a function of task complexity was proposed by Shaw (1964). He suggested that difficult tasks require more analysis and integration than simple tasks. In a centralized or hierarchical network, most of this analysis and integration tends to fall on one person (for example, the central position in the "wheel" structure). This can result in *cognitive overload* or *saturation*, such that the overloaded position impairs the performance of the whole network or group. In decentralized networks (such as the "circle"), the cognitive load is shared more evenly among the members and, although more communications between positions may be needed for successful solution, no member of the network is overloaded.

In addition to efficiency and productivity, a second consequence of differences in communication networks is the morale and satisfaction of the group members. Shaw (1964) argued that when group members have more autonomy and independence, they feel more satisfied. In a centralized network such as the "wheel," most of the group members are dependent on the central member who makes most of the decisions, sends and receives most communications, and calls most of the shots. In a more decentralized network, such as the "circle," each group member has an equal capability to make decisions and to communicate with the other members. Moreover, participants in such networks quickly realize how much control and autonomy they have with respect to the rest of the group. Not surprisingly, most members of centralized networks (with the exception of the central

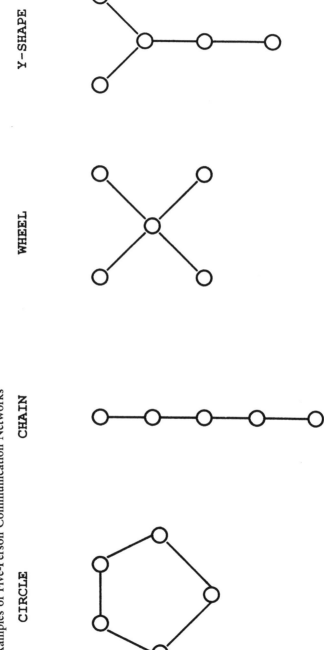

Figure 7.3
Examples of Five-Person Communication Networks

CIRCLE   CHAIN   WHEEL   Y-SHAPE

member) are less happy with the task and the group than members of decentralized networks. The greater satisfaction and morale of decentralized networks may be a contributing factor to the greater efficiency of these networks in addition to the cognitive overload factor.

THE CONTENT OF SOCIAL INTERACTION

There have been many attempts to devise conceptual schemes for the analysis of social interaction. These schemes differ in a number of ways—reflecting the particular biases and interests of the researchers. However, these researchers seem to be talking about the same things, it is just that they view social interaction from different perspectives.

Interaction Process Analysis

One of the most frequently used methods of classifying interactions is Bales's (1950) Interaction Process Analysis (a forerunner of "SYMLOG"—see below). The term *interaction* refers to all words, symbols, and gestures which people use to respond to each other; however, in most research, only verbal behavior is considered. Bales took as his unit of interaction a piece of behavior that can provide enough of a stimulus to elicit a meaningful response from another person. In practice, this is usually a sentence. Each unit or sentence is assigned to only one category. If a group member says, "Let's all get back to work," and laughs after finishing the remark, the statement would be scored as *giving a suggestion* and the laughter that follows the statement would be scored as *showing tension* or *tension release* depending on the nature of the laugh. Table 7.2 shows the twelve Bales's categories together with the interaction profiles for samples of laboratory groups and psychiatric interviews.

The first three categories are *positive reactions* and the last three categories are *negative reactions*. These six categories therefore relate to *socio-emotional activity*. The middle six categories relate to *task activity*, with categories 4–6 representing *problem-solving attempts* or *answers* and categories 7–9 *questions*. The first important feature of Bales's scheme is the distinction between task/instrumental and socio-emotional/expressive activities. Bales perceived the main purpose of a group as reaching some goal; therefore, the main activities of a group should be task activity. However, in pursuit of the goal, difficulties and tensions inevitably arise and these may threaten the functioning and stability of the group. These tensions are manifested in socio-emotional activities such as showing anger. To relieve these tensions, Bales suggested that groups engage in further socio-emotional activities such as tension release or showing solidarity. A second important feature of Bales's scheme is that for every action there is a re-action: a question will produce an answer; asking for an opinion will be

Table 7.2

Interaction Profiles for Laboratory Groups and Psychiatric Interviews

		Percentage of Acts	
		Laboratory Groups	Psychiatric Interviews
Socio-emotional Activity *(Positive)*			
	1. Shows solidarity: jokes, raises other's status, gives help, reward	3.4	0.1
	2. Shows tension release: laughs, shows satisfaction	6.0	0.5
	3. Shows agreement: passive acceptance, understands, concurs, complies	16.5	0.9
Task Activity *(Answers)*			
	4. Gives suggestion: direction, implying autonomy for other	8.0	0.5
	5. Gives opinion: evaluation, analysis, expresses feeling, wish	30.1	16.7
	6. Gives information: orientation, repeats, clarifies, confirms	17.9	56.9
Task Activity *(Questions)*			
	7. Asks for information: orientation, repetition, confirmation	3.5	12.9
	8. Asks for opinion: evaluation, analysis, expression of feeling	2.4	2.8
	9. Asks for suggestion: direction, possible ways of acting	1.1	0.0
Socio-emotional Activity *(Negative)*			
	10. Shows disagreement: passive rejection, formality, withholds help	7.8	0.6
	11. Shows tension: asks for help, withdraws "out of field"	2.7	6.1
	12. Shows antagonism: deflates other's status defends or asserts self	0.7	1.8

Source: Hare, A. P. (1976). *Handbook of small group research* (2nd ed.). New York: Free Press. Copyright © 1976 by The Free Press, an imprint of Simon & Schuster. Reprinted with permission.

followed by giving a suggestion. These forces of action and reaction should result in the group achieving some sort of equilibrium over the long term (at least for successful groups).

For laboratory discussion groups, the main content of the group interactions consists of giving opinion and giving information (categories 5 and 6), which account for about 48 percent of the activities. For the psychiatric interviews, these same two categories account for about 74 percent of the activities. These differences in interaction content reflect the difference in the group task. The laboratory group's task is to discuss a problem and reach a solution within 40 minutes. This is a task that requires a wider range of activities than in the psychiatric interview where the primary purpose is to encourage patients to give personal information for the psychiatrist to evaluate.

A relatively recent reformulation of Bales's scheme is SYMLOG—a *System* for the *Multiple Level Observation of Groups* (Bales & Cohen, 1979). The theory assumes that all interpersonal behavior can be understood in terms of a three-dimensional space, where the three dimensions are Upward-Downward (dominance versus submission), Positive-Negative (friendly versus unfriendly), and Forward-Backward (movement toward the goal versus movement away from the goal). This scheme can be used for coding and analyzing interactions in groups, as in Bales's Interaction Process Analysis, but it can also provide a picture of the social relations in the group by having group members rate each other on adjective rating scales. Thus, a group member's position in the three-dimensional space can be assessed and compared to other group members' positions providing information about the structure and dynamics of the group. In addition to providing hypotheses concerning individual effectiveness in groups, the theory and associated methods have the advantage of providing for the analysis of the relationship of individuals to the group and subgroups to each other. A review of research on SYMLOG is given by Hare (1989).

Exchange and Equity

There has been considerable interest in social psychology in understanding interactions and relationships from the viewpoint of economics. This economics analysis is based on the assumption that people enter into or maintain a social relationship if they can realize some "profit" or maximize their outcomes, so that rewards exceed the costs. Various social resources or commodities can be traded in social exchanges, such as love, status, information, or money.

In Thibaut and Kelley's (1959) social exchange theory, the outcomes (rewards minus costs) of an interaction are compared with a *comparison level* (CL) and with a *comparison level for alternatives* (CL_{ALT}). The CL is a subjective standard based on the average of the outcomes achieved in previous interactions and relationships. If the outcomes of the present interaction exceed the CL, then the participants will evaluate the interaction or relationship positively; but if the present outcomes fall below the CL, the interaction or relationship will be evaluated negatively. The CL_{ALT} is the standard of outcomes available in alternative relationships. If outcomes from the present relationship fall below the CL_{ALT}, the relationship is unstable and a person will be motivated to leave for one which offers better

Table 7.3
Satisfaction and Stability of Relationships as a Function of Outcomes and
Comparison Levels in Exchange Theory

		SATISFACTION WITH RELATIONSHIP	
		SATISFIED	DISSATISFIED
STABILITY OF RELATIONSHIP	STABLE	PRESENT OUTCOMES greater than CL and CL_{ALT}	CL greater than PRESENT OUTCOMES greater than CL_{ALT}
	UNSTABLE	CL_{ALT} greater than PRESENT OUTCOMES greater than CL	CL and CL_{ALT} greater than PRESENT OUTCOMES

outcomes. If outcomes exceed those of the CL_{ALT}, the relationship is stable
and a person will stay put. These differences between outcomes and comparison levels are summarized in Table 7.3.

A variant of social exchange theory is equity theory (Walster, Walster,
& Berscheid, 1978). People in a relationship consider not only their own
rewards and costs but also the rewards and costs of the other person(s).
They like to feel that what they are getting out of a relationship (outcomes)
is proportional to the amount they are putting into the relationship (inputs).
This is the idea of *distributive justice* (Homans, 1958). If the ratio of outcomes to inputs is similar for all people in a relationship, this is an equitable
state of affairs and people feel they are being treated fairly (Adams, 1965).

$$\text{Equity:} \quad \frac{\text{A's outcomes}}{\text{A's inputs}} = \frac{\text{B's outcomes}}{\text{B's inputs}}$$

Interestingly, people feel they are being treated unfairly not only if they are
getting relatively less out of a relationship than they have put in (unfairly
disadvantaged), but also if they are getting relatively *more* out than they
have put in (unfairly advantaged)—although being underbenefited is more
distressing than being overbenefited (Lane & Messé, 1971; see also, Blumberg, 1969).

Intimacy Equilibrium

Research by Argyle and Dean (1965) suggested that individuals try to maintain an equilibrium with regard to the level of intimacy or involvement in an encounter. Close interpersonal distances, greater eye contact, more open postures, warmer tone of voice—and of course topic of conversation—all signal intimate levels of interaction. Individuals can maintain their preferred level of intimacy by altering one or more of these nonverbal and verbal variables. For example, if you felt the interaction was too intimate, you could compensate for too close an interpersonal distance by adopting a more closed posture; or if you felt the topic of conversation was too intimate, you could reduce the amount of eye contact with the other person (or, of course, you could change the topic of conversation).

However, tests of this *compensation* hypothesis have led to some mixed results. Some studies support the hypothesis whereas others do not. In attempting to account for some of the contradictory findings, Patterson (1976) devised a theory that predicts *reciprocal* as well as *compensatory* changes. Patterson argued that changes in intimacy level produce changes in *arousal* that accentuates existing feelings. This arousal may be experienced as a negative feeling (anxiety, embarrassment, discomfort) or as a positive feeling (attraction, comfort, warmth), depending on the situation, the other person, and individual differences. If one person increases the intimacy of the encounter, and this produces negative feelings in the other person, the other person will compensate and try to reduce the negative arousal by lowering the intimacy level. But if a positive feeling is produced, the other person will attempt to maintain or increase the intimacy level by a *reciprocal* reaction.

Self-Disclosure

When people reveal personal information about themselves, they are engaging in self-disclosure. Fisher (1984) defines self-disclosure as "verbal behavior through which individuals truthfully, sincerely, and intentionally communicate novel, ordinarily private information about themselves to one or more addressees." Early recollections of life style are counted and accounts of sexual experience are taken as an especially good indicator of intimate self-disclosure. However, observers' perceptions of self-disclosing behavior are usually based on more than content alone. Variables such as the sex of the speaker and the amount, rate, and affective manner of self-revelations affect the perception of self-disclosure. For example, the same self-disclosure content may be judged to be more intimate in opposite-sex conversation than in same-sex conversation (Cunningham, 1981).

Women tend to engage in more self-disclosure than men, and they tend to talk more about relationships and personal aspects of their lives (Cline,

1989). Although some research shows that people disclose more to strangers than to friends (Derlega, Wilson, & Chaikin, 1976), in most cases self-disclosure is more frequent with friends than with strangers (Rubin & Shenker, 1978). People disclose more to their peers than to their parents, but when they do disclose to their parents they tell their mother more than their father (Balswick & Balkwell, 1977). More self-disclosing responses are given to "high openers"—people who elicit more intimate disclosure because of their greater receptiveness and attentiveness (Miller, Berg, & Archer, 1983). However, ordinary individuals can induce another person to disclose more if they reinforce self-disclosure by, for example, increasing their own disclosure intimacy, or by trading information as an equitable exchange (Rubin, 1975).

Impression Management

Individuals generally use tactical self-presentations as a means of establishing relationships with others that are congruent with their self-image or their preferred ways of dealing with the social world. For example, being liked is the goal of the *ingratiator*, whereas the *self-promoter* is concerned with appearing competent (Jones & Pittman, 1982). Godfrey, Jones, and Lord (1986) found that subjects who were asked to ingratiate themselves with a partner used *reactive* verbal and nonverbal behaviors, whereas those who were asked to act as self-promoters used *proactive* behaviors.

Self-presentations can be determined by, among other things, the particular roles people play. In a group situation, leaders were led to believe that either a task-oriented or a relationship-oriented approach would be most effective in facilitating group performance. Leaders subsequently presented images of themselves to the group that were consistent with the type of leader believed to be most effective (Leary, Robertson, Barnes, & Miller, 1986). People's self-presentations may also be affected by sex-role concerns. In a study by von Baeyer, Sherk, and Zanna (1981), female job applicants were interviewed by a male confederate whose stereotype of the ideal female applicant supposedly conformed closely either to the traditional female stereotype or its opposite. Applicants presented themselves in a traditionally "feminine" manner in their verbal/nonverbal behavior and physical appearance when they knew the interviewer held traditional views of women.

If people are induced to behave in a self-enhancing manner (such as in an interview), this can have carry-over effects in terms of boosting their self-esteem; that is, public displays of self-enhancing behavior can result in changes in private self-evaluations (Jones, Rhodewalt, Berglas, & Skelton, 1981).

Deceptive Communication

Studies of deceptive communication have focused on patterns of communication and nonverbal cues associated with deception. Experimenters ask observers to judge subjects who are telling the truth or lying about some other person, for example, by pretending they like a person who is actually disliked. Cues or clues that a person is engaged in deception include: messages that are ambivalent, discrepant, indifferent, and tense; statements that are spoken slowly and contain many "um's" and "er's;" suppressing leg and foot movements; and using fewer illustrative gestures while increasing voice pitch. Facial cues are not particularly useful in detecting deception because people have greater voluntary control over the face than over other parts of the body (Manstead, Wagner, & MacDonald, 1984).

Persons with higher social skills are better at deception (Riggio, Tucker, & Throckmorton, 1987). However, the lie is easier to detect by the subject if the subject is similar to the liar, for example, similar in physical attractiveness (DePaulo, Tang, & Stone, 1987). If a person *plans* to lie, it may be more difficult (O'Hair, Cody, & McLaughlin, 1981) or less difficult (Littlepage & Pineault, 1985) to detect. (See Chapter 2 of this book on Machiavellianism for further information about deception.)

GROUP DEVELOPMENT

A four-phase sequence can be identified in the development of groups. First, the purpose of the group is defined and the commitment of the members secured. Second, resources or skills must be acquired or provided. Third, appropriate roles must be developed or learned and a sufficiently high level of morale achieved. Fourth, the group works at the task with the coordination of leadership. Eventually these four phases are followed by a fifth, terminal phase, during which the group redefines the relationships between members as the group is disbanded.

In a more fine-grain analysis, phases can be identified, in the same order, within each of the first four phases and in reverse order in the fifth phase. Some persons may drop out of the group at the end of the first phase, if they find that they are not committed to the idea of the group, or at the end of the second phase if they judge that the resources are inadequate. However, the "revolution within the revolution" is most likely to occur near the end of the third phase if they are dissatisfied with the leadership or the role distribution. By this time, they have become committed to the purpose of the group and the resources seem to be adequate. If change does not occur at this point, there is nothing left to do but carry on the work.

Moreland and Levine (1982) outline a model of individual socialization in a group, which is, in effect, a description of group development from the point of view of the individual member, especially if the person joins a group that is already formed. Their model has five phases, each identified with a role type, each marked by a transition point between phases, and each associated with an increase or decrease in commitment to the group (see Figure 7.4).

Figure 7.4
The Process of Group Socialization

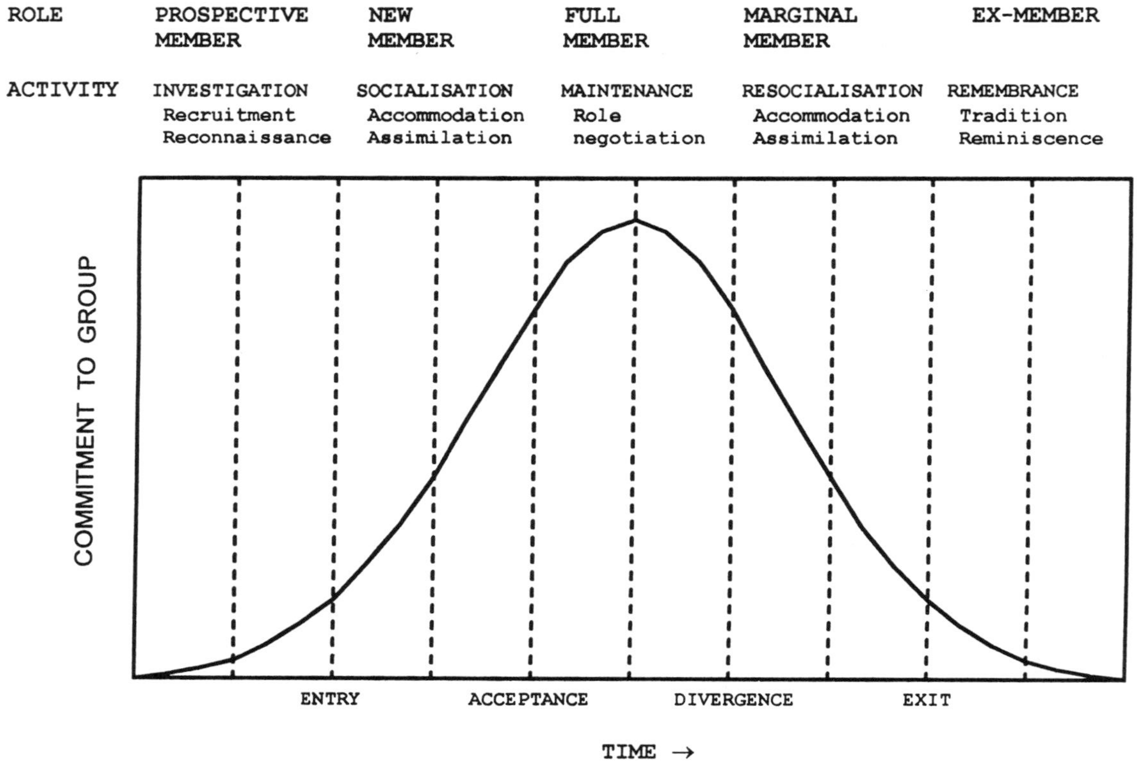

ROLE	PROSPECTIVE MEMBER	NEW MEMBER	FULL MEMBER	MARGINAL MEMBER	EX-MEMBER
ACTIVITY	INVESTIGATION Recruitment Reconnaissance	SOCIALISATION Accommodation Assimilation	MAINTENANCE Role negotiation	RESOCIALISATION Accommodation Assimilation	REMEMBRANCE Tradition Reminiscence

COMMITMENT TO GROUP

ENTRY   ACCEPTANCE   DIVERGENCE   EXIT

TIME →

Source: Moreland, R. L., & Levine, J. M. (1982). Socialization in small groups: Temporal changes in individual-group relations. Advances in Experimental Social Psychology, 15, 137–192. Copyright © 1982 by Academic Press Inc.

1. *Prospective member.* The primary activity is *investigation*, including recruitment and reconnaissance. Following this investigation is the transition point of *entry* to the group.

2. *New member.* The activity here involves *socialization*, including accommodation and assimilation. Successful socialization is the transition point of *acceptance* into the group.

3. *Full member.* This consists of role *maintenance*, involving role negotiation. If this process ends in dissatisfaction, there is a transition point of *divergence*.

4. *Marginal member.* Divergence may be followed by attempts at *resocialization* of an individual who no longer appears to be committed to the group, including accommodation and assimilation. If this resocialization is unsuccessful, the final transition is *exit* from the group.

5. *Ex-member.* A final role after the individual has left the group, this involves *remembrance* on the part of the remaining members about the individual's contribution as part of the group tradition, and reminiscence on the part of the individual.

SUMMARY

The main channels of human communication can be separated into the nonverbal and the verbal. Nonverbal behavior includes gaze and eye contact, facial expression, posture, gesture and touch, spatial behavior, and tone of voice. Nonverbal behavior can be especially powerful in communicating emotions and interpersonal attitudes; and, in conjunction with speech, nonverbal signals regulate conversations by indicating when it is someone else's turn to start or stop talking.

In social interaction, some people talk more than others, and these people also receive the most communications from others in a group. Factors affecting an individual's participation rate include the size of the group, how much other people are participating, and an individual's status (especially leadership status). The physical situation of the group can affect participation rates; a person who occupies a prominent location in the group participates most and is likely to be perceived as a leader. Personality and social factors also affect a person's participation rate.

Early on, an informal hierarchy tends to form in a group based on participation rates, with one or a few members sending and receiving a majority of communications. If a group is to operate effectively, its members must be able to communicate easily and efficiently. Studies have investigated the effects of different communication networks. For simple tasks, it is found that a centralized network is more efficient than a decentralized network. For complex tasks, the situation is reversed. One explanation for this is that central members become overloaded when dealing with difficult tasks. However, whether the task is easy or difficult, group members are happier and morale is higher in decentralized networks.

Studies of the content of interaction patterns in groups suggest a division into task activities and socio-emotional activities. In addition, for every action initiated by a member (such as a question), there is a reaction (such as an answer) from other members. Early research suggested that interactions in groups could be coded into twelve categories to produce an interaction profile for the group. More recent research suggests that only a few dimensions are needed to account for interactions in groups. The three dimensions that are revealed most often are Upward-Downward (dominance), Positive-Negative, and Forward-Backward (acceptance of authority). A very influential approach to understanding social interaction is social exchange. Based on economics, this approach suggests that people enter into or maintain a relationship if they can realize some "profit," that is, where the rewards exceed the costs. If the outcomes of an interaction exceed some comparison level, the participants will evaluate the interaction or relationship positively; but if the outcomes fall below the comparison level, the interaction or relationship will be evaluated negatively. A variant of social exchange theory is equity theory; people like to feel that what they are getting out of a relationship is proportional to the amount they are putting into the relationship. This is the idea of *distributive justice*. If the ratio of outcomes to inputs is similar for all people in a relationship, this is an equitable state of affairs and people feel they are being treated fairly.

At times, individuals try to maintain an equilibrium with regard to the level of intimacy or involvement in an encounter. Individuals can maintain their preferred level of intimacy by altering one or more nonverbal and verbal behaviors. At other times, people may want to increase the intimacy of an interaction, and they can do this by nonverbal means, but a powerful verbal means of increasing the intimacy of an encounter is through self-disclosure. The extent of self-disclosure during conversations is taken as an indication of an especially friendly and trusting relationship. Conversely, people may wish to protect their private selves by putting on a favorable public self-image and managing the impression others have of them. In the extreme, people may lie to achieve their selfish ends (for example, by pretending to like someone whom they actually dislike). However, an individual who is lying may be given away by unintentional patterns of speech or nonverbal cues.

A typical pattern of development in many types of groups includes five phases: obtaining commitment to the goals of the group; supplying resources; developing roles and an appropriate level of morale; carrying out the task with leadership coordination; and a terminal phase as the group is disbanded.

CHAPTER 8

Group Decision Making and Choice Shift

Herbert H. Blumberg

In this chapter we examine the causes of "choice shift" in group decision making—a common finding that, as a result of discussion within a group, nearly everyone's views can shift in the same direction. Then we turn to consider research on jury deliberations. We also look at some ways to prevent group decisions from going horribly wrong.

CHOICE SHIFT

In many studies of group decision making, individuals first express their opinions on a matter—such as legalization of marijuana or reducing the military budget. They then discuss the matter in groups and perhaps are asked to agree on an answer. Finally they express their opinions privately, a second time.

Something odd usually happens in these studies. If group members who start out in rough agreement merely tended to move toward a single position—the majority opinion—we would not be too surprised. After all, we have already seen, in Chapter 4, how strong the forces toward conformity can be. In Sherif's (1935) classic study using the "autokinetic effect," each group of subjects is found to converge on its own narrow range of estimates as to how far a point of light in a darkened room is believed to have "moved." In well-known experiments by Asch and others, subjects often conform to a group's *wrong* estimates, even about clear stimuli such as the length of lines (Asch, 1956); and they may agree with others who have "endorsed" outrageous statements similar to "In a democracy, freedom of speech is not a right but a privilege that must be earned" (Krech, Crutchfield, & Ballachey, 1962).

The oddity about "choice shift"—or "attitude polarization," as it is sometimes called—is as follows. Group members who start out "basically in agreement" will, after discussion, typically converge not merely on the "average" view of their group but on a rather extreme version of this view. That is, they "over-conform" or become polarized. Examples could be eventual agreement that football players ought to make a risky play to avoid a tied game, or that residents in a university dormitory should be *extra* careful to observe fire safety regulations.

These two examples highlight the fact that shift can be in either a risky or conservative direction. In early studies, the changes were called "risky shift" in keeping with what was thought to be the typical direction of change. Even on the original "risky shift"-type questionnaires, some items (it was eventually shown) produced only a conservative shift.

Informational and Normative Influence

The two main causes of shift are "informational" and "normative" influence.

Imagine that a group of four students all favor an arrangement that would provide new students with a personal computer financed from course fees, but that the four students have rather different reasons for their views, and their feelings range from strong to nearly indifferent.

In such a situation, shifts in opinion—following group discussion—occur for two main reasons: "persuasive arguments" and "social comparison." The persuasive arguments (or *informational*) explanation accounts for the largest choice-shift effects. "People are found to be sensitive to the number of arguments in a particular direction as well as to the novelty and persuasiveness of these arguments" (Hare, Blumberg, Davies, & Kent, 1994, p. 202). A clear, precise description of this effect is as follows.

There exists a pool of arguments for each issue. . . . Each person who considers the issue will have knowledge of a sample of the pool of arguments, which will determine his or her initial attitude. During the group discussion, individual arguments are discussed and become fully shared. Because participants are more likely to express arguments that favor their initial attitude, a large pool of arguments favoring the group's initial inclination will be shared among all group members. Each individual participant learns new arguments in favor of his or her initial viewpoint and, as a result, attitude polarization occurs. (Brauer, Judd, & Gilner, 1995, p. 1015, summarizing work of Burnstein & Vinokur, 1977, and others)

The following is the "social comparison" (or *normative*) explanation.

Individual group members polarize when they realize that others share their opinions to a greater extent than they had thought (Myers & Lamm, 1976). Many of us have the desire to be perceived [favorably]. . . . As Roger Brown (1974) pointed out, "to be virtuous . . . is to be different from the mean—in the right direction and to the right degree" (p. 469). When all members of an interacting group engage in the same social comparison process, the result is an average shift in the [same] direction of the predominant attitude. (Brauer, Judd, & Gilner, 1995, p. 1015)

The two main forces toward change—informational and normative—have long been well known to those who study attitude change or conformity in general (Deutsch & Gerard, 1955). Even outside of a group context, we might change our views about providing students with computers in the face of new substantive information about the effects of such a policy (which we have read about in a magazine article, for instance) or newly publicized "norms" found in social surveys (suggesting, for instance, a favorable attitude by most—or by very few—members of a social group with whom we strongly identify).

In theory, we might expect choice shift to follow from other forms of influence, having to do with values and goals (Hare, 1983). Shift would be likely if group members were made aware that a particular position was especially consistent, or inconsistent, with their basic values or goals (such as, for freedom or health or money or planetary survival). However, this awareness would not move all group members in the same direction, which is what is usually meant by choice shift, unless group members shared the values or goals and were all, at the same time, confronted with an awareness of their relevance. No doubt this would be most likely if the values or goals were "packaged" in an influential message to a group, that is, imbedded in an informational or normative context.

Repeated Expressions

Both of these explanations, persuasive arguments and social comparison, relate to small groups in which we hear a variety of arguments and where, too, we express our own opinions repeatedly. Do we shift our opinions because of what we hear or because of what we say? These two possibilities were varied systematically in an ingenious pair of experiments by Brauer, Judd, and Gilner (1995). In one study, subjects joined with others who agreed with them on several (but not all) issues. "Discussion" was carefully, and openly, orchestrated as to who spoke when, and about which issue. It turned out that people are influenced *both* by the frequency with which they themselves express an attitude, *and* by the number of other people whom they hear expressing a similar attitude.

Effects were particularly strong in an experimental condition (in a second study) where subjects rehearsed each other's arguments. A participant in each group was instructed to use the arguments of the other group members as much as possible (perhaps prefaced by phrases like, "As Jennifer pointed out earlier, . . ."), provided that they agreed with the person on the issue.

Clearly, attitude polarization "is very much a social process, being enhanced where one hears others integrate one's own arguments," thereby validating each other's ideas, aspirations, and opinions (Brauer, Judd, & Gilner, 1995, p. 1027).

We have noted that polarization (choice shift) is strongest when group members start out in general agreement. As was also true in Asch's conformity work and Milgram's studies of obedience, the presence of even a single dissenting member in a decision-making group can moderate the polarization effect (Williams & Taormina, 1993).

Choice Shift, Attributes, and Prototypes

Just what (if anything) is it that group members conform to, when they shift their views? As we have seen, it is in part a collection of arguments and partly an almost mythical, ideal member of the group.

To digress for a moment: a somewhat similar distinction can be made for most categories, including concrete ones such as fruit, or furniture, or even close friends. In a sense, "fruit" is represented by a collection of attributes such as soft, edible, sweet, with seeds, etc. (no one of which is found in *all* fruit). But we also share an "image" or *prototype* of what we mean by fruit, and could probably agree that (if we were forced to choose) some examples, such as an apple, are "better" representations than others, such as a watermelon (Brown, 1986). (Not that an apple tastes better, just that it is more "fruit-like.")

When a collection of arguments is shaped into a "view," one thing is clear: people do not usually arrive at a view by rating every argument on a particular issue, and then entering a set of ratings and weights into a calculator or computer! Rather, they maintain a rough impression which *simulates* an exact tally. Presumably this "tally" is partly a "sum" of the arguments one hears and partly an "average." That is, to hear only a collection of very weak arguments in favor of your own position might actually "weaken" your view. (At least this is what one might infer from studies in another area of social psychology—namely, how people combine trait information to form overall opinions of people.)

When arguments are collected into one's overall impression, we might, alternatively, associate this impression as being, not a "collection of arguments," but a prototype, or a particularly good "image"—either of ideal group members and how they would feel about, say, providing computers for students, or an ideal image of the view or feeling itself.

This may sound rather curious. It is one thing to imagine a very typical fruit, another to say we conform to a "prototypical group member." Nevertheless, McCarty and colleagues explain and extend the view that people "are conforming to a shared in-group norm, . . . [being] the position most *prototypical* of the group" (McCarty et al., 1992, p. 3). Moreover, for choice shift to occur, the group members must start out generally agreeing about their position, and that agreement must be away from the neutral point of the relevant scale. So if the issue in question is whether to provide computers to new students, the group must all fall roughly on the same side of the scale (be it "for" or "against"), and the scale as a whole must represent a range of viable positions. In other words, the group in question forms an "in-group;" everyone is a little surprised to learn how much they agree about "what side of the scale they fall on."

As of 1995, studies of choice shift were being published at the rate of approximately 25 per year. As has been true for about 30 years, interest seems to be based not just on group polarization as such, but also on the ability of this topic and method to provide a "foothold" for studying and understanding the individual and social aspects of group decision making. "Mock jury" studies, too, help in this understanding. We turn to these next.

SIMULATED JURIES

To understand how juries reach their verdicts is of both practical and theoretical interest. Detailed international publicity of the 1995 O. J. Simpson trial in the United States increased public awareness of this long-standing issue. In order not to interfere with the judicial process itself, and also to permit controlled experimental designs, much research has used "mock juries"—groups of people, often selected in exactly the same way as real juries, who take part in a simulated trial or in some aspects of one. Other studies have been based on computer simulations or on information from ex-jurors or from "retrospective analysis" of court records (Tindale & Davis, 1983).

According to findings from studies of choice shift (discussed above), we would expect that a jury which begins its deliberations in general agreement as to the innocence or guilt of the accused is likely to reach a conclusion that matches its initial view but that is moreover particularly strong or firm. If we think about it in this context, typical choice-shift findings are very plausible. Suppose you start out moderately confident that the accused is innocent, and then hear several people all agreeing with you, to various degrees. This is likely to increase your initial resolve. That is, the discussion will probably shift your moderate belief in the innocence to an even stronger one.

Perhaps surprisingly, most of the jury research does not really examine the rather fine gradations of belief that are used in the study of choice shift. At least, however, the research does confirm that a jury's leaning at the start of deliberation is a very good predictor of final verdict.

Prediction of verdict has in fact been a focus of research. For instance, is the outcome much affected by the personality and other background variables of the jurors, by the characteristics of others involved in the trial, or by group composition, jury size, or other variables. For instance, high authoritarianism—a personality trait associated with inflexibility, ethnocentrism, and obedience to authority—is associated with jurors being conviction-prone.

Size and Decision Rule

When apparent guilt is low, the size of a jury—six or twelve persons— seems to have little effect on its likelihood to convict. But when apparent guilt is high, six-person juries seem especially conviction-prone (Valenti & Downing, 1974, 1975).

Does it matter whether the requirement for a verdict is "unanimity" or some form of "majority rule?" Acquittal rates may be unaffected, but under a unanimity rule there may be fewer convictions and more hung (undecided) juries.

Two-Stage Decision Formation

Group deliberations can be helpful if a task is complicated or demanding. We know from studies of person perception that impressions can be formed in two quick stages, (2) drawing an immediate face-value inference and (2) adjusting that inference according to extenuating circumstances.

Kerwin and Shaffer (1994) have examined the effects of deliberation on jurors' ability to disregard inadmissible testimony. Subjects (312 undergraduates), read a transcript of a (made-up) case of someone on trial for the armed robbery of a liquor store. The prosecution based its case on the rather weak testimony of an eyewitness. In addition, a police officer testified that a bag with the robbery weapon and money were found in the defendant's apartment; and this testimony then was—or was not—ruled as inadmissible because the search of the apartment was illegal. Next, subjects gave a predeliberation opinion as to how likely they thought it was that the defendant had actually committed the crime and how definitely they would urge conviction or acquittal. In each group (admissible and inadmissible evidence): 25 subjects served as "individual" jurors and the remaining subjects were divided into 24 juries of four to six subjects each that were asked to try to reach a unanimous verdict. Finally, all subjects were asked again about their beliefs as to innocence. The results supported the view that, compared to individuals on their own, juries (after deliberation) were more likely to follow judicial instructions to ignore inadmissible evidence.

The authors speculate that deliberation increases the accountability that jury members feel toward one another, permits the expression of minority views and divergent thinking, and enhances involvement and seriousness toward the decision-making task. In more general studies of group problem solving, groups do better than the average individual mainly because even one person who is confident about having a correct or proper answer can share it with other group members (Hare, Blumberg, Davies, & Kent, 1994, p. 265). In the experiment on inadmissable evidence, it may simply be that a group is likely to have at least one member who will call the group's attention to the judge's instructions.

The effects of group discussion do, however, depend on the nature of the available communication network, as we shall see in the following section.

CLUSTERING AND GROUPTHINK

The communications network might be viewed as part of the physical setting (see Chapter 1) if there are spatial or other constraints on who can speak with whom. In any case, classic studies suggest that decision making is more egalitarian and satisfying for everyone in networks where everyone can communicate with everyone else (Leavitt, 1951) (see also, Chapter 7). In particular, of course, we are likely to be most influenced by those who are closest to us.

According to Latané's (1981) theory of dynamic social impact, the total impact of a group of people on an individual is the product of their strength, immediacy, and number. If others are of high status, are nearby, and numerous, they will have a greater effect. Over time, one can expect stable diversity of opinions in a population (despite a possible reduction in the minority's size), and the emergence of clusters of like-minded people (Latané & Jackson, 1994). Conceptually similar work has been done both with real groups and computer simulations. Latané, Nowak, and Liu (1994) describe the following instance of computer simulation.

Imagine that 400 people are brought together in one place to discuss an issue. Figure [8.1] . . . is an aerial view showing the distribution of attitudes in two such groups *before* the start of discussion, with the open faces . . . representing people who hold the majority viewpoint and the solid faces . . . those in the minority. . . . The placement of the faces represents their location in physical space, which is important because people are not allowed to move about, and their voices can be heard only so far. Naturally, neighbors can see and hear each other more clearly than more distant pairs. The majority and minority are randomly distributed, since the issue is new and location randomly assigned. Finally, the people differ in how wise and knowledgeable they are—some being both very persuasive to those who hold opposing positions and supportive to those who share their opinion, while others are less influential. (p. 2)

Figure 8.2 shows sample distributions of attitudes in the same two groups after simulated "discussions" according to different models of influence. The authors developed various quantitative measures. Under a wide range

Figure 8.1
The Initial, Random, Distribution of Attitudes in Two Groups, Rounds of 400 People, Each with a 30 Percent Minority

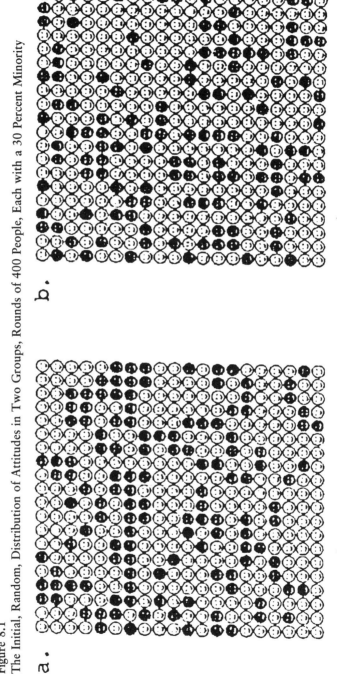

Source: Latané, B., Nowak, A., & Liu, J. H. (1994). Measuring emergent social phenomena: Dynamism, polarization, and clustering as order parameters of social systems. *Behavioral Science, 39,* 2; reprinted by permission.

Figure 8.2
Equilibrium Distributions of Attitudes after Six Rounds of Influence

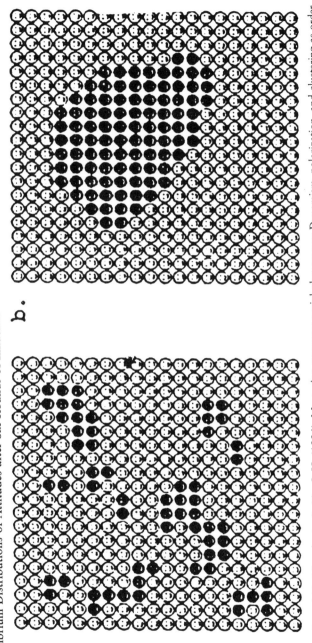

Source: Latané, B., Nowak, A., & Liu, J. H. (1994). Measuring emergent social phenomena: Dynamism, polarization, and clustering as order parameters of social systems. *Behavioral Science, 39,* 6; reprinted by permission.

of circumstances, discussion did lead, not to unification, but to incomplete polarization (increase or decrease of a minority position over time—but the minority does not disappear altogether) and clustering.

Groupthink

If a decision-making group is isolated from opinions other than those of its own members, a pathological condition that Janis (1982) named "groupthink" may develop. A likely example is found in Saddam Hussein—leader of Iraq for an extended period, including the abortive annexation of Kuwait—who surrounded himself with a group of close "advisers" but would not tolerate any dissenting advice from them (Blumberg & French, 1994). He made a well-known series of cruel and disastrous decisions (as have others, of course).

The characteristics of groupthink include:

[A] shared illusion of invulnerability, fostering optimism and risk taking; rationalizations which discount warnings that might lead to reconsidering a continuation of past policy decisions; inflated faith in the group's morality; stereotyped views of opponents as being inept or as being too evil for negotiation; pressure against any dissenting "disloyal" group members; a resulting shared illusion of unanimity; and "self-appointed mindguards" "who protect the group from adverse information." (Hare, Blumberg, Davies, & Kent, 1994, pp. 204-205, describing Janis's work)

Fortunately, Janis and Mann (1992) have also derived recommendations for *good* decision making. The reconsiderations are not unlike "consensus" decision making, in which dissent is accommodated rather than overridden (Hare, 1973). They conclude that, for equivocal situations, decision making that is *moderately* complex is likely to yield the best outcomes for everyone concerned. Ideally, to the best of his or her ability, the good decision maker does the following:

—surveys a wide range of objectives, taking account of the multiplicity of values

—canvasses a wide range of alternative courses of action

—correctly takes account of new information or expert judgment, even if it does not support an initially preferred course of action

—reconsiders the positive and negative consequences of originally unacceptable alternatives

—carefully examines the costs and risks of negative, as well as positive, potential consequences of the chosen alternative

—makes detailed provisions for implementing and monitoring the chosen course, with special attention to contingency plans for possible problems. (Adapted from Janis & Mann, 1992, pp. 36–37)

Janis and Mann also have provided various data pertinent to their views. For instance, in independent ratings of 19 international crises since 1945 in which the United States was involved, both international and American outcomes were more positive in crises showing fewer groupthink-like symptoms of defective U.S. policy making.

SUMMARY

"Choice shift" is found when individuals (who are roughly in agreement about the answer to a problem or dilemma) first give their private responses, then discuss the matter and try to reach a group decision, and finally give their "post-deliberation" private responses. Not only do the group members tend to converge onto a narrow range of response, which is what one would expect from research on conformity, but the response also polarizes. That is, most individuals move to a more extreme response, in the same direction as their initial view.

For example, if the initial responses to a dilemma represent a moderate consensus that someone should accept a particular job offer, then, after discussion of the matter, most group members are likely to feel this way even more strongly.

Such shifts occur partly because the group members expose one another to additional arguments in favor of their viewpoint (the informational influence of "persuasive arguments"), and partly because the individuals wish to conform to a group with which they identify (the normative influence of "social comparison"). The effects result both from individuals hearing others put a particular view forward and from "hearing" themselves express their own opinion.

The position that people adopt may be seen either as a collection of arguments or else as a prototype or "image" of the position held by a (real or hypothetical) "ideal" member of the group.

Studies of simulated juries suggest that the pre-deliberation view held by a majority of jurors is likely to become the jury's eventual verdict. A decision to convict may be more likely in smaller juries and in those not required to reach a unanimous decision. Not surprisingly, deliberation may be especially helpful if a case is particularly complicated—for example, because some evidence must be disregarded as inadmissible.

Over time, groups may reach a "stable diversity of opinion," with clusters of like-minded people emerging. This is particularly likely in a setting where, as is commonly the case, there are spatial constraints as to who can speak with whom.

Good group decision making is most likely in settings where members are encouraged to consider a diversity of viewpoints, to evaluate the probable effects of various options, and to monitor the effects of their decisions.

PART V

Interactive Modes

CHAPTER 9

Cooperation, Competition, and Conflict Resolution

Herbert H. Blumberg

This chapter covers various topics related to cooperation and conflict resolution. Let us start by considering an adaptation of Elliot Aronson's "jigsaw classroom," itself a tried and tested educational method in which groups of students learn set material which has been divided into "pieces" distributed within each group. Typically, compared to traditional teaching in which students are sometimes competing with each other or simply learning "in isolation," this form of cooperative learning reaps social as well as academic gains (Aronson et al., 1978).

COOPERATION VERSUS COMPETITION

In an adaptation of the jigsaw procedure, Slavin (1991) arranged for students to work in teams of four or five members.

All students read a common narrative, such as a book chapter, a short story, or a biography. However, each student receives a topic (such as "climate" in a unit on France) on which to become an expert. Students with the same topics meet in expert groups to discuss them, after which they return to their teams to teach what they have learned to their teammates. Then students take individual quizzes, which result in team [improvement] scores. . . . Teams that meet preset standards earn certificates. (Slavin, 1991, p. 75)

Reviewing this and other research on cooperative learning, Slavin concludes that, provided group goals are combined with individual accountability, the achievement effects of cooperative learning have been consistently positive regardless of grade level (2–12), academic level, and urban-suburban-rural school status. Moreover, positive effects apply to a wide variety of outcomes such as self-esteem, acceptance of minority group members, and attitudes toward school.

Contact Hypothesis

The positive findings from jigsaw-classroom and similar studies are in fact a special case of the "contact hypothesis" (discussed in more detail in Chapter 12): that intergroup contact—for instance, by successful interracial teams of people (who are "mindful" of their colleagues)—"reduces prejudice under specific conditions, such as equal-status members working together with support from authority (e.g., teachers), and with rewards based on group performance" (research by Cook as described by Hare, Blumberg, Davies, and Kent, 1994, p. 215).

If gains are rewarded, by marks or payment or certificates, for instance, it does seem important that the rewards simply be regarded as an indicator of achievement rather than looming so large as to be an "intrinsic goal" in themselves (Schneider, Hastorf, & Ellsworth, 1979, pp. 87–90; Kohn, 1991).

Reward Structure

The satisfaction of group members (in other research) does depend partly on how rewards are distributed. "Equity theory," developed by Hatfield (1983) and other social psychologists, suggests that people prefer rewards to be distributed fairly; but *fairly* can mean "proportional to individual contributions" (as equity theorists usually suggest), or it can mean "equally to each group member" or "winner takes all" or "according to need."

Research on cooperation/competition, carried out by Deutsch (1990) and others, suggests that, when individual or group task performance depends on effective social cooperation, most subjects initially prefer rewards to be distributed according to each person's size of contribution. Perhaps not surprisingly, however, the subjects who turn out later to be good performers, and also those "with a sense of power . . . and a more conservative political orientation," may prefer "winner takes all." And the poor performers, as well as those having a more favorable attitude toward fellow group members, may prefer rewards to be distributed according to "equality" or "need." When it comes to making a decision and voting on the system of rewards, subjects' preference for "equality" increases. The reward system affects attitudes but not necessarily productivity, at least not when all subjects receive at least a basic payment in addition to distributed bonuses. Productivity *is* enhanced, however, if these bonuses are paid according to achievement rather than "effort."

Inducing Cooperation

The advantages of working together for common benefits are often unmistakable. Perhaps unfortunately, however, we are not always in the position of the teacher or experimenter who can *decide* that procedures are to be "cooperative." How can we induce possible adversaries to join in a common effort? The question can arise among classmates or indeed among groups of all sizes including nations. No single "formula" will always work, but Patchen (1987), reviewing a substantial body of research, concluded that the best general advice is to reciprocate what the other party or parties are doing, but throw in a generous dash of "unilateral initiative" every now and again to break out of "competitive lock-ins."

Other studies suggest a diverse array of things that affect relevant behavior. Cooperation may be enhanced if "art music or mood music" is playing or if people have just heard some good news (Chertock, 1974; Hornstein, LaKind, Frankel, & Manne, 1975). The nature of rewards may induce cooperation or competition (see, for instance, the discussion of Prisoners Dilemma in Chapter 10). In Sherif's (1966) famous "Robber's Cave" experiment, discussed in detail in Chapter 12, groups of competing boys in summer camp were finally brought together by events in which "everyone gained" by working together on common problems such as mending a "failure" in the camp's water supply. Sherif called such important common objectives "superordinate goals." In general, cooperation is especially likely when people have a *goal* of mutual cooperation and an *expectation* that the other parties have a similar goal (Pruitt, 1983b).

In-Group Identity

We have already noted that greater reduction in prejudice results when individuals are "mindful" of the others in their group (Langer, Bashner, & Chanowitz, 1985). An experiment carried out by Bettencourt, Brewer, Croak, and Miller (1992) is worth describing in some detail. Ninety-six female subjects were randomly "identified" as being overestimators or underestimators. Then eight-person groups—four previously unacquainted people from each of the two "categories"—were divided, first, into two homogeneous teams (four underestimators vs. four overestimators) for one task and then, for the main part of the experiment, into heterogeneous teams (two from each category in each team) for a second problem-solving task.

In earlier research, when identification with even a trivial category (similar to the underestimators or overestimators) has been emphasized, people are known to show bias in favor of others who share "their own category" (Tajfel, 1970) (see also, Chapter 12). Such emphasis was maintained in the present experiment by having the eight subjects in each session wear large badges bearing the word UNDER or OVER, plus the number 1, 2, 3, or 4. The experimenter explained that these codes ensured confidentiality when subjects came to evaluate each other.

When team members were asked to evaluate each person's work, ingroup bias was evident. Underestimators favored other underestimators on their team, and overestimators favored overestimators. This was true in evaluations not only of the quality of work but also of the friendliness of others. Such bias was largely absent, however, in those groups that had been randomly assigned to experimental groups having either of two properties. Bias was in fact reversed, in favor of out-group members, when *both* properties were present. The first bias-damping property was a reward structure that induced cooperative orientation. When subjects were told that they would be eligible for a small monetary reward if *both* of two teams achieved a certain standard, there was even less bias against outgroup members of *their own* team than if the monetary reward was available only to the better-scoring team. The second bias-damping property was an "interpersonal focus" rather than a task focus. Those teams assigned to the interpersonal focus were told, "During this task it is very important that you form an accurate impression of what your fellow team members must really be like;" for task-oriented teams, emphasis was given to forming an accurate impression of the quality of answers. Although the picture is more complicated (see, for instance, Ruscher, Fiske, Miki, & Van Manen, 1991), we can conclude that social identity is less likely to cause bias and discrimination in groups if a cooperative interpersonal orientation is emphasized and rewarded.

THE MANAGEMENT AND RESOLUTION
OF CONFLICT

Although conflicts are no doubt more likely to arise in competitive settings than in cooperative ones, disagreements can of course arise within (and between) almost any groups. Three dimensions of social interaction—similar to the "SYMLOG" dimensions (Bales & Cohen, 1979) discussed in Chapter 7—provide reminders of some important distinctions among conflicts, and help us to understand how they might be managed or, even better, resolved.

Conflicts vary in dominance or size, which is the first dimension. This can refer to the verbosity or power of individual participants, to the number of participants involved, or to the complexity of the conflict itself. Some conflicts are small, single-issue disputes within a family or work group, whereas others are extremely complicated matters involving a host of groups, small and large, such as the international Cold War of the 1950s through the 1980s. One of the questions about a multi-issue conflict is whether to deal with one problem at a time or to seek a single grand solution. Fisher (1971) wrote convincingly about the advantages of "fractionating conflict," that is, breaking it into manageable portions and then dealing with these portions one at a time. On the other hand, experiments on multi-issue bargaining suggest the usefulness of keeping options open on several issues at once, so that they can be "traded off" until one finds a viable "package" of solutions (see also the discussion of bargaining in Chapter 10). One possibility, sometimes, is to find provisional solutions for several issues but to keep options open temporarily until a full agreement is reached.

Conflicts also vary along a positive-negative dimension. Although we think of conflicts as generally being nastier than competitions and lacking "routine procedures" for solution, some conflicts can be viewed more positively. Different scientists in a community of scholars may have conflicting theories about the origins of the universe, for instance, but their common or "superordinate" goal is, hopefully and ultimately, to concur on the truth.

Certainly many researchers and practitioners have advised that what appear to be "win-lose" or "zero-sum" conflicts—where one party's gains represent another's losses—should, if possible, be recast as "win-win," by finding a creative solution in which all parties gain something.

If a conflict is too "hot" for parties to discuss a solution, they may be able to begin with less threatening topics, such as discussion of the conditions or criteria for an acceptable solution (Likert & Likert, 1978). Another practical suggestion, once a possible solution has been found, is to avoid "sufficing;" that is, to continue to explore for even better solutions.

An intriguing third dimension, task-social, does not seem to have attracted much research as regards conflict resolution. We shall return to this later. First, let us look at some practical advice for groups trying to resolve a conflict.

Research-Based Advice

Deutsch (1983) has summarized findings from research done by himself and others, as follows.

1. Few conflicts are intrinsically and inevitably win-lose conflicts. . . . There has been developing a technology of how to help people maintain an awareness of their common interests even as they deal with their opposing interests.

2. If the conflict is not by its nature a win-lose conflict, one should develop and maintain a cooperative problem-solving orientation that focuses on the interests of the different parties (and not their positions) . . .

3. A full, open, honest, and mutually respectful communication process should be encouraged . . .

4. A creative development of a wide range of options for potentially solving the

problem of the diverging interests of the conflicting parties should be fostered. . . .

5. [T]here are resources and effective procedures for dealing with many of the common problems and impasses that often cause a conflict to degenerate into a destructive process. There are potentially helpful third parties . . . (M. Deutsch, 1983, pp. 450–451)

Dimensions

Some writers distinguish among different ways of handling interpersonal conflict—such as avoiding, accommodating, compromising, problem solving, and various forms of fighting. It may be helpful to be aware of each of these modes, but Van de Vliert and Euwema (1994) conclude that they can all be reliably distinguished on the basis of just two factors—agreeableness and activeness—which are very similar to the dominance and positive-negative dimensions described above. Activeness here refers to how parties act rather than to the complexity of the conflict itself.

Van de Vliert and Euwema carried out a role-playing experiment among 82 Dutch police officers who were doing a four-day course in conflict management as part of their in-service training. Subjects participated individually in a videotaped encounter, where they were asked to act "as naturally as possible" in the part of a station sergeant. The other party in each encounter was an actor taking the part of a subordinate or superior officer who had taken away and used a police car for more than an hour without reporting this to the station sergeant. In a confrontation with the sergeant (the subject), the actor escalated the conflict through three stages—trivialization ("I don't think that that's much of a problem"), underlying policy ("These rules are too bureaucratic. We must be able to improvise"), and personal attack ("Blame yourself if things went wrong").

Independent ratings were made of the subject's conflict-handling style and of agreeableness and activeness. Although the different styles could be reliably distinguished on the basis of agreeableness and activeness, the results leave open the question of which behavior patterns are most effective. Other research, however—with ratings of (genuine) accounts in which people have responded to real or threatened violence—suggests that a moderately dominant, moderately positive response is likely to give the best outcomes (Blumberg, 1988/1992).

An approach called "GRIT" provides an example of how a moderately positive-dominant approach can reverse the "vicious escalating spirals of negative behavior" that one sometimes sees. Developed in the 1960s by the eminent experimental psychologist Charles Osgood (1962), GRIT stands for *Graduated Reciprocated Initiatives for Tension-reduction*. The idea is that at least one of the antagonist parties should announce beforehand, and carry out, a diverse series of modest positive initiatives that show good intentions but do not in any way threaten the security of one's position. A factious neighbor might make a gift of a useful paperback book on gardening. Or a country might provide humanitarian aid to its rival. One also invites the other party or parties to reciprocate in some way. The initiatives are always carried out, but (true to "stimulus-response reward theories") if they are not reciprocated, one slows the pace. If they are reciprocated, one steps up this "arms race in reverse" by announcing more major acts. Perhaps the other party will view the initiatives as a mere publicity stunt, but even so will likewise feel obliged to reciprocate.

Incidentally, as "psycholinguists," Osgood and colleagues also developed the semantic differential, a carefully tested scheme for differentiating the meaning of objects along three independent dimensions: positive-negative evaluation, potency, and activity (Osgood, Suci, & Tannenbaum, 1957). When rocks, for instance, are rated on "bi-polar adjective scales" (to measure their "cognitive loadings"), nearly everyone finds them strong, inactive, and neutral on positive-negative. For reducing tensions, Osgood pointed out that the acronym GRIT is itself intended to convey the appropriate cognitive loadings, or meaning, of the approach: "grit" sounds rather assertive (strong and active, in contrast to "passive" resistance) and neutral (clearly more positive than most of the behavior in a feud). The dimensions of the semantic differential are similar to, but not quite the same as, those of SYMLOG and were primarily designed for rating objects rather than social interaction (see Chapter 7). Both schemes can be "mapped" onto the "big five" personality dimensions (but see, for example, Benet & Waller, 1995). Nevertheless, in SYMLOG terms, the GRIT approach is indeed deliberately rather dominant-positive, which generally seems the best stance for de-escalating conflict.

Procedures

To turn to a more "analytic" approach: Clarke (1993) delineates a (somewhat one-sided) 10-step process for the successful termination of conflicts. The following description is adapted from Clarke's work, originally framed in international terms. In order to achieve a good outcome, it would presumably be essential to add to these steps the advice of Janis and Mann for avoiding "groupthink," described in Chapter 8.

Step 1. Define the problem. What is the nature of the dispute? How important is the dispute to each party? What are both sides' objectives?

Step 2. Define "settlement"/post-conflict situation (strategic vision). What do we want the situation to look like after the conflict phase is completed?

Step 3. Analyze courses of action. Conduct a cost-benefit analysis for the direct and indirect effects of each option. Establish the upper limits on the power to be used.

Step 4. Select a course of action that will achieve the "victory criteria" within the upper limits of power that have been decided upon.

Step 5. Synchronize the courses of action selected from the above analysis. Define decision points (conditions) for changing of ends, ways, or means. (Preempt, escalate or intensify, do nothing, quit.)

Step 6. Execute the plan/strategy.

Step 7. Evaluate to determine if the plan is unfolding as envisioned.

Step 8. Based on the evaluation either return to step 2 or if "victory" has been achieved then proceed to:

Step 9. Execute the post-hostility process planned for.

Step 10. Settlement. (Adapted from pp. 44–45)

Similar steps—but with an aura of more cooperation between disputants—emerge from a flowchart model of conflict resolution, developed by Littlefield, Love, Peck, and Wertheim (1993).

A Third Dimension

In theory, one would expect a third dimension to emerge in the analysis of conflict resolution, namely, "instrumentally controlled vs. emotionally expressive" (Hare, 1983, p. 509). Some findings here are probably waiting to be uncovered! For instance, perhaps good solutions require a mixture of intellect and emotion.

Anyone interested in researching this might look at the effects of parties approaching conflict resolution with varying degrees (and mixtures) of being serious and objective rather than emotional, of being oriented to the task at hand rather than to the social needs of participants, and of conforming to expectations rather than acting in unexpected or random ways.

Negotiation

A possibly conforming, "expected" procedure is for conflicting parties to negotiate, although negotiation itself can be done with varying degrees of regularity or innovation. Given the leadership findings reported in Chapter 6, one might expect to find an interaction between a negotiator's sex and optimal manner, with men being perceived as better negotiators if they rely relatively more heavily on instrumentally controlled (that is, task-oriented) strategies.

The late Jeffrey Rubin made major contributions to the field of conflict resolution, and among these are some empirically derived recommendations for negotiation. Several prescriptions are described succinctly in a summary of Rubin's advice:

(a) be aware of the tightropes that confront both parties, (b) avoid the need to impress others, (c) maintain moderate sensitivity to the moves and gestures of the other party, (d) encourage moves that allow the other negotiator to feel competent, (e) avoid commitments to positions of intransigence, and (f) maintain sensitivity to the intensity of the conflict. (Rubin, 1983/1984)

The three main psychological approaches to understanding negotiation have focused on individual differences, motivation, and cognition (Thompson, 1990). One of the clearest findings—from motivational studies—is that overly high aspirations can block agreement. This is probably not surprising but does serve as a salutary reminder of the need for moderation.

Cognitive approaches analyze information-processing models and help identify sources of bias that hinder negotiations. A common example of such bias is the assumption that the other party's interests are completely opposed to one's own needs.

THIRD PARTIES

Negotiation is often seen in settings having "third parties." Third parties can, for instance, be invited to provide mediation—services such as facilitating communication between disputants and helping to find suitable compromise solutions—or arbitration, directed toward solutions that are binding.

Three generalizations emerged in Rubin's (1980) review of relevant research: (1) third parties can help disputants "save face," because concessions can be attributed to the independent mediator's suggestions; (2) techniques that are effective in low-intensity conflicts may fail or even be counterproductive in very hostile disputes; and (3) mediators may sometimes be unwelcome, so it is important that they have or find an "invited entry."

A number of social scientists—including Carl Rogers (1982), Herbert Kelman (1992), Leonard Doob (1970), John Burton (1979), and others—have highlighted the value of bringing together disputants (or their representatives) in informal small-group workshops, preferably under the auspices of a prominent third-party, in a nonthreatening, reasonably secluded setting. There, participants can say things "off the record," can explore what they and their adversaries "really want," and, if need be, can communicate with each other indirectly through good-willed third parties. The "Camp David" talks between Egyptian and Israeli leaders—mediated by Jimmy Carter, then President of the United States—provide a prominent example (Hare & Naveh, 1985).

COLLECTIVE DILEMMAS

Collective dilemmas can represent a particularly challenging "conflict" to resolve. Problems can arise not through the "fault" of the parties concerned but due to an entrapping reward structure.

A colorful although artificial example is the "dollar auction," where participants are asked to bid for a dollar bill. The dollar goes to the highest bidder, but it is explained that *both* of the two highest bidders must pay out their bid to the "auctioneer" experimenter. Bidders can readily be found at low amounts—10 cents, 15 cents, and so on. Typically, the first "moment of truth" comes when the bids exceed 50 cents; that is, the auctioneer is guaranteed a profit. A second moment of truth arises when the individual bids exceed a dollar and, indeed, then go much higher! The procedure was devised by Shubik, studied extensively by Teger, and analyzed lucidly by Rubin (1981), who offers some general advice about social traps:

Set limits on your involvement and commitment in advance.

Once you set a limit, stick to it.

Avoid looking to other people to see what you should do.

Beware of your need to impress others.

Remind yourself of the costs involved.

Remain vigilant. (Rubin, 1981, as extracted in Hare, Blumberg, Davies, & Kent, 1994, p. 233)

Of course, this advice might not help much when we are unaware that we are in a social trap. Perhaps there is a scarce resource that we are "rewarded" for over-using. To take an example at a larger level than the small group: only in recent years have the adverse environmental effects of automobiles been widely appreciated—pollution, congestion and, perhaps especially, the depletion of petroleum. Collectively we would be better off if, instead of driving, people used trains, buses, bicycles, and their feet. Even with this awareness, many people use their cars because, with everyone else doing so, public transportation is sometimes inadequate.

A similar situation can arise in small groups if individuals are in effect rewarded for acting individually rather than pooling resources for the common good. The prisoner's dilemma game, discussed in the next chapter, represents an especially heavily researched form of collective dilemma. Co-operative learning procedures such as jigsaw classroom, mentioned near the start of this chapter, can help delineate reward structures in which "everyone wins."

REVIEWS AND SOURCES OF PRACTICAL ADVICE

O'Donnell and O'Kelly (1994) describe and contrast a variety of cooperative-learning techniques for the classroom and explain how to deal with problems that can arise. The techniques include not only the promotion of peer tutoring and individual rehearsal within an overall "traditional teacher presentation and student recitation" framework, but also investigation and problem solving within established cooperative groups. For a bibliography and structural framework of prosocial behavior, see Kent and Blumberg (1988/1992b). For psychological research related to how we can cooperate to achieve a sustainable ecology, see McKenzie-Mohr and Oskamp (1995) and Staub and Green (1992).

For an outstanding review of classic work in the area of conflict resolution and negotiation (a topic related to peace psychology), see Deutsch (1986); see also, other chapters in the same volume and also Deutsch (1973). Johnson et al. (1981) provide a meta-analytic review comparing cooperation to various forms of competition. Rubin's (1980, 1983) work, cited in this chapter, is well worth reading. Likewise, that of Fisher and Ury (1981). For practical advice on handling crises see, for instance, Parry (1990).

For an excellent review of psychological theories of two-party negotiation, see Thompson (1990). For additional practical advice, see Leritz (1987). For a review that covers both negotiation and mediation, see Carnevale and Pruitt (1992).

SUMMARY

Cooperative educational techniques, such as the jigsaw classroom, can not only foster good interpersonal relations (including the reduction of prejudice) but also usually yield better learning.

If one does get caught up in a hostile relationship, or even an "arms race," it may be possible to induce cooperation by carrying out a carefully graduated series of positive initiatives (GRIT strategy).

Various example sets of helpful suggestions for dealing with conflict are included in the text of the chapter.

Three major dimensions of conflict are dominance (size and complexity of conflict or activeness of participants), positive-negative evaluation ("conflict" suggests negative activity, although to solve difficulties productively can be a necessary growth experience), and task-serious versus social-emotional emphasis. A moderately positive, moderately dominant approach to conflict resolution seems to work best. Sometimes a third party—a mediator or arbitrator, for instance—can help.

CHAPTER 10

Bargaining, Coalitions, and Games

Herbert H. Blumberg

In recent decades, there has been a steady flow of small-groups studies in which subjects bargain with one another as individuals, or join forces to form winning groups, or play "matrix games" in which they learn (or fail to learn) how to cooperate.

Indeed, our understanding of the basic processes of bargaining, coalition formation, and prisoners' dilemma and other games may have outstripped efforts to apply this understanding to the "real world." More research in applying the findings would still be most welcome!

The present chapter displays and explains three basic experimental procedures dealing, respectively, with bargaining, coalitions, and games. Each section begins with an introductory anecdote, followed by a description of the sample experimental procedure. Each example can itself be used at three levels: as a textbook or classroom demonstration, as a template for experiments, and as a representation of real-life phenomena. Finally, for each area, I briefly consider a multidimensional ("SYMLOG-based") analysis of the area (Bales & Cohen, 1979) and look at research developments.

The names, at least, of the three areas are memorable. By shifting the words around, and permitting "game" to be abbreviated as "ge," one arrives at the phrase *COAL-BARGE* as an abbreviation for "coalitions, bargaining, and games." Visualize several groups of subjects sitting around small tables to play the various procedures, and imagine that these tables themselves are on the deck of a rather sooty barge which is otherwise used to carry coal down the river to a nearby old-fashioned electricity power station. This initial practice at stretching your imagination (to visualize a coal-barge) may be useful as you also try to imagine the full meaning and applicability of the experiments I am about to describe.

BARGAINING

Anyone who has studied the shelves in a supermarket will realize that (usually!) it works out cheaper to buy things in larger packages. A half-gallon container of milk is usually a better value than a pint, a quart, or a liter; and a gallon bottle is a better value still, if you can open and pour it without spilling the milk, and can finish it before it spoils.

A further truth is available to you if (for example) you have ever been part of a small urban food co-op and, going along with a neighbor, have taken a turn at trudging down to an early-morning wholesale vegetable market in search of three bags of onions, two boxes of bananas, and a variety of other like items. The truth is this. Yes, there may well be considerable savings to be made from bulk buying, but the *potential* extent of the savings is not immediately apparent—unlike the more recent and more prosaic bulk-buy warehouse clubs. In many wholesale vegetable markets, prices are generally not displayed on or near the bags of fruit and vegetables, so you need to ask various vendors what the prices are and how the cost varies with quantity. Some of the questions may be difficult to formulate. If it is near to closing time, will the last eight trays of "very ripe" strawberries be only slightly more expensive than four of them? Could your co-op actually use all eight?

In negotiating a purchase, you are free to try to bargain, that is, to offer less than the asking price. Some economic and psychological matters complicate the process however. You might not know exactly how much the wholesalers themselves have had to pay nor what they regard as a fair profit.

It may also be unclear what their *time* is worth. If they are very busy, they may find it costly (of time) to sell "just" two or three bags of potatoes and even more costly to have protracted discussions about the matter. During slack periods, however, some may positively welcome discussions about their trade and its economics. If particular vendors are chronically less busy, however, you may wonder why. (High prices for the given quality? Merely a narrow specialty—selling only parsnips and mushrooms? Very talkative personality?) Your own time also has a value, of course, and the extent to which you enjoy the experience and value a break from other commitments must enter into the calculation.

The main features of the wholesale-market example do show up in typical experiments on bargaining. In principle, moreover, the research is meant to extend to more abstract forms of interpersonal bargaining, such as small groups deciding among alternatives—for instance, a household planning where to spend a holiday or a research team allocating and prioritizing a set of tasks.

Let us look, in turn, at two sets of figures, similar to those used by Kelley and Schenitzki (1972, pp. 300, 327); they themselves adapted their first set of figures from Siegel and Fouraker (1960).

Tables 10.1 and 10.2 can both be used in classroom demonstrations of bargaining. The procedures are not original with me, but I have successfully tested them many times and in a variety of classroom settings. You are urged to try these out, either in the classroom or with a partner but, even if you don't, then simply reading the description will mean that the exercise will serve you as a textbook demonstration. First, the procedure; then, the rationale.

First Bargaining Procedure (Adapted)

Subjects play in pairs and are randomly assigned the roles of seller and buyer. In the example shown in Table 10.1, the seller could be viewed as the vegetable wholesaler, and the buyer would be the purchaser for the food co-op. The procedure can be carried out either with the entire table in front of both players (full information) or with each player seeing only his or her "own half" of the table (incomplete information).

A shorthand account of each play is recorded by means of the buyer and seller passing a single sheet of paper back and forth between them. To start, the buyer makes an initial offer. The seller either accepts the offer, or else notes an alternative offer and passes this back to the buyer. The play continues until an offer is accepted. Sometimes one "round" is followed by more rounds.

The buyer might begin by offering to purchase 3 bags at 30 units (pennies?) each, for example; the table shows that the buyer's profit, if such an offer were accepted, would be 750 pennies. (In our example, "profit" might mean how much the co-op would save compared to buying the same items at a local supermarket.) The seller, however, would be obliged to reject an offer of 3 bags at 30 units each, because the tables show a blank (i.e., a loss), which is not permitted. So the seller would make an alternative offer for the buyer to consider.

Rationale

The figures in the table itself represent a dependent variable—the payoff structure. The figures in Table 10.1 are, as it happens, arranged in a reasonably plausible way: (1) as the price goes up, the seller's profit increases and the buyer's profit decreases; (2) as quantity increases, the buyer's and seller's joint total profit first increases and then decreases, so that there is an optimal intermediate quantity. We can imagine that larger quantities are advantageous to both parties, up to a point; but there may be high transportation costs *per unit* if the seller has to make special loading arrangements and, for the buyer, there is a point beyond which a larger quantity is useless. The items may spoil before use and, especially if the price is high, the buyer will be unable to resell the excess at a profit.

The procedure can be (and has been) used to test a wide variety of variables. These include, among others, the following three categories, presented here with some sample findings. (Some of these are as cited by Hare, Blumberg, Davies, & Kent, 1994, chapter 10.)

1. *Background variables.* Among major demographic and individual variables are: age, sex, personality, etc., of the players, and interactive background matters, such as whether they know each other beforehand.

   For instance, females bargainers have, in some studies, been found to be more cooperative than males and to reach the same number of agreements but more quickly. People who imagine themselves to have high personal strength tend to be tougher bargainers, which sometimes means that they get more profits, but also can make it less likely that they will reach agreement at all, particularly if their toughness is unyielding over time.

2. *Process and outcome variables.* How do the players go about bargaining, what strategies do they use, and with what results? Does "tough bargaining" lead to better outcomes for self? When do the two players together achieve maximum joint profit (MJP)?

   One strategy is particularly worth noting here—it could be called "systematically exploring successive frontiers of diminishing profits." In other words, particularly if players only see their own half of the profit tables, either player might begin by trying out all of the offers which are most profitable to self, and gradually work down to less profitable levels, until the other player finds an offer acceptable. If even one player does this systematically, both are likely to wind up better off than if players take shortcuts in exploring the matrix or agree "too quickly."

3. *Independent variables.* These include the nature and arrangement of the tables, whether the players have full information, whether there are real rewards, and the rules of the game. These variables relate to questions such as: How many rounds are played? Are offers made by one player at a time, as described above, or does the seller make offers about price and the buyer make offers about quantity? Is there a price penalty for taking too much time? Can the procedure be adapted for more than two players at a time?

Having a limited amount of help can facilitate agreement, for instance, a third party who offers advice. Even *anticipation* that a third party is to be forthcoming may cause bargainers to be more cooperative. Oddly, if you know that the third party is affiliated to the *other* side, this could make agreement more likely, because it may lower your outcome expectations and lead you to accept more compromise (Conlon & Ross, 1993).

Representing other people (as when you are buying for a food co-op?) could lead to harder bargaining so that "you don't let the others down." Alternatively, "reasonable" solutions may be more likely if you have the

Table 10.1
Profit Tables

Seller's Profit Table

Price (per sack)	Quantity (e.g., no. of sacks)			
	8	9	10	11
240	1190	1350	1430	1430
230	1120	1260	1320	1300
220	1050	1170	1210	1170
210	980	1080	1100	1040
200	910	990	990	910
190	840	900	880	780

Buyer's Profit Table

Price (per sack)	Quantity (e.g., no. of sacks)			
	8	9	10	11
240				
230				
220				
210	50	0		
200	120	90	33	
190	190	180	143	91

221	253	270	260	180	650	770	810	770	180
351	363	360	330	170	520	660	720	700	170
481	473	450	400	160	390	550	630	630	160
611	583	540	470	150	260	440	540	560	150
741	693	630	540	140	130	330	450	490	140
871	803	720	610	130	0	220	360	420	130
1001	913	810	680	120		110	270	350	120
1131	1023	900	750	110		0	180	280	110
1261	1133	990	820	100			90	210	100

Source: An original table incorporating principles used by Siegel & Fouraker (1960), Appendix B, pp. 113–115, and adapted by Kelley & Schenitski (1972), p. 300.

165

Table 10.2
Rewards in Multi-Issue Bargaining

Payoff Table for Player I

	Issue		
	1	2	3
A	1	21	11
B	11	21	21
C	19	21	29
D	24	21	34
E	28	20	38
F	34	20	44
G	44	20	54
H	51	19	61

Payoff Table for Player II

	Issue		
	1	2	3
A	20	11	100
B	19	18	94
C	18	23	27
D	16	27	77
E	13	29	61
F	9	34	38
G	8	40	32
H	7	45	24

Source: An original table incorporating principles used by Kelley & Schenitski (1972), p. 327.

"knowledge" that you are representing other people ("constituents") who expect you to behave cooperatively.

Experiments and Real-Life Paradigms

The demonstrations can be run as experiments virtually unaltered. Typically, real rewards are offered. Each pair might, for instance, carry out three rounds of bargaining and earn a penny for every ten points of own (tabled) profit in the agreed sales.

One can also test procedures not ordinarily used in the classroom demonstrations, such as seeing how players react to various programmed strategies used by their "partners." Whether the results reflect real-life bargaining is itself an empirical question, which largely still remains to be answered.

Multi-Issue Variant

Table 10.1 "looks" more like the wholesale-vegetable example, and Table 10.2 better fits the situation of a work partnership or a household trying to decide on various issues.

In the latter case, issue 1 might be "where to spend a holiday weekend." Issue 2 could be "what color should we paint the living room?" Issue 3 perhaps relates to various schemes for allocating household tasks. Notice that, in this example, the various lettered alternatives, A through H (in Table 10.2), would take on different meanings for the various issues. For issue 1 (holidays), A might represent camping in a very rural area, B might mean renting a cottage in the moors, C could be a seashore resort, and so on; whereas for issue 2 (room color), A through H would represent various colors of paint.

The figures in Table 10.2 represent "metaphorical rewards" (e.g., "how much" each player would like the various possible holidays or room colors). Given the particular numbers in the Table, the two players appear to have very different preference hierarchies, and they attach different levels of importance to the various issues. For instance, player 1 might not have much preference among room colors: issue 2 has less impact for player 1 (reward range 28 to 32) than for player 2 (range 16 to 68).

The procedure for this game is similar to that for the basic bargaining game of Table 10.1. When there is more than one issue, however, an offer may encompass more than one issue, and a round does not end until the players have agreed on an alternative for each issue. Player 1 might begin by "offering" 1-A (option A for issue 1) plus 3-A. Player 2 might reject the offer, and propose 1-H plus 3-A. And the offers and counteroffers would proceed from there.

One question that arises is whether it is better to settle one issue at a time or to wait until there is a "package" which both parties find acceptable. Profit levels are generally higher if players seek a suitable package before finally agreeing on any of the constituent issues, because such bargaining affords the opportunity to "keep options open" for trading off one issue against another. For particularly complicated or protracted situations, however, it may be easier to reach agreement by settling one issue at a time.

Dimensional Analysis and Additional Research

Better outcomes would be expected when bargainers are moderately assertive, friendly (or even humorous!), and task-oriented. In SYMLOG terms, that means being fairly dominant, positive, and forward. Recall that if even one player takes the trouble to explore the task's payoff matrix systematically, both are likely to wind up better off than otherwise. Ironically, if players are so friendly that they do not wish to "impose" such exploration on one another, the outcome may suffer. Promises and threats (if nonhostile) may have positive effects, but penalties may have negative ones. (For specific sources of the foregoing general findings, see Hare, Blumberg, Davies, & Kent, 1994, chapter 10.)

If you are especially assertive, what effect does that have on others? Where sellers have marked competition—in car sales, for instance—a dominant buyer may simply achieve a better purchase price (Cialdini, Bickman, & Cacioppo, 1979). However, when both parties have *moderately* high aspirations, and where their needs are, in principle, compatible, it is helpful if even one of the parties adopts a "problem-solving" orientation, seeking a "formula" for resolving their situation. That is, at least one bargainer does either or both of the following: (1) seeks the other party's reaction to a large variety of tentatively advanced options (perhaps through trial and error), or (2) requests and provides valid information about profits (information exchange). Such an orientation encourages the other party to do likewise (Pruitt & Lewis, 1975).

In fact, researchers of late have continued to explore the advantages of what is now called Mutual Gains Bargaining (MGB)—training bargainers to look for solutions in which all parties benefit. Joint training of both sides (e.g., labor and management) can include matters such as (1) looking for solutions that are within everybody's "acceptance latitude," (2) having open creative "brainstorming" sessions to seek a variety of possible solutions, (3) considering how to balance the demands of all parties and their constituents (see, for instance, Ancona, Friedman, & Kolb, 1991).

Research has provided many concrete suggestions about successful bargaining, but they are not well organized into systematic theory. It is probably still true that, as Chertkoff and Esser (1983, p. 158) put it, "What seems to be needed in bargaining research are theories of greater specificity and precision and research of greater theoretical relevance."

Sometimes bargaining takes place between coalitions rather than between individual parties; indeed, bargaining may be involved in the process of *forming* coalitions.

COALITIONS

On August 2, 1990, Iraq invaded Kuwait; within seven hours troops occupied the capital (ACCESS & Simpson, 1994). Later in the chain of events, a coalition of countries, most notably including the United States, acting with the agreement of the United Nations (if not under its aegis), repelled the invaders and freed Kuwait.

The parties to these events were a rather large group of nations rather than a small group of people, but the war does illustrate some of the principles of coalition formation; and the most visible policy makers—George Bush, Saddam Hussein, and others—did form a fairly small group that moreover, arguably, had the electronic and diplomatic equivalent of face-to-face interaction.

We can observe that one party (Kuwait) was not in a position to repel the invasion, but that the pooled resources of countries allied in the purpose were more than adequate for the purpose. The events also help to explain some puzzling features of coalition formation. The resources needed to "win" may be very different from the rewards which the winner acquires. The United States acting on its own clearly would have had the sheer power to overcome Iraq, but in doing so would no doubt have accumulated so much ill will among countries in the Middle East for intruding in their affairs that its probable goal of safeguarding its interests in regional oil would have been poorly met. The larger and more legitimate coalition had "more power than it needed," but it also carried a distribution of rewards that was more satisfactory to the nations concerned, apart from Iraq.

Certain other aspects of the war were more relevant to "bargaining when one has to satisfy one's constituency," a topic already discussed above, than to coalition formation. These include the relatively hidden but effective control of Western media and the arguably insufficient trial of nonviolent sanctions against Iraq (see Blumberg & French, 1994).

Demonstration

A classroom demonstration of coalition formation can be based on a classic study by Gamson (1961), as described by Stryker (1972). Class members are divided into groups of five players, and any people left over are assigned the roles of observers and scorekeepers. Each group sits around a table and is asked to play the roles of five political candidates (designated by the five colors shown in Table 10.3) who need to form coalitions in order to win an election. Within each group, every player has a large

Table 10.3
Demonstration of Coalition Formation: Initial Distribution of Resources and Payoffs for Three Experimental Situations

Situa-tion		Player (Color)				
		Red	Yellow	Blue	Green	White
1	Votes	20	20	20	20	20
	Jobs	100	100	100	100	100
2	Votes	17	25	17	25	17
	Jobs	100	100	100	100	100
3	Votes	15	35	35	6	10
	Jobs	90	100	0	90	0

Source: Gamson, W.A. (1961). An experimental test of a theory of coalition formation. *American Sociological Review, 26,* 565–573.

card indicating to which one of the five colors he or she has been assigned; each player also has five little cards, one for each of the five colors. Each group plays one or more rounds.

The object of a round is to form a winning coalition—a group of players holding 51 or more of the 100 available votes. As a "reward," the winning coalition divides among its members a certain number of points, indicated by the number of patronage "jobs" shown in Table 10.3. If time permits, each group plays one or more rounds for each of the three situations shown in Table 10.3.

To start a round, one of the players or observers gives a starting signal. Each player holds up a small card showing the color of the person she or he wishes to bargain with—holding up one's own color means that one does not wish to bargain at that signal. If there are no reciprocal choices, then the starting signal is simply given again. If there are any reciprocal choices (e.g., yellow chooses blue and blue chooses yellow), the members concerned attempt to reach agreement on the following question: "If we should form part of a winning coalition, how would we divide the rewards—at least as regards the two of us?" If they can agree on a division of rewards, then they become a coalition for the remainder of that round and play as a partnership under one of the two colors. If yellow and blue formed a coalition, for instance, then one of their colored cards (say blue— it doesn't matter which, but they must tell the other players which one) would drop out from the remainder of that round.

To continue the round, the starting signal is then given again. The round ends when a winning coalition is formed, that is, one which controls at least 51 votes.

Several predictions can be "tested" in the demonstration. One is that the quickest and smallest winning coalitions are the most likely. In Situation 1, if yellow and blue have formed an interim coalition (with 40 votes between them), then the winning coalition is likely to include yellow-blue and one other player rather than for a coalition among all of the other three players to take place.

Another prediction is that the most likely winning coalitions are the "cheapest" ones, that is, those with (a little more than) the minimum number of winning votes. Thus, in Situation 2, a red-yellow coalition (42 votes, needing only 9 more to win) is more likely to join with blue (17 votes) than with green (25 votes), because green, having more "power" than blue, would probably demand a larger share of the reward.

A further principle that may get demonstrated is the irony of "pivotal power" or "weakness is strength." In Situation 3, for example, if interim red-yellow and blue-white coalitions have formed, then green is likely to be able to command a much larger share of the rewards than its mere six votes would suggest, because green would hold a balance of power, for which the two interim coalitions could bid. Notice, however, that there is a point beyond which green's "asking price" would be too high, for the two coalitions could, if necessary, simply join with each other to win.

All three of the demonstrations in this chapter may (correctly) seem "artificial" to some students, and there are several answers to this point. At least they do demonstrate the main concepts, which can otherwise be elusive. True, in discussion, people often point out ways in which the demonstration "differs from reality." Usually, however, the differences can actually be built into a revised version of the experiment. In any case, the demonstration may help to form interesting questions that might otherwise go unasked and therefore unanswered.

This demonstration can also serve as a template for experiments, usually employing real rewards. Subjects may be told that at the end of the session, members of the winning coalitions will accumulate cash prizes in which each "patronage job" which they have earned will be worth a certain amount of money.

As in the case of bargaining, experiments have included a wide variety of background, process, and independent variables. Many of the studies in the latter two categories—dealing with experimental process and independent manipulation of reward structure and other experimental conditions—have been designed to test various theories of coalition formation.

Background Variables

A wide array of these has been studied, but their effects tend to be small or to occur only under certain conditions (Hare, Blumberg, Davies, & Kent, 1994, chapter 10). For example, how well players like each other affected coalition formation only when the players' resources (like jobs and votes in the above demonstration) were similar across players.

Background variables may contribute to the individual differences in results. As the classroom demonstrations in this chapter readily demonstrate, a single predictable outcome is unlikely. The same conditions can lead to a wide variety of results. In the present case, the goal is to understand the "distribution of coalitions that occur" under specific conditions.

Theories

Particular attention has been paid to various theories of coalition formation—which coalitions are most likely to form, and how rewards are likely to be divided (Komorita & Kravitz, 1983). The results are difficult to summarize simply, but some relevant factors, such as simplicity, small size, and minimum necessary resources, are manifest in the "predictions" already described above.

Players' expectations about rewards may change, and changed expectations may affect what actually happens. At the outset, the "wealthiest" players may seek rewards proportional to their resources (a "proportionality" norm of equity), and the players with fewer resources may feel that a fair share is simply an equal share ("equality" norm). Early divisions of rewards may fall somewhere in the middle between proportionality and equality.

As additional rounds and situations are experienced, players form expectations about the maximum reward they can expect in each of various possible coalitions. These expectations help to determine which coalitions in fact become stably reformed, and what rewards are expected by the various members of the winning coalitions.

With coalition formation in real life, prior acquaintance and similarity of purpose or ideology would appear to be important, but it seems difficult to demonstrate this in experimental studies of coalition formation. A worthwhile challenge would be to try bringing together three largely separate research areas: friendship (Davies & Blumberg, 1988), helping (Kent & Blumberg, 1988/1992b), and coalitions.

Dimensional Analysis and Additional Research

Although many studies have been concerned with how people go about forming coalitions, the "SYMLOG" dimensions have apparently not been examined systematically: what are the effects of being friendly or unfriendly, dominant or inactive, serious about the task versus unpredictable and emotional?

As in bargaining, one would presume that it is best to be moderately positive-dominant-serious. Friendliness invites reciprocation, and acting together is almost the essence of coalitions. If one is not at least moderately assertive, one might simply get overlooked! Finally, one needs a certain amount of predictive and serious concern with the task at hand in order to be a productive party to a coalition.

Any variables which predict social interaction, such as mutual positive perception of self and another, may also predict the formation of coalitions or cliques (Virk, Aggarwal, & Bhan, 1983).

Surely, being negative and dominant toward other parties is to invite the formation of a coalition *against* one's self—that is what happened to Saddam Hussein on invading Kuwait. Aggression does not always precipitate an opposing winning coalition, however. Intergroup historical examples might include China's annexation of Tibet, or American treatment of Native Americans in the nineteenth century. What determined the outcomes in these cases or in interpersonal examples you might be familiar with?

Whether people cooperate or compete may of course follow from the "reward structure" of a situation rather than from personality or the "tone of social interaction." The much-studied "prisoners' dilemma" and similar

Table 10.4
Payoff Matrix for Prisoners' Dilemma (or Commuters' Dilemma)

		Others' choice	
		Cooperate (train)	Defect (Car)
Your choice	Cooperate (train)	+10 for you; +10 for others	+2 for you; +12 for others
	Defect (car)	+12 for you +2 for others	+5 for you; +5 for others

"games" provide laboratory paradigms for studying cooperation versus competition.

PRISONERS' DILEMMA AND OTHER GAMES

Whenever we decide to drive somewhere rather than take public transportation, we are potentially engaged in a large-scale prisoners' dilemma game.

If everyone took the train, when feasible, there would surely be a wider and more frequent service, and substantial amounts of relatively scarce fuel would be conserved for future needs. In short, we (and the next generation) would probably nearly all be better off. Let's say our rewards would be +10 on some arbitrary scale. As things are, many people seem to drive much of the time and, despite the heavy traffic and wasted fuel, often get to their destinations more quickly than they could by train. Perhaps the rewards for driving—if that is what nearly everyone is doing, mainly on crowded roads—are often around +5 on the same arbitrary scale.

What happens when most people drive but a substantial minority go by train? If we leave aside the ecological satisfaction and comfort of the train journey: those who do drive have the benefit of less crowded roads and fairly quick door-to-door journeys, but there is relatively little fuel conservation for the population as a whole. In the short run, perhaps drivers' rewards would be +12 in this situation. Those who use the limited number of trains do at least get to their destinations, possibly at a high price and with little population-wide conservation of fuel. Perhaps their rewards are +2.

Let us look at a "payoff matrix" for this situation, and also see how it can apply to small groups. Table 10.4 displays the rewards associated with the situation. (The figures in this example have been unashamedly adjusted to fit the paradigm.) Clearly the best joint outcome, and nearly the best individual outcomes, take place when everyone agrees to take the train. Unfortunately, in reaching a decision, you could reason as follows. Others will do one of two things: (1) they will take the train, in which case I will be better off driving (in the first column of figures, you get only +10 for taking the train but +12 for driving); or (2) they will drive, in which case I would *again* be better off driving (last column of figures, you get only +2 for the train but +5 for driving). Like you, everyone could reason that way, and, in the absence of appropriate schemes of incentives for train travel, all would wind up in the comparatively undesirable lower right cell of the table. This table may help (a little) to explain why freeways and motorways can be overflowing, while trains in many places are infrequent or nonexistent.

The prisoners' dilemma itself follows a similar logic. The following is a hypothetical paradigm attributed to A. W. Tucker.

Two men suspected of a crime have been taken into custody and separated. The district attorney is confident that the two together have committed the crime but he does not have evidence that is adequate to convict them. He points out to each prisoner alone that each has two alternatives: to confess to the crime the police are sure they have committed or not to confess. If they both do not confess the district attorney states that he will book them on some minor charge such as illegal possession of weapons and each will get one year in the penitentiary. If both confess they will be prosecuted but the district attorney will recommend less than the most severe sentence; both will get eight years in the penitentiary. However, if one confesses and the other does not then the one who confesses will receive lenient treatment for turning state's evidence while the other will get the maximum penalty. The lenient treatment might mean six months in jail and the maximum might be twenty years. (Brown, 1965, p. 738)

The figures from both the car-train situation and the prisoners' dilemma itself can be readily translated into classroom demonstrations or laboratory experiments. In each case, subjects work in pairs. In a series of trials, each pair member must take the part of one of the players and choose one of the options, using figures such as those in Table 10.4.

In the case of the prisoner's dilemma, the rewards are framed as penalties. It is straightforward, however, to begin by "giving" each subject a set amount of money to play with; in every trial, each player forfeits some of the money according to the penalties associated with the pair's joint choices.

What will induce players to cooperate with each other? One can look at the same classes of variables used to investigate bargaining and coalitions.

Background variables include sex, personality, and prior acquaintance. Mainly these give conditional or interaction effects—such as males, but not females, being more cooperative if their partner is described as being of low status (Clark, 1983). Also, there are cross-cultural differences in co-operation as well as in bargaining and coalition formation (see, for instance, Polley, 1989, and Sparkes, 1991).

Process variables, including the strategies employed by the players, can make a big difference in outcomes. Often players take their cues from their partners' actions. As noted in Chapter 9, one strategy that is relatively successful in inducing cooperation is: "tit-for-tat" (mimicking your partner's most recent choice) but with an added bias toward cooperation (see also, Axelrod, 1980).

Independent experimental variables have included, for instance: varying the figures in the payoff matrix, or the numbers of players or choices, or the nature of the rewards, or the possibly divergent information available to each player. Sometimes an apparent prisoners' dilemma is really a *perceptual* dilemma, in which the players both wish to cooperate but believe that the other does not (see, e.g., Plous, 1987).

Classification of Experimental Games

Literally hundreds of studies have been (and are still being) carried out using the prisoners' dilemma and similar paradigms. Pruitt (1983b) has offered a useful classification scheme of five types of experimental games, including the three major paradigms covered in the present chapter plus two others. One of these two other types is locomotion games (Deutsch, 1973): parties move forward on an actual or virtual game board—possibly some paths can be traversed by only one party at a time, creating divergent interests, or players may accumulate pegs of different colors, which enable them to earn points or steal points or "disarm," for instance. The remaining type of game is the social trap, "in which there is a strong temptation to compete and yet the typical cost of competition is greater than the fruits of that competition" (Pruitt, 1983b, p. 108).

Probably the most colorful social-trap paradigm is the money auction" (see the discussion of collective dilemmas in Chapter 9). As in the prisoners' dilemma, the outcomes would be better (for the subjects) if only they could all have agreed to cooperate. Perhaps the bidding could have begun (and ended) with one person offering 10 cents and everybody splitting the dollar!

Pruitt's (1983b) chapter concentrates mainly on prisoners' dilemma and similar games. In an effort to inject additional theory into the area, Pruitt puts forward the "goal/expectation hypothesis." A wide array of findings can be predicted simply by positing that cooperation is most likely when two conditions are met: both players have a *goal* of achieving mutual cooperation and an *expectation* that the other will also cooperate.

SYMLOG Dimensions and Additional Findings

The prediction here is similar to that suggested for bargaining and coalitions, but Pruitt's goal/expectation hypothesis helps one understand some possible underlying mechanisms. The familiar prediction, using SYMLOG dimensions, is that cooperation is more likely when players are moderately positive/dominant/task-oriented. If players acted in a negative way, one might infer that their goals were unlikely to be cooperative. If players were submissive (uncommunicative), one would simply not know what their goals were, and one might perhaps hesitate to cooperate blindly. Third, if they were highly emotional, unpredictable, and unconcerned with the task at hand, one again would not infer "reliable cooperativeness." In the opposite directions: if another is *extremely* friendly, this may appear sarcastic or suspect; if the other is highly dominant, one might feel that there is no basis for cooperation; and if someone is *too* task-oriented, one might fear that the person is inhuman or might be unresponsive to social needs in future situations requiring cooperation. Thus, the presumed effects of different styles of social interaction are not mysterious but make sense in terms of how people plausibly respond to one another.

SUMMARY

Bargaining is likely to be most effective if at least one party "explores the successive frontiers of diminishing profit," that is, begins by proposing all of the options that are most profitable to self, and gradually tries out less profitable options, until a solution is found which is within the latitudes of acceptance of all parties concerned. With repeated experience, parties may know what sorts of solutions are likely to be effective. This is just as well, because systematic bargaining can be very time-consuming.

Parties who negotiate are not necessarily individuals but may be coalitions of individuals. The process of forming coalitions may itself entail bargaining. Typically, the most likely coalitions are those that can be formed most readily or without much "excessive" power (because an overly powerful ally, brought into a winning coalition, may command a large share of the rewards). A party that is relatively weak "on paper" but that holds a "balance of pivotal power" may be able to demand disproportionately large rewards.

In some cases, cooperation between parties may be in everybody's interests, but the "reward structure" (or apparent reward structure) of a situation may lead to noncooperative choices. As is the case with bargaining and coalition formation, the likelihood of cooperation in these "prisoners' dilemmas" and analogous situations may depend on people's backgrounds, on the strategies they employ, and on the reward structure and other particulars of the experimental procedure.

In general, cooperation is most likely when parties have mutual cooperation as a goal and expect that others do as well. Successful outcomes are often more likely if people are at least moderately friendly, assertive, and task-oriented.

PART VI

The Group and the Situation

CHAPTER 11

The Group and the Organization

A. Paul Hare

The mission and values of an organization are important influences on the social interaction in a small group. Organizations that deliver social services place more emphasis on interpersonal relations, while manufacturing organizations are more concerned with the relationships to objects. Cooperation among small-group members is more difficult in organizations that value individual performance. The function of the group in relation to the organization determines the appropriate leadership style, degree of role specialization, level of morale, and amount of cohesiveness required for the group task. While the organization affects the small group, the group may also have an influence on the organization. It may set informal norms that reduce organizational output, or it may be the key to organizational effectiveness.

THEORIES FOR SMALL GROUPS AND ORGANIZATIONS

The theories for small groups, usually of less that 30 members, are the same as those for organizations, for small networks, and for large networks (Hare, 1993). Alvarez and Robin (1992), for example, use functional theory (AGIL) for the analysis of both small groups and organizations. The typical definition of an organization is similar to that proposed by Barnard (1938, p. 73): "The consciously coordinated activities of two or more people." For example, Robey (1986, p. 16), in a textbook on designing organizations, defines an organization as "a system of roles and a stream of activities designed to accomplish shared purposes." The definition of a small group has been given in the Introduction to this book; however, as a reminder, a typical definition is that of Shaw who has written several editions of a popular text on group dynamics. After reviewing some 80 definitions of a group, he concluded that a group is: "two or more persons who are interacting with one another in such a manner that each person influences and is influenced by each other person" (Shaw, 1976, p. 446).

The main difference between "small" and "large" is in the number of members. Although organizations are usually composed of a number of small groups, even small groups can have identifiable subgroups within them. Given the use of electronic media of communication between individuals through phone, FAX, and computer, restrictions of spatial arrangements are overcome (McCann & Galbraith, 1981, pp. 71–72). Communication networks as "information systems" have characteristics similar to those of groups and organizations even though the members do not share the same physical space (Finholt & Sproull, 1990). Tichy (1981, p. 237) identified a number of roles in networks including the gatekeeper, liaison, opinion leader, and cosmopolite.

Small networks may be in the form of cliques, cabals, coalitions, or other types. Tichy (1981, p. 228) defines a "clique" as a set of persons who pursue a broad range of purposes over a long period of time, especially to meet expressive and affectional needs. In contrast, he defines a "coalition" as a temporary alliance for limited purposes. In a study of the informal structure in a factory, Burns (1955) contrasted "cliques," which allowed members who were partial failures some protection and chance to withdraw from the institution, with "cabals," which offered the possibility of "illegitimate" control to members who wished to move up in the organization. Homans labels the interaction in informal groups, that is not proscribed by formal work organizational roles, as "elementary social behavior." He observes that "elementary social behavior . . . is not driven out by institutionalization but survives alongside it, acquiring new reason for existence from it" (Homans, 1961, p. 391).

There is a special interest in "teams." However, there is usually no essential difference between the definitions given for groups and for teams (see Sundstrom and Altman, 1989, p. 176, or Larson and La Fasto, 1989, p. 19). All teams are groups, but not all groups are teams. There is an implication that teams have more clearly defined roles, higher morale, and greater productivity (Bassin, 1988, pp. 65–88; Francis & Young, 1979, pp. 6–7; Patten, 1988, p. 15). Shaplin (1964, p. 61) has noted that teams are formally organized and highly structured, for example, a surgical team in a hospital, a football team, or a police antiterrorist team. Small groups may be formal or informal. Many groups have limited role differentiation and their decision making depends primarily on individual contributions, for example, a jury, a board of trustees, or a personnel evaluation board. If a team does have minimal role differentiation, for example, a wrestling or debating team, the team is likely to be in competition with other teams and to represent some larger organization. The applied literature offers advice for managers on how to make their work groups into teams (Herrick, 1990; Tannenbaum & Yukl, 1992).

Some definitions of a group, such as that of Shaw, would seem to apply more to informal groups. However, other definitions, such as that of Cartwright and Zander in their classic text on group dynamics, stress the fact that members of a "full-fledged" group also have a system of interlocking roles and work toward a common goal (Cartwright & Zander, 1968, p. 48). Although Robey stresses the formal aspects, organizations also have their informal side. Research on organizations tends to focus on the formal side, and research on small groups tends to focus on informal or "elementary" behavior. However, small groups can also be formally organized, especially if they are part of larger formal organizations, and informal networks of individuals can function as organizations (Hare, 1993, p. 62).

In terms of functional theory, both fully functioning small groups and large organizations share the following characteristics (Hare, 1982, p. 20):

1. the members are committed to a set of values that define the overall pattern of activity;

2. the members have accumulated or generated the resources necessary for the task at hand;

3. the members have worked out an appropriate form of role differentiation and developed a sufficient level of morale for the task; and

4. the members have sufficient control, in the form of leadership, to coordinate the use of resources by the members playing their roles in the interest of the group's (or organization's) values.

An additional reason for viewing small groups as small organizations is that much of the research conducted to understand interaction in organizations has actually focused on small groups of persons. Many observers see the small group as a "microcosm" of larger organizations and indeed of whole societies (Slater, 1966). Much of the research cited in all major texts on organizations—for example, on authoritarian and democratic group atmospheres (White & Lippitt, 1960), on communication networks (Leavitt, 1951), on conformity to norms (Asch, 1955), and on situational leadership (Fiedler, 1967)—was all done on small groups.

REFERENCES TO SMALL GROUPS IN ORGANIZATIONAL BEHAVIOR TEXTS

Information about small groups typically appears in textbooks on organizational behavior in the following three ways.

1. In chapters on leadership, where most of the research evidence is from studies in small groups. However, this is appropriate for the organizational context. The effective organizational leader usually deals with a small number of persons, in a face-to-face situation, who are his or her "direct reports." These persons in turn pass on orders to their direct reports.

2. In chapters on decision making, since many management decisions are made in small groups. The "group dynamics" can lead either to "creative problem solving," providing "integrative solutions" (Follett, 1924; Pruitt, 1983a) or to "groupthink," when group members fail to be critical enough to examine the evidence (Janis, 1982).

3. In chapters on productivity where the influence, on organizational productivity, of the norms of the informal small group is noted (Taylor, 1903; Miner, 1992). Often the advantages of having individuals work alone are compared to those of having individuals work in a group, or having small "autonomous groups," for example, to assemble automobiles, as in the Volvo experiment (Katz & Kahn, 1978), or to make suggestions for more effective production using the "quality circles" developed in Japanese industry (Kosower, 1987; Porras & Silvers, 1991).

In handbooks on organizational behavior, there may be a chapter on the small group. However, most of the material in the chapter concerns the internal dynamics of the small group. There is very little attention given to the impact of the organizational context on the group or the influence of the small group on the organization (Golembiewski, 1965; Hare, 1993). Yet the small group plays an important part in organizations because the small group provides a link between the "micro-system" in which the individual is present and the "macro-system" that forms the organization (Golembiewski, 1965, p. 113), although in the 1990s more emphasis was being placed on the "macro-system" than on the "micro-system" (O'Reilly, 1991). Nemeth and Staw (1989) suggest using insights from small-group research for the analysis of organizations and vice versa.

INFLUENCE OF THE ORGANIZATION ON THE SMALL GROUP

The main influence of the organization upon the small group is to set the goal or the mission. Most formal small groups exist in organizations, which become part of the "external system," that includes the society and the environment, setting boundary conditions on the behavior in the small group (Homans, 1950, p. 316).

The boundary conditions may influence the ability of a group to make good decisions. Aldag and Fuller (1993) suggest that one of the factors that led to the "groupthink" decisions described by Janis (1982) was the insulation of the group within the organization. They identify three other classes of antecedents that may be influenced by the organization and can influence decision making:

1. decision characteristics (importance, time pressure, structure, procedural requirements, task characteristics);
2. group structure (cohesiveness, leader power, phase of group development); and
3. decision-making context (organizational political norms, prior goal attainment, external threat).

The introduction of advanced manufacturing technology, such as computers, can also affect the work of a small group (Susman, 1990). With regard to the group task, more skill may be required of members, and there may be more task interdependence if two or more workers share the same machine. However, the new technology may make it possible to give the workers timely feedback on their performance and thus reduce costs. With regard to the group dynamics, the introduction of advanced manufacturing technology tends to strengthen group boundaries and make the task more meaningful to the members, especially when the workgroup is able to identify with a completed product. However, time pressure may reduce the time available for solving social-emotional problems related to group performance.

The introduction of computers for communication between members of a small group or network in an organization makes it possible for several persons in the group to send messages to all the others at the same time rather than waiting to take turns as they would in a face-to-face group. Thus, "brainstorming" can become "electronic brainstorming" with a reduction in the effects of "production blocking" and "evaluation apprehension" experienced especially in larger face-to-face groups (Gallupe et al., 1992).

A company may create "cells" (groups of workers) on the shop floor by arranging equipment for some part of the production in close proximity. Members of the same "cell" can then work as a unit to produce their particular part of the manufactured item. Plants with cells are more likely to adopt a "just-in-time" manufacturing philosophy, where items are not stockpiled. Cellular manufacturers place greater responsibility upon shop floor workers. They provide more cross training and job enlargement. They use employee involvement programs as a tool for problem solving and continuous improvement of production processes. There are fewer labor grades, resulting in a flatter hierarchy of labor skills with more workers in the same grade. However, there is greater managerial control over the manufacturing process and the pace of production with a focus on increasing flexibility and maintaining effective process control (Magjuka & Schmenner, 1993).

The "boundary conditions" imposed by the external system may be set in the form of norms governing behavior in roles, or by physical arrangements of the space available for work (Sundstrom & Altman, 1989). An example of the latter is given by Homans in his description of the "bank wiring observation room" experiment that was part of the study at the Western Electric Company (Roethlisberger & Dickson, 1939). In that experiment, the workers who were placed in the front of the room formed one informal clique, and those in the back of the room formed another (Homans, 1950, pp. 70–72).

A more recent example is the "open plan" for offices, an innovation of the 1960s. Internal walls in office building were either removed altogether or replaced with a few partitions. The intention was to facilitate communication, heighten accessibility of fellow workers, and minimize hierarchical barriers. However, the arrangement did not solve workers' attempts to regulate privacy. Workers in open-plan offices complained about the lack of visual and acoustic privacy, compared to workers in conventional walled offices (Sundstrom, Herbert, & Brown, 1982). Homans notes that informal behavior arising in response to the physical arrangement of the work space or to other aspects of the task may come to be formalized in norms for the group. These norms, in turn, will change more slowly than the behavior of the group members (Homans, 1950, p. 412).

Robey (1986, pp. 241–271) describes several types of groups or teams that derive their function from the organizational context: liaison groups, product development teams, a matrix group formed of representatives of different departments, and a "skunk works," a small group of people given freedom to come up with good ideas. Harrison and Connors (1984) describe several types of teams whose mission requires them to operate in "exotic environments," those on space capsules, super tankers, and weather stations.

In the literature on groups in organizations, the term "group" is often used interchangeably with "team." A third term that appears in the literature is that of a "crew," which typically refers to a group of persons managing some form of technology, especially forms of transportation such as boats, aircraft, or spacecraft.

Using the functional (AGIL) cybernetic hierarchy, it is possible to make some distinctions between the different types of groups (Hare, 1992, pp. 19–21). "A" includes resources and equipment. "G" refers to management for specific tasks, by coordinating resources and roles. "I" combines the rules for work with considerations of morale. "L" refers to the overall values, and includes creativity that redefines the task and the situation. Crews of boats, planes, or spaceships can be placed at the bottom of the cybernetic hierarchy (A level) since their function is bound to a particular type of equipment or technology. Change the technology and you change the nature of the team. Aircrews are an example, where a large amount of information about the conditions of the plane and the weather must be processed in a short period of time (Foushee, 1984).

Moving up, at the "G" level are work teams in business, manufacturing, health, and education. These teams are bound to a product, an object, or the care or education of a person. Change the nature of the product or the service provided and the team must be reorganized. At the "I" level would be sports teams that are rule-driven. They produce nothing. However, the playing field is usually swarming with referees to ensure that the game is played within the rules. Change the rules and you have a new game (Kew, 1987).

At the top of the hierarchy, the "L" level, are scientific research and development teams. They are not bound by existing equipment, product, or rules. Their task is to develop new concepts and to discover new relationships between old or new concepts. Wolpert and Richards (1988, p. 9), writing about "a passion for science," suggest that: "perhaps it is, above all, the thrill of ideas that binds scientists together, it is the passion that drives them and enables them to survive."

In addition to sorting crews and teams by functional specialty (AGIL), they can be classified according to the amount of (1) integration and (2) role differentiation required. Although some merge the two continua (Dyer, 1987), they can be kept separate to form at least a two-by-two table of types of teams that are either high or low on each characteristic. Olmsted made this type of distinction for types of group leadership in his analysis of group activity (Olmsted, 1959; see also Olmsted & Hare, 1978, p. 14). Sundstrom and Altman (1989, p. 185) have also used this double dichotomy in their typology of work teams.

Sports teams provide the easiest example of this type of classification. Golf teams are low on both integration and role differentiation. Synchronized swimming teams are high on integration but low on differentiation since all swimmers perform the same activity within a prescribed pattern created by the placement of the swimmers. Track teams are low on integration but high on differentiation, with each member of the team performing a different skill at a different time. Football teams (American style) are high on both the need for integration and differentiation. Each type of team requires a different leader style, a different mix of task and social-emotional functions, and thus different solutions to the four functional problems. For some teams, the main function of the members is to support the activity of the central person, such as the surgeon in a surgical team or the pilot of an airplane.

In sum, the organization sets the overall value framework. Group habits are shaped by the organizational context (Gersick & Hackman, 1990). Organizational members' performance is controlled through the leaders of small groups (Kerr & Slocom, 1981, p. 128). High-performance teams must pay attention to the external factors in the organization, including identifying and establishing relationships with persons who are critical for their performance. In order to be seen as a winning team, team members must let others know that they are winning (Isgar & Isgar, 1993).

INFLUENCE OF THE SMALL GROUP ON THE ORGANIZATION

Small, autonomous groups can be the key to productivity if they are involved in problem solving (Susman, 1990). Ancona and Caldwell (1992) report that cross-functional teams can be a blessing or a curse for new product development. The diversity needed for new product design may result in difficulties in communication between team members. However, articles in popular business magazines, such as the *Harvard Business Review*, recommend the formation of teams with a small number of members with complementary skills. These teams can be used for a company's "critical delivery points," where the cost and value of the company's products and services are most directly determined, for example, for the management of accounts, customer service, and product design (Katzenbach & Smith, 1993). Another name for the type of mixed team that is focused on change is the "task force" (Beer, Eisenstat, & Spector, 1990).

The small group sets norms for productivity. Consultants who work with a "human relations" framework try to align the group's norms with those of the organization (Moch & Seashore, 1981, p. 218). The early Western Electric studies demonstrated that the norms of the informal small group can either raise productivity, as in the "test room" (Hare, 1967), or lower it, as in the "bank wiring room" (Roethlisberger & Dickson, 1939; Homans, 1950, p. 79). Norms can also camouflage the amount of conflict in a group which may be leading to reduced productivity (Sinclair, 1992). More recent research confirms the early Western Electric studies—informal networks can cut through formal reporting procedures to "jump start" stalled initiatives and meet extraordinary deadlines. However, they can just as easily sabotage a company's best laid plans by blocking communication and fomenting opposition (Krackhardt & Hansen, 1993). Blocking may be due simply to the constraint on groups that members can talk only in turn (Stroebe & Diehl, 1994).

Rather than leave the informal networks to chance formation, it has been proposed that they be consciously composed by the chief executive office and senior executives of a company. The members of the network would be drawn from across the company's functions, business units, and geography, and from different levels in the hierarchy. The networks would function to build trust, encourage evaluation of business problems from a broad perspective of customers and the company rather than follow narrow functional or departmental interests (Charan, 1991).

The small group that constitutes the management team in an organization is especially important. Eisenhardt and Schoonhoven (1990) conducted a longitudinal study of factors affecting growth in 98 semiconductor firms in the United States. They found that the firms had greater sales growth when the top management teams were composed of people who had worked together more in the past, when the teams were larger, and when the teams were composed of people with varying amounts of industry experience. In a study of a sample of Fortune 500 companies, the firms most likely to undergo changes in corporate strategy had top management teams with members who were younger, had shorter organization tenure, higher team work, higher educational level, higher educational specialization heterogeneity, and higher academic training in the sciences (Wiersema & Bantel, 1992).

Another group that is important is the board of directors for a company. If the board is composed of members who are independent and drawn from persons outside the company, then the top managers are likely to be rewarded on the basis of objective performance criteria. However, there is a tendency to maximize short run gains, with more diversified products, and place less emphasis on research and development. If the board of directors is drawn from the inside, the managers will be rewarded by open and subjective appraisal of the quality of the production process (Baysinger & Hoskisson, 1990).

VARIATIONS IN GROUP ROLES: AN EXAMPLE FROM SOUTH AFRICAN MINES

Just as individuals can play different roles in small groups, so groups can play different roles in organizations. Some of these roles are formal, some informal, and some dramaturgical. Just as individuals may be present or absent in a small group, so groups that play roles in organizations may already exist, or they may be formed or arise to meet a special need and then disband. Groups that already exist may maintain the same structure but change their function to meet a specific set of conditions.

An example of variations in roles is provided by the contrasts in a series of events that occurred during protests in two South African mines in 1970. In each case, the mine represents the organization. Some of the groups are relatively small: the managers, the police, and the dance team. However, the number of miners directly involved in each mine was over 1000 out of a total number of miners of about 6000.

The occasion of the protest was a notice that the homeland chief of one of the tribes of miners had changed the conditions concerning the amount of their pay that would be withheld until they returned to their homeland. Usually miners would live and work at the mines for all but about two weeks during the year when they could return to their homelands. There are records of "disturbances" in eleven mines. Two of the mines have been selected for contrast—one with the most creative management and one with the least. The disturbances took place over a period of two weeks where the management was least creative, and two and a half weeks where the management was creative. In both mines, the events of the first few days were about the same—the management took the initiative to notify the miners of the change, and the senior Black miners who were the formal spokesmen for the mines passed the word along. However, in the most creative case, both management and senior Blacks made an active effort to be sure that the miners understood the change; while in the least creative case, the senior Blacks were instructed not to tell the men, but merely to answer questions if asked.

In the least creative case, the miners who were affected by the change in pay protested, led by the members of their dance team. The dance team is composed of a group of young men who ordinarily perform tribal dances on various public occasions. Thus they are accustomed to expressing the themes of their tribe. However, this is usually done in a joyous fashion, whereas here they led the miners in a hostile attack on police who had been called in to the mine since a protest was feared. Over a period of several days, there were continuing clashes between police and miners. A small informal group of eight spokesmen for the miners met mine officials. They indicated that their grievance was with their homeland government and not the mine, and that many of the men wished to go home. The management said they would assist anyone wishing to leave. However, fighting continued, now between different tribal groups of miners. The management insisted that the miners go back to work or go home. The police then brought the miners under control. The disturbances left seven miners dead and 26 injured. Three-thousand miners were discharged. There was considerable damage to the hostel where the miners lived.

In the most creative case, the chief of the senior Blacks and a small group of three to seven spokesmen for the miners carried out discussions with the management and held meetings with the miners involved. The management tried to negotiate with the homeland chief. When they were not able to secure any changes of conditions, the miners proposed sending a 21-man delegation to their homeland and requested that one of the White managers accompany them. The mine management provided transportation for the trip. After meeting the Minister of Finance for the homeland, the delegation returned with a change in the conditions of pay that was satisfactory for the miners. No one died, there were no injuries, and no miners left the mine.

In the mine with the least creative management, the formal roles of management, senior Blacks, and police were played with no change in structure or function. The group of spokesmen for the miners played an informal role with a new structure and function. The dance team maintained their traditional structure. However, they performed their dramaturgical function as theme carriers for their tribe by leading a hostile attack rather than by representing traditional values. In the most creative case, the management and senior Blacks maintained their formal roles with their usual structure, but changed their function to that of mediators. The informal group of spokesmen had a new structure and function.

THE SMALL GROUP AS AN INSTRUMENT OF ORGANIZATIONAL CHANGE

Most of the proposals for bringing about organization change are implemented through small numbers of managers or workers in groups to learn new ways of decision making (Huse & Cummings, 1985) often with computer-supported decision-making systems (Poole & DeSanctis, 1992). New types of small groups, such as "quality circles," may be introduced as a continuing source of evaluation and new ideas (Buch, 1992). When the problem in an organization is diagnosed as a lack of sensitivity to interpersonal relations, managers and workers may be taken through experiences of "sensitivity training" (Van Buskirk & McGrath, 1993).

Proposals for change may deal mainly with the cognitive aspects of group performance as in "reconceptualization" (Friedman & Lipshitz, 1992) or through attempts to maximize all major functions in a group (Cummings, 1981). Unfortunately, in many team building workshops, tasks that are used to stimulate "creative problem solving" do not permit the solutions at the highest levels of creativity. In addition, "team building" may be achieved through providing groups with real experiences of changing group methods, rather than by using "workshops" (Hare, 1992, pp. 57–61).

SUMMARY

The social-psychological theories that apply to behavior in small groups also apply to behavior in organizations, as well as to small networks and large networks. This is especially true when the persons in the network are connected through computer-video communication. Both groups and networks may be either formal (having roles designated by their organization) or informal (with roles developed to satisfy the needs of the members in cliques or cabals or to facilitate the achievement of organizational goals).

The main influence of the organization on the small group is to define the mission of the group. The organization is part of the "external system" of the group that includes the society and the environment. In addition to setting the goal for the group, the organization may also have an influence by providing facilities for the task, including the design of the work space and means for electronic communication, or by setting norms for the types of roles that may be played.

In terms of functional theory, some groups are bound more by their equipment (such as aircrews), some by the product (such as manufacturing groups), and some by the rules of the game (such as sports teams). Some groups are not bound by any existing equipment, product, or rules, but have a task to develop new concepts and discover new relationships (such as scientific research teams). Within each type of group, a further differentiation can be made according to the amount of integration and role differentiation required.

Small groups or informal networks can be the key to increased productivity if they are involved in problem solving, or they can develop norms that are counter to those of the organization and decrease productivity. Just as individuals can play different roles in small groups, so small groups can play different roles in organizations. Some of these roles are formal, some informal, and some dramaturgical. An example from South African mines indicates that some roles may remain constant, and others may change, especially during periods of crisis for the organization.

Most of the systems for implementing organizational change involve small groups, for example, by introducing "quality circles" for workers or "team building" for managers.

CHAPTER 12

Intergroup Relations

Martin F. Davies

One of the most enduring topics in social psychology is the study of prejudice and attitudes toward other groups (mainly racial groups). Attitudes in general can be defined in terms of a cognitive component (knowledge and beliefs), an affective component (emotions and feelings), and a behavioral component. Attitudes toward groups can be similarly described in terms of a cognitive component (stereotypes), an affective component (prejudice), and a behavioral component (discrimination).

STEREOTYPING, PREJUDICE, AND DISCRIMINATION

Stereotypes are beliefs about the attributes and behaviors of a whole social group. The grouping can be based on age, sex, race, occupation, physical attractiveness, and so on. In an early study, Katz and Braly (1933) asked North American college students to identify personality characteristics associated with different racial groups. Those characteristics which most people agreed applied to a group were taken as the stereotype of the group. *Prejudice* is the tendency to prejudge members of a social group in terms of feelings and emotional reactions. Although we can have a positive attitude to some groups and a negative attitude to others, prejudice is the term usually applied when one group evaluates another group in a negative fashion. *Discrimination* is the tendency to act in a biased way toward members of a social group; typically, discrimination is taken as behaving negatively toward members of a group.

The Authoritarian Personality

An early explanation of prejudice and discrimination was the idea of a prejudiced personality. The main work here is the *authoritarian personality*.

Table 12.1
Dimensions of the F-Scale

Dimension	Description
Conventionalism	rigid adherence to conventional middle-class values
Authoritarian submission	submissive, uncritical attitude toward idealized moral authority of the ingroup
Authoritarian aggression	tendency to condemn & punish people who violate conventional values
Anti-intraception	opposition to the creative, imaginative, tender-minded
Superstition & stereotypy	belief in the mystical forces determining fate; tendency to think in dogmatic & rigid ways
Power & toughness	preoccupation with dominance-submission, strength-weakness; idealization of power figures
Destructiveness	generalized hostility
Projectivity	belief in dangerous forces: projection of unacceptable urges onto others
Sexual repression	exaggerated concern with sex

Adorno, Frenkel-Brunswik, Levinson, and Sanford (1950) suggested that people's political and social attitudes stemmed from deep-lying trends in personality. Based on ideas from Freudian theory, they argued that personality development involves the repression and redirection of unacceptable urges. Parents are the main agents in this developmental process. In normal development, there is a healthy balance between discipline and allowing the child self-expression. In the authoritarian personality, however, the child is subjected to harsh discipline and an overemphasis on conformity to conventional social norms. As a result, the child displaces its natural aggression away from the parents (because of fears of further discipline) and onto alternative targets. Typically, these targets are weaker than or inferior to the self—for example, members of minority groups. The authoritarian personality syndrome consists of (among other things) over-dependence on power and authority figures (symbolizing the parents) and hostility to members of subordinate groups.

A tendency toward authoritarianism is measured by the F-scale which was originally devised by Adorno, Frenkel-Brunswik, Levinson, and Sanford (1950) to measure fascist tendencies. The nine dimensions of the F-scale are shown in Table 12.1. Using the F-scale personality test, the researchers found that authoritarians had a repressed childhood, repressed aggression, were deferent toward authority, and were dogmatic and conservative. However, later work suggested that the F-scale was not particularly valid; for example, people who simply agreed with the questionnaire items tended to get a higher F-score. Also, it was found that extreme left-wing as well as extreme right-wing people scored high on the F-scale.

The personality explanation for prejudice has been criticized because it omits social and cultural forces that can give rise to prejudice. Pettigrew (1958) compared Whites in South Africa, the southern United States and the northern United States and found that although Whites in South Africa and the southern United States were more prejudiced toward Blacks than those in the northern United States, they did not differ in terms of authoritarianism as measured by the F-scale. Pettigrew argued that prejudice may come about because of cultural norms legitimizing negative attitudes and behavior. This explanation suggests that prejudice and racism may be commonplace in particular societies at particular times. Historically, significant changes in attitudes to social groups have been observed within a generation (for example, American attitudes toward Japanese during World War II). Such changes in prejudice are difficult to explain in terms of wholesale changes in people's personality.

Frustration-Aggression

The frustration-aggression hypothesis of Dollard et al. (1939) was also derived from psychoanalytic theories but, unlike the authoritarian personality explanation, this explanation was able to account for historical changes in prejudice. According to Dollard et al., aggression is due to frustration. Frustration occurs when a person's attempt to reach a goal is interfered with. The resulting state of tension needs to be resolved, and aggression is one way of releasing the tension. If the aggression cannot be directed at the source of the frustration, for example, because the source is too powerful, then it is displaced onto a weaker target or scapegoat. Prejudice is therefore the displacement of aggression onto minority groups. To account for historical changes in prejudice, Dollard et al. noted that social and cultural factors such as economic depression and hardship can give rise to frustration and hence to prejudice. Hovland and Sears (1940) found a correlation between the price of cotton in the southern United States (an indicator of the state of the economy) and the number of lynchings of Blacks (an indicator of prejudice and racism); the lower the price of cotton, the more lynchings occurred. However, this correlational evidence does not mean that economic changes cause changes in prejudice. Experimental studies of frustration and aggression show that frustration does not always result in aggression, and that aggression can be due to factors other than frustration (Berkowitz, 1962). Not surprisingly, therefore, the findings on frustration and prejudice are inconsistent.

Belief Dissimilarity

A third explanation of prejudice is in terms of belief dissimilarity. Rokeach (1960) argued that an important determinant of a person's attitude toward another is the similarity or congruence of belief systems. We like people who share our beliefs and opinions because they validate our view of the social world. Conversely, we dislike people who do not share our world view. Rokeach believed that prejudice is not due directly to membership of different social groups but to differences in attitudes and beliefs associated with different groups. He tested his ideas by having subjects make judgments of stimulus persons who differed in both ethnic group and belief similarity. Although racial similarity-dissimilarity had an effect on attitudes to and liking for another person, belief similarity-dissimilarity was found to have a stronger effect (Rokeach & Mezei, 1966).

There are, however, a number of criticisms of Rokeach's theory. First, Rokeach did not claim that belief similarity-dissimilarity would account for prejudice when there are strong social and cultural forces legitimizing prejudice. In these cases, he argued that any effects of belief dissimilarity would be outweighed by group membership. This seems to be a major qualification of the theory since it rules out many, if not most, cases of prejudice and racism. Second, it is not clear that the experimental paradigm which Rokeach employed has anything to say about *intergroup* prejudice; the subjects in Rokeach's experiments were reacting to information about *one* member of a different group. This individualistic orientation suggests that Rokeach was studying inter*personal* attraction rather than inter*group* prejudice. When the experimental setup is designed to focus on *group* differences, it turns out that group membership has stronger effects than belief dissimilarity.

For example, Billig and Tajfel (1973) had children allocate rewards to other children who were either similar to them (on the basis that they preferred the same kinds of painting) or for whom no similarity information was provided. In one condition, group membership was emphasized by categorizing the other children as belonging to the same group (X) or a different group (Y), whereas in a second condition group membership was not mentioned (i.e., the children were not categorized into X and Y groups). As can be seen from Figure 12.1, although belief similarity resulted in more ingroup favoritism, the effect of categorization into groups was much greater.

INTERGROUP CONFLICT

Stereotyping, prejudice, and discrimination can be seen as particular cases of intergroup relations. One pervasive feature of research on prejudice

Figure 12.1
Ingroup Favoritism as a Function of Belief Similarity and Group Membership

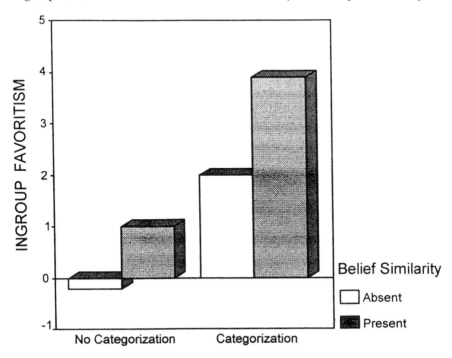

Source: Billig, M. G., & Tajfel, H. (1973). Social categorization and similarity in intergroup behaviour. *European Journal of Social Psychology, 3,* 27–52. Copyright © 1973. Reprinted by permission of John Wiley & Sons, Ltd.

is that it takes an individualistic approach to intergroup relations; it is concerned with an individual's beliefs, feelings, and reaction to another social group. More recent research on intergroup relations has recognized that an intergroup perspective is needed to understand phenomena that occur within and between groups. Most research on intergroup relations has dealt with the case where the goals and interests of one group are set against the goals and interests of another group, as, for example, in labor-management relations or disputes about territory between two neighboring countries. A typical outcome in such cases is *intergroup conflict.* However, intergroup relations do not inevitably involve conflict; if two groups are working toward the same shared goal, then intergroup cooperation can occur. (See also, Chapters 9 and 10.)

Realistic Conflict

Sherif (1967) was the first researcher to investigate intergroup relations from an explicitly group perspective. He believed that one cannot extrapolate from the properties of individuals to the characteristics of group situations. A key element of Sherif's analysis was that a group member's attitude and behavior toward another group is determined by the goals of one group relative to those of the other group. This is the basis of *realistic conflict theory*. If these goals conflict, then the group's interests are best served by adopting a competitive orientation toward the outgroup, and this can result in prejudice, discrimination, and actual conflict *between* the groups. In addition, the group's goal is likely to be achieved if group members adopt favorable attitudes toward other ingroup members, resulting in increased morale and cohesion *within* the groups. If the goals of the different groups coincide, however, then the group's interests are best served by adopting a cooperative orientation toward the outgroup. Such a cooperative orientation increases the likelihood of achieving the groups' goal.

Sherif carried out a series of studies of boys at summer camps in the United States; these studies have come to be known as the Robber's Cave experiments, after the name of the site of the camps (Sherif et al., 1961). The studies followed the activities of groups of boys over a period of weeks, and were designed to evaluate changes in attitudes and behavior as a result of changes in intergroup relations. The design consisted of three phases: group formation, intergroup conflict, and conflict reduction. The adults in charge of the summer camps were the researchers, and the boys who took part in the studies were white, middle class, about 12 years old, and had been selected so that they were well-adjusted and from stable home environments (thus eliminating any psychopathic or deviant cases). The boys were not acquainted with each other before they arrived at the camp, so that there was no existing friendship or animosity which could affect their group behavior.

Group Formation. In the first phase, the boys were split into two experimental groups, with the two groups matched as carefully as possible (on physical and psychological attributes). For some days, the boys in each group engaged in various activities without having much to do with the other group. As in other small group situations, the groups developed a structure and evolved mini-cultures with their own group symbols and names. Although there was little contact between the two groups, the observers noted that group members tended to make favorable comparisons between their own group and the other group. That is, a little bit of ingroup favoritism existed even before there was any actual conflict of interest.

Intergroup Conflict and Competition. The second phase consisted of a series of intergroup contests (e.g., softball, tug-of-war). The winner of these contests was to receive a cup, and each member of the successful group would be given a brand-new penknife. The losing group would receive nothing. Thus, an objective conflict of interest was established in this phase. The groups were now interdependent, whereas previously they had been independent. After the commencement of this phase, the boys' behavior

Figure 12.2
Ingroup Bias after Intergroup Competition

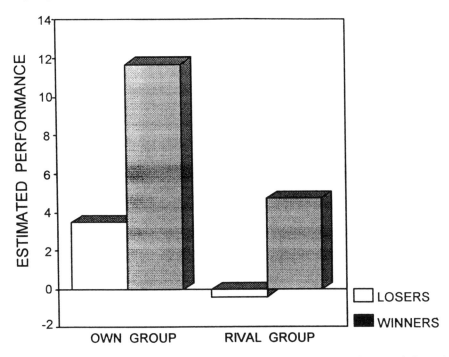

Source: Based on Sherif, M. (1967). *Group conflict and cooperation.* London: Routledge and
    Kegan Paul. Figure 5.2. Copyright © 1967 International Thomson Publishing Services
    Ltd.

changed dramatically. Whereas in the first phase, the two groups had co-
existed more or less peacefully, they now became two hostile factions, den-
igrating the outgroup, and sometimes physically attacking it. By instituting
competitive games, Sherif et al. established systematic and consistent ingroup favoritism and prejudice against the outgroup. This can be seen in
Figure 12.2, where group members overestimated the performance of their
own group members relative to rival group members. In addition, it was
found that members of the winning group tended to show more bias than
members of the losing group. Changes also took place *within* the groups;
they became more cohesive and the leadership structure changed so that a
more aggressive boy assumed the leader role.

   These findings show how the behavior of a group of ordinary well-
adjusted boys could change as the nature of intergroup relations changed.
These changes in behavior were too widespread and too rapid to be explained by enduring personality traits. In addition, members of the winning
group showed more denigration of the outgroup than did members of the
losing group who should have been the more frustrated by being denied

the prizes. Thus, explanations in terms of the authoritarian personality or frustration-aggression are not sufficient to explain the findings. Studies by Blake and Mouton (1962) also found that groups in competition tended to overvalue their own group compared to the outgroup, and Kahn and Ryen (1972) found that members of winning teams showed more ingroup bias than members of losing teams.

Another interesting aspect of Sherif's study is that it shows how intergroup relations can affect *intra*group behavior. When two groups come into conflict, each group becomes more tightly knit and cohesive. Julian, Bishop, and Fiedler (1966) confirmed this finding in a study of army recruits training under competitive or noncompetitive regimes. The competitive groups showed greater solidarity and higher morale. Similarly, the finding that intergroup conflict can change the internal structure of a group was confirmed by Sherif and Sherif (1964) in a study of urban youth gangs showing that a clearer dominance hierarchy emerged under intergroup conflict.

Conflict Reduction: Superordinate Goals

By introducing a real conflict of interest between the boys in the summer camp studies, Sherif showed how ingroup favoritism and prejudice against the outgroup can develop. According to realistic conflict theory, the way to reduce intergroup conflict is to establish a state of positive interdependence between the groups, that is, to instill a sense of cooperation so that each group's interests are best served by working toward a shared goal. Sherif et al. (1961) therefore devised a strategy of working toward *superordinate goals*. These are goals that both groups want to reach but which are not attainable by one group working on its own; they are attainable only by both groups working together. In one example, Sherif et al. arranged for the camp truck to break down a number of miles from the camp base. As the boys were getting hungry, it was imperative that the truck should be started without delay! Unfortunately for the boys (but fortunately for Sherif's theory), the truck was too heavy for either one of the groups to move on its own. The interests of both groups were therefore served by cooperating to achieve the superordinate goal of getting the truck started. Following a number of such incidents designed to produce intergroup cooperation, there was a marked reduction in intergroup hostility and also in ingroup favoritism. As shown in Figure 12.3, relative to the intergroup conflict phase, ingroup friendship choices decreased and outgroup friendship choices increased after a series of superordinate goals.

A number of subsequent studies have confirmed the finding that working toward superordinate goals reduces intergroup conflict (Brown & Abrams, 1986; Ryen & Kahn, 1975). However, some studies have shown that working toward superordinate goals does not always lead to a reduction in conflict. First and most obvious is how successful the groups are in achiev-

Figure 12.3
Friendship Choices after Superordinate Goals

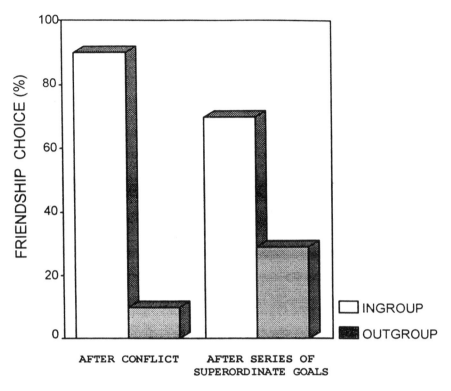

Source: Based on Sherif, M. (1967). *Group conflict and cooperation.* London: Routledge and
     Kegan Paul. Figure 5.3. Copyright © 1967 International Thomson Publishing Services
     Ltd.

ing their shared goal. In the summer camp studies, the superordinate goals
were always achieved. Therefore, it could be that success itself rather than
cooperation led to a reduction in conflict. Worchel, Andreoli, and Folger
(1977) had groups work together to achieve a superordinate goal such that
half the groups succeeded whereas the other half failed. Prior to this, the
groups had either been working cooperatively, competitively, or independently. The researchers suspected that the previous history of relations between the groups would affect their reactions to success and failure when
working together to reach a joint goal. In all cases, working toward a
superordinate goal improved intergroup relations except for the previously
competitive groups who failed to reach the goal. Further work by Worchel
and Norvell (1980) showed that unsuccessful intergroup cooperation leads
to poorer intergroup relations if the failure is attributed to the outgroup.

A second limit on the effectiveness of working toward superordinate goals is that prolonged cooperation between groups can lead to a blurring of the boundaries between the groups (Gaertner, Mann, Murrell, & Dovidio, 1989). Reducing the boundaries or barriers between groups would seem like a surefire way of reducing intergroup conflict, but in fact groups have an interest in maintaining their distinctive identities and they may react adversely to the blurring of distinctions between groups. For example, Brown and Wade (1987) had groups work cooperatively toward a superordinate goal, but they varied the extent to which the groups had distinctive roles to play in working toward the goal. They found that groups who had distinctive roles exhibited more positive intergroup relations than those whose group contributions were overlapping.

The Contact Hypothesis

Since prejudice is a negative attitude toward an outgroup, there is usually little contact between different groups, and little opportunity to meet actual members of the outgroup. Different ethnic groups may be kept apart by intergroup prejudice and hostility as well as by educational, occupational, and cultural divisions. A commonsense idea is that relations between groups would be improved if there was more contact between them: social isolation only reinforces people's prejudices and ignorance of others. This thinking was an important element in the landmark decision by the U.S. Supreme Court in 1954 banning racial segregation in schools. It was felt that such segregation impairs the opportunity for improvement in minority groups and perpetuates ethnic prejudice and intolerance. School desegregation should increase intergroup contact and improve intergroup relations.

Allport's (1954) analysis of the *contact hypothesis* suggested that contact alone would not improve intergroup relations. He argued that there were three important preconditions for contact to have a beneficial effect.

1. Contact should be prolonged and involve cooperative activity rather than be casual and purposeless. This echoes Sherif's summer camp findings.
2. There should be official institutional support for integration. Legal and institutional support for desegregation does not directly reduce prejudice but it provides a social climate that fosters the development of more favorable intergroup relations.
3. Contact should be between equal status people and groups. Contact between group members of unequal status can simply reinforce prejudice (as in the case of slaves and the slave owner).

Research on Allport's contact hypothesis has generally provided support for his ideas (Amir, 1976). However, there are a number of important unresolved issues (Hewstone & Brown, 1986; Miller & Brewer, 1984). The first of these issues centers on the role of contact in reducing ignorance about other groups and in reducing perceived differences between the groups (Pettigrew, 1971). The idea is that increased intergroup contact should make people realize that they are more similar than they thought, and this increased similarity should lead to greater liking. However, if the groups are in fact quite different in attitudes, values, and beliefs, increased contact will only highlight these differences and lead to less liking and more prejudice (Bochner, 1982). But lack of knowledge may not be the main cause of intergroup prejudice and hostility. Realistic conflict theory suggests that groups may in fact have an accurate picture of each others' interests. If these interests conflict, then additional knowledge about the other group resulting from increased contact does not change the situation.

A second problem with the contact hypothesis is the extent to which contact with a few outgroup members generalizes to the group as a whole. Cook (1978) concluded that cooperative encounters between members of different groups often improves attitudes between the particular participants but does little to change attitudes to the outgroup as a whole. In typical encounters, participants are reacting to each other on an *interpersonal* basis not on an *intergroup* basis. Any favorable reactions to outgroup members could be attributed to the individual rather than to the whole group. This suggests that contact should improve attitudes between groups if group membership is emphasized rather than deemphasized. Wilder (1984) provided support for the idea that increased salience of group membership is important. In a cooperative task, students interacted with a person from a rival college who behaved either in a constructive manner or a critical manner. In one condition, this contact person was portrayed as a typical member of the rival college, whereas in another condition, the contact person was portrayed as atypical of the college. As shown in Figure 12.4, Wilder found that ratings of the outgroup as a whole were more positive only when the contact person behaved in a pleasant manner *and* was seen as a typical college member.

A contrary position was proposed by Miller, Brewer, and Edwards (1985) who argued that making group membership salient can heighten the differences between groups and increase intergroup conflict. They recommend that intergroup contact should emphasize the participants' unique personal attributes and socio-emotional aspects of the encounter rather than group attributes and task-oriented activities. Confirmation for these ideas was obtained by Miller, Brewer, and Edwards (1985) in experimental situations using artificially constructed groupings, but there is doubt about whether such contact would improve intergroup attitudes for existing groups where group membership is conspicuous (as in multiracial groups).

Social Categorization

Although Sherif's realistic conflict theory has been very influential in explaining intergroup relations, some research has shown that conflict of in-

Figure 12.4
Rating of a Rival College after Contact with a Typical or Atypical Member

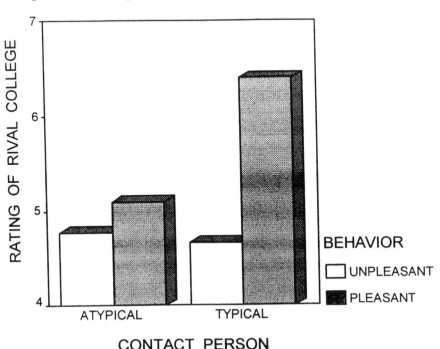

Source: Wilder, D. A. (1984). Intergroup contact: The typical member and the exception to
the rule. *Journal of Experimental Social Psychology*, 20, 177–194. Copyright © 1984 by
Academic Press Inc.

terest is not a necessary precondition for the appearance of intergroup
prejudice and hostility. Intergroup discrimination can occur when the
groups' goals are not interdependent (Rabbie & Horwitz, 1969), when the
groups are not competing with each other (Ferguson & Kelley, 1964), or
even when the groups are working in a cooperative relationship (Rabbie
& DeBrey, 1971).

The Minimal Group Paradigm. One apparently extreme suggestion is that
mere group membership is sufficient to trigger intergroup discrimination.
Tajfel devised a *minimal group paradigm* to investigate the effects of mere
group membership (Tajfel, Billig, Bundy, & Flament, 1971). Schoolboys
were assigned to one of two groups on a purely random basis, but ostensibly on the basis of their expressed preference for paintings by one of two
abstract artists, Paul Klee or Vassily Kandinsky. The only thing each boy
knew was which group he himself had been assigned to; the identity of
other members of the ingroup and members of the outgroup was concealed

by giving code numbers to participants. Under the guise of a study of decision-making, each boy was required to distribute money between pairs of recipients (excluding self) identified only by code number and group membership. The task of allocating money was performed a number of times to see what effect different pairings of ingroup-outgroup members had. The choices open to the allocator were represented in matrices such as those shown in Table 12.2. One pair of numbers was to be chosen by the allocator as the distribution of money to the pair of recipients.

The results showed that the allocations were generally fair, i.e., there was no extreme favoritism toward the ingroup (such as "18 for Klee"/"5 for Kandinsky" in Matrix 1), but there was a consistent tendency to favor the ingroup over the outgroup (such as 13 for Klee/10 for Kandinsky). This tendency to give more to ingroupers than to outgroupers occurred even when ingroupers would be worse off in absolute terms. For example, in Matrix 2, members of the Kandinsky group would choose the 11/12 option which gives the ingroup an advantage of one over the outgroup, but which is quite a bit less than the maximum amount available for the ingroup (the 25/19 choice).

Using this very minimal group situation, numerous studies have confirmed that the mere assignment of people to arbitrary social categories is sufficient to produce intergroup bias and discrimination (Brewer & Kramer, 1985; Hogg & Abrams, 1988; Tajfel, 1982). However, there has been debate about the interpretation of these minimal group findings. One question is whether participants are really trying to be fair (equal rewards) rather than showing ingroup favoritism. The choices typically observed are not the most extremely favorable to the ingroup, but, taken over a large number of participants, there is always a bias toward the ingroup. Turner (1980) suggests that the intergroup discrimination observed is something of a compromise between ingroup favoritism and fairness. Another issue is the artificiality of the minimal group paradigm. Participants are allocated to groups on a flimsy and arbitrary basis; there is no interaction with group members; the identity of other members is not known; and there are no previous relationships within or between the groups. How useful is the paradigm to our understanding of real groups? One argument is that the very artificiality of the situation is a benefit in that it allows us to see group processes operating uncontaminated by confusing or confounding factors (Turner, 1981). What the minimal group situation shows is that intergroup discrimination can occur just by categorization into groups; in the "real world" other factors, such as past history, attitudes, and beliefs, etc., can make intergroup discrimination worse.

How can the minimal group effect be explained? The original explanation (Tajfel, Billig, Bundy, & Flament, 1971) was in terms of *norms*. Dividing people into two groups invokes notions of teams and games, and implies a norm of competition so that "team" members are motivated to

Table 12.2
Sample Matrices of Reward Allocations in the Minimal Group Paradigm

Reward Numbers

Matrix 1

Member 72 of Klee group	18	17	16	15	14	13	12	11	10	9	8	7	6	5
Member 47 of Kandinsky group	5	6	7	8	9	10	11	12	13	14	15	16	17	18

Matrix 2

Member 74 of Klee group	25	23	21	19	17	15	13	11	9	7	5	3	1
Member 44 of Kandinsky group	19	18	17	16	15	14	13	12	11	10	9	8	7

Source: Taifel, M., Billig, G., Bundy, R. P., & Flament, C. (1971). Social categorization and intergroup behavior. *European Journal of Social Psychology, 1,* 149–178. Copyright © 1971. Reprinted by permission of John Wiley & Sons, Ltd.

win for their side. However, this competitive norm is not so extreme that the other side is wiped out (by extremely biased allocations). Rather, a second norm of fairness (a typically British norm!) tempers any tendency to win at all costs. However, the problem with this explanation (as with most normative theories) is that it cannot predict in advance when different norms will become more or less salient. There are a number of possible norms that could be invoked in intergroup situations apart from fairness and competitiveness, such as maximization of profit and equity. The norm explanation is really only a redescription of the findings. In addition, a normative account is too general since it explains the behavior of *all* members of a society or culture, whereas intergroup discrimination varies across members of the same society depending on the group task, the relations between group members, the situation, and so on.

Categorical Differentiation. A more cognitive explanation for the minimal group findings is in terms of *categorical differentiation* (Doise, 1978). Tajfel and Wilkes (1963) had earlier shown that applying a simple categorization (such as red/green) to physical stimuli (such as lengths of lines) resulted in distorted judgments so that the differences between stimuli in different categories were accentuated. Tajfel argued that the complexity of the real world can be simplified by the process of categorization. By noting the similarities and differences between stimuli, people, and events, we can handle the mass of information with which we are presented efficiently and economically by assigning similar things to the same category and different things to other categories. This classification of things into same/different categories results in differences between the categories being accentuated and differences within the categories being minimized. In the minimal group situation, the participants have little to go on in making their allocations except for group membership. The Klee/Kandinsky classification is the only basis on which participants can allocate rewards, and the process of categorical differentiation means that differences between the ingroup and the outgroup are accentuated. This process results in some interesting predictions. When there are two dimensions of classification, such as race and gender, then both between-group accentuation and within-group minimization can occur. For example, in a comparison of black males and white males, there should be accentuation effects due to different ethnicity but minimization effects due to same gender. Such "criss-cross" categorization leads to less intergroup discrimination than if only one dimension of classification is present (Deschamps & Doise, 1978; Vanbeselaere, 1987). On the other hand, when there is a double ingroup/outgroup comparison, intergroup discrimination is increased rather than reduced due to the accentuation effects of two categories (Brown & Turner, 1979).

The process of within-group minimization or homogenization suggests that people should see the outgroup as more homogeneous than the ingroup—"*they* all look alike, whereas *we* are diverse" (Brigham & Malpass,

1985: Quattrone, 1986). One explanation for this is that we are more familiar with ingroup members than with outgroup members, and so we make finer discriminations among ingroup members (Wilder, 1986). However, the outgroup homogeneity effect occurs when people report similar amounts of familiarity with ingroup and outgroup members (Jones, Wood, & Quattrone, 1981). Stephan (1977) found that children in both segregated (low intergroup familiarity) and integrated schools (higher intergroup familiarity) judged their *own* groups as more homogeneous than outgroups. The difference between Stephan's study and previous studies was that he studied two minority groups (Blacks and Chicanos) whereas previous studies have looked at majority (usually white) and minority groups. Therefore, majority/minority status may be contributing to the outgroup homogeneity effect. To test this, Simon and Brown (1987) carried out a minimal group study where the relative size of the groups was varied and participants were asked to judge the variability of both ingroup and outgroup. It was found that members of majority groups showed the usual outgroup homogeneity effect, whereas members of minority groups showed an opposite ingroup homogeneity effect—the outgroup was seen as more variable than the ingroup. What may be happening here is that minority groups emphasize their sense of belonging to the group (their *social identity*) by perceiving a greater degree of similarity and cohesion among ingroup members.

Social Identity

One problem with categorical differentiation is that it does not explain an important asymmetry in intergroup relations. Not only does an ingroup differentiate itself from the outgroup, but such differentiation is always *favorable* to the ingroup—accentuation of between-group differences is in the direction of positive ingroup distinctiveness. *Social identity theory* proposes that an important part of our identity resides in our membership of various groups. Categorization not only serves to separate other people into different groups, it also serves to define who we are in relation to these groups. Since we want to have a positive sense of self, it follows that we should evaluate those groups of which we are a part (and which define our identity) in a more favorable way than groups that we do not belong to. If our own group is judged to be better than other groups, then we can feel better about our own identity. People should be motivated, therefore, to make comparisons so that the ingroup is seen to be better than other groups; this is what Tajfel (1978) called "the establishment of positive distinctiveness."

In the minimal group paradigm, there is nothing to distinguish between the groups except group membership. Being an arbitrary distinction, this group membership does not initially contribute anything to a sense of positive identity. Ingroup members can establish a way of appearing better than the outgroup only through the differential allocation of rewards to ingroup and outgroup members. (Note that we prefer to establish such a positive *difference* rather than allocating the maximum reward to the ingroup.) One consequence of this line of reasoning is that exhibiting ingroup favoritism should result in an increase in self-esteem. Oakes and Turner (1980) found that participants in the minimal group paradigm who made the usual intergroup reward allocations showed higher self-esteem than those who were not given the opportunity of allocating rewards. Moreover, Lemyre and Smith (1985) showed that it was engaging in *intergroup* discrimination that increased self-esteem; subjects who allocated rewards to two ingroupers or two outgroupers did not have higher self-esteem than control subjects who did not make reward allocations.

An important feature of social identity theory is that it distinguishes between social and personal identity in an attempt to explain group and intergroup phenomena in terms of social processes rather than in terms of personality or interpersonal processes. Whereas the authoritarian personality, frustration-aggression theory, or belief dissimilarity theory try to explain intergroup relations in terms of individualistic processes, social identity theory suggests that an explicit group perspective is required to understand intergroup relations.

What if you are a member of a minority group? Frequently, you will be disadvantaged economically, socially, and politically, and if you compare yourself to the majority group, most of the time the comparisons will be unfavorable. How, therefore, do members of minority groups maintain a positive sense of identity? Tajfel and Turner (1979) suggest three possibilities.

First, members of a disadvantaged minority group may try to leave the group to join the advantaged majority group. This can occur by psychologically distancing yourself from the minority group and identifying with the majority group (Clark & Clark, 1947). However, such a strategy is unlikely to be successful if the divisions between groups are clear-cut, such as between different racial groups.

A second strategy is to make comparisons which are favorable to your group. This could involve making comparisons to other disadvantaged minority groups rather than with the advantaged majority group. Alternatively, a minority group could make comparisons on particular dimensions which are favorable to them. For example, if the economic status and attainment of a minority group is lower than the majority group, a positive sense of identity could be maintained by emphasizing the fact that family life is more fulfilling and rewarding.

A third strategy is to challenge the dominance of the majority group by instigating political and social change. This takes us into complex territory for social psychologists; Tajfel and Turner suggest that social circumstances must be seen already to be changing for this strategy to be a viable one. If the social system is widely believed to be unfair and untenable, then social change may be a more concrete rather than psychological way of improving the conditions of disadvantaged minority groups.

SUMMARY

Attitudes toward groups can be described in terms of stereotypes, prejudice, and discrimination. Stereotypes are beliefs about the attributes and behaviors of a whole social group, prejudice is the tendency to judge members of a social group in terms of negative feelings and reactions, and discrimination is negative behavior toward another social group.

One explanation of prejudice and discrimination is the authoritarian personality—a type of person who is overdependent on authority figures and hostile to members of subordinate groups. A second explanation that can account for historical changes in prejudice is the frustration-aggression hypothesis: social and cultural factors such as economic hardship give rise to frustration which produces aggression in the form of prejudice. However, frustration does not always result in aggression, and aggression can be due to factors other than frustration. A third explanation of prejudice is in terms of belief dissimilarity: we dislike people who do not share our view of the social world. Prejudice is not due directly to membership of different social groups but to differences in beliefs associated with different groups. However, this explanation seems to apply to inter*personal* relations rather than inter*group* relations. When intergroup judgments are involved, group membership has much stronger effects than belief dissimilarity.

An explicitly intergroup approach is Sherif's realistic conflict theory: if the goals of different groups conflict, then the group's interests are best served by adopting a competitive orientation which results in prejudice and discrimination toward the outgroup. A successful way to reduce intergroup conflict is to introduce a cooperative motive so that the group's interests are best served by working toward a shared goal. This is the strategy of working toward superordinate goals, that is, goals which are not attainable by one group working on its own, only by both groups working together.

A commonsense idea is that relations between groups would be improved if there was more contact between them. However, contact alone is not enough. What is required is that the contact should be prolonged, involving cooperative activity, should be supported by official institutions, and should be between equal status people and groups. However, lack of knowledge may not be the main cause of intergroup prejudice and hostility. Realistic conflict theory suggests that groups may in fact have an accurate picture of each others' interests. Also, cooperative encounters between members of different groups may improve attitudes between the particular individuals but do little to change attitudes to the group as a whole. Some evidence seems to show that emphasizing group membership improves intergroup relations, but other evidence suggests that deemphasizing group membership leads to better intergroup relations.

A more recent explanation of intergroup conflict is that the mere assignment of people to arbitrary social categories is sufficient to produce intergroup bias and discrimination. Classification of people or things into same/different categories results in differences between the categories being accentuated and differences within the categories being minimized. In the minimal group paradigm—where people are assigned to groups on an arbitrary basis—the accentuation of differences between groups is seen in the favoring of the ingroup at the expense of the outgroup.

This process of categorization, however, does not explain why the accentuation of between-group differences is always in the direction of positive ingroup distinctiveness. Social identity theory proposes that an important part of our identity resides in our membership of groups, and that we can attain a positive sense of self by judging our own group as better than other groups. In the minimal group paradigm, people who engage in intergroup discrimination show a more positive sense of self.

This explanation would suggest that members of minority groups would always be psychologically disadvantaged compared to the dominant majority group. However, minority groups can attain a positive sense of identity by comparing themselves favorably to other disadvantaged minority groups, or by comparing themselves on particular dimensions which favor their group. A more radical solution for improving the lot of disadvantaged minority groups is to challenge the dominant majority group by attempting social and political change.

For Further Reading

Further reading for all of the topics in this book—although to a lesser extent for Chapters 11 and 12—can be found in *Small group research: A handbook* (Hare, Blumberg, Davies, & Kent, 1994). That volume focuses on work from 1975 until the late 1980s. For a detailed account of earlier work, see the previous handbook (Hare, 1976).

For collections of classic research, see *Small groups and social interaction* (Blumberg, Hare, Kent, & Davies, 1983, two volumes). Covering an earlier period— Hare, Borgatta, and Bales (1965); and, from a group dynamics approach, Cartwright and Zander (1968).

In addition, the following general works have been called to our attention: Barker, Wahlers, and Watson (1995); Cathcart, Samovar, and Henman (1996); Hogg and Moreland (1993); Paulus, Seta, and Baron (1995).

A selection of works relevant to specific chapters is as follows:

Chapter 1, "Physical Situation." See Hare, Blumberg, Davies, & Kent (1994, chapter 1).

Chapter 2, "Personality and Social Characteristics." See Hare, Blumberg, Davies, & Kent (1994, chapter 2).

Chapter 3, "Presence of Others." Guerin (1993).

Chapter 4, "Conformity." Turner (1991). Also, Miller, Collins, and Brief (1995).

Chapter 5, "Roles and Relationships." Duck (1992, 1993); Hendrick (1989).

Chapter 6, "Leadership." Hollander (1985). Also, Ayman, Chemers, & Fiedler (1995); Dansereau, Yammarino, and Markham (1995).

Chapter 7, "Social Interaction." Bales and Cohen (1979); Kenny (1996); Tubbs (1995).

Chapter 8, "Group Decision Making and Choice Shift." Myers and Lamm (1976) provide a summary and integration of the basic research on choice shift, as of the mid-1970s. Brown (1986) provides a good account of categories and prototypes; see also Bruner, Goodnow, and Austin (1956, pp. 1–49), and Rosch et al. (1976).

Chapter 9, "Cooperation, Competition, and Conflict Resolution." Carnevale and Pruitt (1992); Deutsch (1986); see also other chapters in the same volume and also Deutsch (1973); Fisher and Ury (1981); Glance and Huberman (1994); Johnson et al. (1981); Leritz (1987); O'Donnell and O'Kelly (1994); Parry (1990); Rubin (1980, 1983); and Thompson (1990).

Chapter 10, "Bargaining, Coalitions, and Games." For a review of the now-classic research in these areas, including two of the three demonstrations featured in this chapter, see McClintock (1972, chapters 9, 10, and 11). See also Axelrod and Dion (1988); Brams (1990).

Chapter 11, "The Group and the Organization." Alvarez and Robin (1992); Guzzo and Dickson (1996); Hare (1993); O'Reilly (1991); Worchel, Wood, and Simpson (1991).

Chapter 12, "Intergroup Relations." Deaux (1995); Deaux, Dane, and Wrightsman (1993, chapter 13); Katz and Taylor (1988); Langer, Bashner, and Chanowitz (1985); Stephan and Brigham (1985); Unger and Crawford (1992); Winstead and Derlega (1993).

Bibliography

Abele, A. (1982). Hilfsbereitschaft in Abhangigkeit von Aufgaben- und sozialer Struktur der Situation. Ein Experiment zum Interventionsverhalten [Readiness to help in relation to the problem and social structure of the situation: An experiment on intervention behavior]. *Zeitschrift fur Experimentelle und Angewandte Psychologie, 29,* 1–23.

Abelson, R. P. (1981). Psychological status of the script concept. *American Psychologist, 36,* 715–729.

Abrams, D., & Hogg, M. A. (1990). Social identification, self-categorization and social influence. *European Review of Social Psychology, 1,* 195–228.

ACCESS, & Simpson, J. (1994). Chronology of events. In H. H. Blumberg & C. C. French (Eds.), *The Persian Gulf War: Views from the social and behavioral sciences* (pp. 27–40). Lanham, MD: University Press of America.

Adams, J. (1965). Inequity in social exchange. *Advances in Experimental Social Psychology, 2,* 267–299.

Adato, A. (1975). Leave-taking: A study of commonsense knowledge of social structure. *Anthropological Quarterly, 48,* 255–271.

Adorno, T. W., Frenkel-Brunswik, E., Levinson, D., & Sanford, N. (1950). *The authoritarian personality.* New York: Harper.

Ahmed, S. M. (1979). Invasion of personal space: A study of departure time as affected by sex of the intruder and saliency condition. *Perceptual and Motor Skills, 49,* 85–86.

Aldag, R. J., & Fuller, S. R. (1993). Beyond fiasco: A reappraisal of the groupthink phenomenon and a new model of group decision processes. *Psychological Bulletin, 113,* 533–552.

Allen, K. M., Blascovich, J., Tomaka, J., & Kelsey, R. M. (1991). Presence of human friends and pet dogs as moderators of autonomic responses to stress in women. *Journal of Personality and Social Psychology, 61,* 582–589.

Allen, V. L., & Wilder, D. A. (1979). Social support in absentia: The effect of an absentee partner on conformity. *Human Relations, 32,* 103–111.

Allport, F. H. (1924). *Social psychology.* Boston: Houghton Mifflin.

Allport, G. W. (1954). *The nature of prejudice.* Reading, MA: Addison-Wesley.

Altman, I. (1975). *The environment and social behavior.* Monterey, CA: Brooks/ Cole.

Altman, I., & Haythorn, W. W. (1967). The effects of social isolation and group composition on performance. *Human Relations, 20,* 313–340.

Alvarez, R., & Robin, L. (1992). Organizational structure. In E. F. Borgatta & M. L. Borgatta (Eds.), *Encyclopedia of sociology* (Vol. 3, pp. 1394–1404). New York: Macmillan.

Amato, P. R. (1983). Helping behavior in urban and rural environments: Field studies based on a taxonomic organization of helping episodes. *Journal of Personality and Social Psychology, 45,* 571–586.

Amir, Y. (1976). The role of intergroup contact in change of prejudice and ethnic relations. In P. A. Katz (Ed.), *Towards the elimination of racism* (pp. 245– 308). New York: Pergamon.

Ancona, D. G., & Caldwell, D. E. (1992). Cross-functional teams: Blessing or curse for new product development? In T. A. Kochan & M. Useem (Eds.), *Transforming organizations* (pp. 154–166). New York: Oxford University Press.

Ancona, D. G., Friedman, R. A., & Kolb, D. M. (1991). The group and what happens on the way to "yes." *Negotiation Journal, 7,* 155–173.

Anderson, L. R., & Blanchard, P. N. (1982). Sex differences in task and social-emotional behavior. *Basic and Applied Social Psychology, 3,* 109–139.

Apple, W., & Hecht, K. (1982). Speaking emotionally: The relation between verbal and vocal communication of affect. *Journal of Personality and Social Psychology, 42,* 864–875.

Arbuthnot, J., & Wayner, M. (1982). Minority influence: Effects of size, conversion, and sex. *Journal of Psychology, 111,* 285–295.

Argyle, M., & Dean, J. (1965). Eye-contact, distance, and affiliation. *Sociometry, 28,* 289–304.

Argyle, M., & Ingham, R. (1972). Gaze, mutual gaze, and proximity. *Semiotica, 6,* 32–49.

Aries, E. J. (1976). Interaction patterns and themes of male, female and mixed groups. *Small Group Behavior, 7,* 7–18.

Aronson, E., Blaney, N., Stephan, C., Sikes, J., & Snapp, M. (1978). *The jigsaw classroom.* Beverly Hills, CA: Sage.

Asch, S. E. (1951). Effects of group pressure upon the modification and distortion of judgments. In H. Guetzkow (Ed.), *Groups, leadership, and men* (pp. 177– 190). Pittsburgh: Carnegie Press. [See also, e.g., Cartwright & Zander, 1960.]

Asch, S. E. (1955). Opinions and social pressure. *Scientific American, 193*(5), 31– 35.

Asch, S. E. (1956). Studies of independence and conformity: A minority of one against a unanimous majority. *Psychological Monographs, 70* (9, Whole No. 416).

Austin, W. (1979). Sex differences in bystander intervention in a theft. *Journal of Personality and Social Psychology, 37,* 2110–2120.

Axelrod, R. (1980). Effective choice in the prisoner's dilemma. *Journal of Conflict Resolution, 24,* 3–25.

Axelrod, R., & Dion, D. (1988). The further evolution of cooperation. *Science, 242,* 1385–1390.

Ayman, R., Chemers, M. M., & Fiedler, F. (1995). The contingency model of leadership effectiveness: Its level of analysis. *Leadership Quarterly, 6,* 147–167.

Baird, J. E. (1976). Sex differences in group communication: A review of relevant research. *Quarterly Journal of Speech, 62,* 179–192.

Bales, R. F. (1950). *Interaction process analysis: A method for the study of small groups.* Reading, MA: Addison-Wesley.

Bales, R. F. (1953). The equilibrium problem in small groups. In T. Parsons, R. F. Bales, & E. A. Shils (Eds.), *Working papers in the theory of action* (pp. 111–161). Glencoe, IL: Free Press.

Bales, R. F. (1983). SYMLOG: A practical approach to the study of groups. In H. H. Blumberg, A. P. Hare, V. Kent, & M. F. Davies (Eds.), *Small groups and social interaction* (Vol. 2, pp. 499–523). Chichester, England: John Wiley.

Bales, R. F. (c. 1987). *SYMLOG and leadership theories.* Unpublished manuscript.

Bales, R. F., & Cohen, S. P. (1979). *SYMLOG: A system for the multiple level observation of groups.* New York: Free Press.

Bales, R. F., & Slater, P. E. (1955). Role differentiation in small decision-making groups. In T. Parsons & R. F. Bales (Eds.), *Family, socialization, and interaction process* (pp. 259–306). Glencoe, IL: Free Press.

Bales, R. F., Strodtbeck, F. L., Mills, T. M., & Roseborough, M. E. (1951). Channels of communication in small groups. *American Sociological Review, 16,* 461–468.

Balswick, J. O., & Balkwell, J. W. (1977). Self-disclosure to same- and opposite-sex parents: An empirical test of insights from role theory. *Social Psychology Quarterly, 40,* 282–286.

Barker, L. L., Wahlers, K. J., & Watson, K. W. (1995). *Groups in process: An introduction to small group communication* (5th ed.). Boston: Allyn and Bacon.

Barnard, C. I. (1938). *The functions of the executive.* Cambridge, MA: Harvard University Press.

Baron, R. A., & Bell, P. A. (1976). Aggression and heat: The influence of ambient temperature, negative affect, and a cooling drink on physical aggression. *Journal of Personality and Social Psychology, 33,* 245–255.

Baron, R. A., & Ransberger, V. M. (1978). Ambient temperature and the occurrence of collective violence: The "long, hot summer" revisited. *Journal of Personality and Social Psychology, 36,* 351–360.

Baron, R. S. (1986). Distraction-conflict theory: Progress and problems. *Advances in Experimental Social Psychology, 19,* 1–40.

Bartol, K. M., & Butterfield, D. A. (1976). Sex effects in evaluating leaders. *Journal of Applied Psychology, 61,* 446–454.

Bass, B. M. (1990). *Bass & Stogdill's handbook of leadership research: Theory, research and applications* (3rd ed.). New York: The Free Press.

Bassin, M. (1988). Teamwork at General Foods: New & improved. *Personnel Journal, 67*(5), 62–70.

Bauer, G. P., Schlottmann, R. S., Bates, J. V., & Masters, M. A. (1983). Effect of state and trait anxiety and prestige of model on imitation. *Psychological Reports, 52,* 375–382.

Baum, A., Aiello, J. R., & Calesnick, L. E. (1978). Crowding and personal control: Social density and the development of learned helplessness. *Journal of Personality and Social Psychology, 36,* 1000–1011.

Baum, A., & Davis, G. E. (1980). Reducing the stress of high density living; an architectural intervention. *Journal of Personality and Social Psychology, 38,* 471–481.

Baum, A., Harpin, R. E., & Valins, S. (1975). The role of group phenomena in the experience of crowding. *Environment and Behavior, 7,* 185–198.

Baum, A., & Valins, S. (1977). *Architecture and social behavior: Psychological studies of social density.* Hillsdale, NJ: Erlbaum.

Baumeister, R. F. (1982). A self-presentational view of social phenomena. *Psychological Bulletin, 91,* 3–26.

Baysinger, B., & Hoskisson, R. E. (1990). The composition of boards of directors and strategic control: Effects on corporate strategy. *Academy of Management Review, 15,* 72–87.

Beaman, A. L., Cole, C. M., Preston, M., Klentz, B., & Steblay, N. M. (1983). Fifteen years of foot-in-the-door research: A meta-analysis. *Personality and Social Psychology Bulletin, 9,* 181–196.

Beattie, G. (1977). The dynamics of interruption and the filled pause. *British Journal of Social and Clinical Psychology, 16,* 283–284.

Becker, F. D. (1973). Study of spatial markers. *Journal of Personality and Social Psychology, 26,* 439–445.

Beer, M., Eisenstat, R. A., & Spector, B. (1990). Why change programs don't produce change. *Harvard Business Review, 68*(6), 158–166.

Benet, V., & Waller, N. G. (1995). The big seven model of personality description: Evidence for its cross-cultural generality in a Spanish sample. *Journal of Personality and Social Psychology, 69,* 701–718.

Ben-Yoav, O., Hollander, E. P., & Carnevale, P. J. (1983). Leader legitimacy, leader-follower interaction, and followers' ratings of the leader. *Journal of Social Psychology, 121,* 111–115.

Berger, J., Cohen, B. P., & Zelditch, M. (1966). Status characteristics and expectation states. In J. Berger, M. Zelditch, & B. Anderson (Eds.), *Sociological theories in progress* (Vol. 1, pp. 29–46). Boston: Houghton Mifflin.

Berger, J., Fisek, M. H., Norman, R. Z., & Zelditch, M. (1977). *Status characteristics and social interaction: An expectation-states approach.* New York: Elsevier.

Berger, J., Rosenholtz, S. J., & Zelditch, M. (1980). Status organizing processes. *Annual Review of Sociology, 6,* 479–508.

Berger, M. M. (1958). Nonverbal communications in group psychotherapy. *International Journal of Group Psychotherapy, 8,* 161–178.

Berger, S. M., Carli, L. C., Garcia, R., & Brady, J. J. (1982). Audience effects in anticipatory learning: A comparison of drive and practice-inhibition analyses. *Journal of Personality and Social Psychology, 42,* 478–486.

Berkowitz, L. (1962). *Aggression: A social psychological analysis.* New York: McGraw Hill.

Berkowitz, L. (1978). Decreased helpfulness with increased group size through lessening the effects of the needy individual's dependency. *Journal of Personality, 46,* 299–310.

Bettencourt, B. A., Brewer, M. B., Croak, M. R., & Miller, N. (1992). Cooperation and the reduction of intergroup bias: The role of reward structure and social orientation. *Journal of Experimental Social Psychology, 28,* 301–319.

Billig, M. G., & Tajfel, H. (1973). Social categorization and similarity in intergroup behaviour. *European Journal of Social Psychology, 3,* 27–52.

Blake, R. R., & Mouton, J. S. (1962). Overevaluation of own group's product in intergroup competition. *Journal of Abnormal and Social Psychology, 64,* 237–238.

Blake, R. R., & Mouton, J. S. (1982). Theory and research for developing a science of leadership. *Journal of Applied Behavioral Science, 18,* 275–291.

Blank, T. O., Staff, I., & Shaver, P. (1976). Social facilitation of word associations: Further questions. *Journal of Personality and Social Psychology, 34,* 725–733.

Blumberg, H. H. (1969). On being liked more than you like. *Journal of Personality and Social Psychology, 11,* 121–128.

Blumberg, H. H. (1988/1992). Nonviolent responses to violence. *Social and Behavioral Sciences Documents, 18*(2), 38–39. [Ms. No. 2871, 91 pp.]

Blumberg, H. H. (1993). Perception and misperception of others: Social-cognition implications for peace education. *Educational and Psychological Interactions* (115), 1–22.

Blumberg, H. H. (1994). Peace psychology, peacemaking, and related areas: A review of topics covered in recent publications. Paper presented at the meeting of the International Congress of Applied Psychology, Madrid, July.

Blumberg, H. H., & French, C. C. (Eds.). (1994). *The Persian Gulf War: Views from the social and behavioral sciences.* Lanham, MD: University Press of America.

Blumberg, H. H., Hare, A. P., Kent, V., & Davies, M. F. (Eds.). (1983). *Small groups and social interaction* (2 vols.). Chichester, England: John Wiley.

Bochner, A. P., di Salvo, V., & Jonas, T. (1975). A computer-assisted analysis of small group process: An investigation of two Machiavellian groups. *Small Group Behavior, 6,* 187–203.

Bochner, S. (1982). The social psychology of cross-cultural relations. In S. Bochner (Ed.), *Cultures in contact: Studies in cross-cultural interaction* (pp. 5–44). Oxford: Pergamon.

Bond, C. F. (1982). Social facilitation: A self-presentational view. *Journal of Personality and Social Psychology, 42,* 1042–1050.

Bond, C. F., & Titus, L. J. (1983). Social facilitation: A meta-analysis of 241 studies. *Psychological Bulletin, 94,* 265–292.

Bond, M. H., & Shiraishi, D. (1974). The effect of body lean and status of an interviewer on the non-verbal behavior of Japanese interviewees. *International Journal of Psychology, 9,* 117–128.

Borden, R. J. (1980). Audience influence. In P. B. Paulus (Ed.), *Psychology of group influence* (pp. 99–131). Hillsdale, NJ: Erlbaum.

Borgatta, E. F., & Bales, R. F. (1953). The consistency of subject behavior and the reliability of scoring in interaction process analysis. *American Sociological Review, 18,* 566–569.

Borges, M. A., & Penta, J. M. (1977). Effects of third party intercession on bystander intervention. *Journal of Social Psychology, 103,* 27–32.

Bradley, P. H. (1978). Pressure for uniformity: An experimental study of deviate responses in group discussions of policy. *Small Group Behavior, 9,* 149–160.

Bradley, P. H., MacHamon, C., & Harris, A. M. (1976). Dissent in small groups. *Journal of Communication, 26,* 155–159.

Brams, S. J. (1990). *Negotiation games: Applying game theory to bargaining and arbitration.* New York: Routledge.

Brauer, M., Judd, C. M., & Gilner, M. D. (1995). The effects of repeated expressions on attitude polarization during group discussions. *Journal of Personality and Social Psychology, 68,* 1014–1029.

Bray, R. M., Johnson, D., & Chilstrom, J. T. (1982). Social influence by group members with minority opinions: A comparison of Hollander and Moscovici. *Journal of Personality and Social Psychology, 43,* 78–88.

Bray, R. M., Kerr, N. L., & Atkin, R. S. (1978). Effects of group size, problem difficulty, and sex on group performance and member reactions. *Journal of Personality and Social Psychology, 36,* 1224–1240.

Bray, R. M., & Noble, A. M. (1978). Authoritarianism and decisions of mock juries: Evidence of jury bias and group polarization. *Journal of Personality and Social Psychology, 36,* 1424–1430.

Brehm, S. S., & Brehm, J. W. (1981). *Psychological reactance: A theory of freedom and control.* New York: Academic Press.

Brewer, M. B., & Kramer, R. M. (1985). The psychology of intergroup attitudes and behavior. *Annual Review of Psychology, 36,* 219–243.

Brigham, J. C., & Malpass, R. S. (1985). The role of experience and contact in the recognition of faces of own- and other-race persons. *Journal of Social Issues, 41*(3), 139–156.

Brown, R. (1965). *Social psychology.* New York: Free Press.

Brown, R. (1986). *Social psychology: The second edition.* New York: Free Press.

Brown, R. (1988). *Group processes: Dynamics within and between groups.* Oxford: Blackwell.

Brown, R. J., & Abrams, D. (1986). The effects of intergroup similarity and goal interdependence on intergroup attitudes and task performance. *Journal of Experimental Social Psychology, 22,* 78–92.

Brown, R. J., & Turner, J. C. (1979). The criss-cross categorization effect in intergroup discrimination. *British Journal of Social and Clinical Psychology, 18,* 371–383.

Brown, R. J., & Wade, G. S. (1987). Superordinate goals and intergroup behaviour: The effects of role ambiguity and status on intergroup attitudes and task performance. *European Journal of Social Psychology, 17,* 131–142.

Bruner, J., Goodnow, S., & Austin, G. (1956). *A study of thinking.* New York: Wiley.

Buch, K. (1992). Quality circles and employee withdrawal behaviors: A cross-organizational study. *Journal of Applied Behavioral Science, 28,* 62–73.

Bull, P. E., & Brown, R. (1977). The role of postural change in dyadic conversations. *British Journal of Social and Clinical Psychology, 16,* 29–33.

Burger, J. (1986). Increasing compliance by improving the deal: The that's-not-all technique. *Journal of Personality and Social Psychology, 31,* 277–283.

Burger, J. M., & Petty, R. E. (1981). The low-ball compliance technique: Task or person commitment? *Journal of Personality and Social Psychology, 40,* 492–500.

Burke, R. J., Firth, J., & McGrattan, C. (1974). Husband-wife compatibility and the management of stress. *Journal of Social Psychology, 94,* 243–252.

Burns, T. (1955). The reference of conduct in small groups: Cliques and cabals in occupational milieux. *Human Relations, 8,* 467–486.

Burnstein, E., & Vinokur, A. (1977). Persuasive argumentation and social comparison as determinants of attitude polarization. *Journal of Experimental Social Psychology, 13,* 315–332.

Burton, J. (1979). *Deviance, terrorism and war: The process of solving unsolved social and political problems.* Oxford: Martin Robertson.

Butler, D., & Geis, F. L. (1990). Nonverbal affect responses to male and female leaders: Implications for leadership evaluations. *Journal of Personality and Social Psychology, 58,* 48–59.

Cacioppo, J. T., Petty, R. E., & Losch, M. E. (1986). Attributions of responsibility for helping and doing harm: Evidence for confusion of responsibility. *Journal of Personality and Social Psychology, 50,* 100–105.

Calhoun, J. B. (1962). Population density and social pathology. *Scientific American, 206*(2), 139–148.

Campbell, J. D., Tesser, A., & Fairey, P. J. (1986). Conformity and attention to the stimulus: Some temporal and contextual dynamics. *Journal of Personality and Social Psychology, 51,* 315–324.

Carlsmith, J. M., & Anderson, C. A. (1979). Ambient temperature and the occurrence of collective violence: A new analysis. *Journal of Personality and Social Psychology, 37,* 337–344.

Carnevale, P. J., & Pruitt, D. G. (1992). Negotiation and mediation. *Annual Review of Psychology, 43,* 531–582.

Carter, I. F., & Nixon, M. (1949). An investigation of the relationship between four criteria of leadership ability for three different tasks. *Journal of Psychology, 27,* 245–261.

Cartwright, D., & Zander, A. F. (Eds.). (1953). *Group dynamics, research and theory.* Evanston, IL: Row, Peterson.

Cartwright, D., & Zander, A. F. (Eds.). (1960). *Group dynamics: Research and theory* (2nd ed.). New York: Row, Peterson/Harper & Row.

Cartwright, D., & Zander, A. (Eds.). (1968). *Group dynamics: Research and theory* (3rd ed.). New York: Harper & Row.

Cathcart, R. S., Samovar, L. A., & Henman, L. D. (Eds.). (1996). *Small group communication: Theory & practice* (7th ed.). Madison, WI: Brown & Benchmark.

Cattell, R. B. (1947). Confirmation and clarification of primary personality factors. *Psychometrika, 12,* 197–220.

Chaiken, S., Liberman, A., & Eagly, A. H. (1989). Heuristic and systematic information processing within and beyond the persuasion context. In J. S. Uleman

& J. A. Bargh (Eds.), *Unintended thought* (pp. 212–252). New York: Guilford.

Chaiken, S., & Stangor, C. (1987). Attitudes and attitude change. *Annual Review of Psychology, 38,* 575–630.

Charan, R. (1991). How networks reshape organizations—for results. *Harvard Business Review, 69*(5), 104–115.

Cheek, J. M., & Buss, A. H. (1981). Shyness and sociability. *Journal of Personality and Social Psychology, 41,* 330–339.

Chemers, M. M., Hays, R. B., Rhodewalt, F., & Wysocki, J. (1985). A person-environment analysis of job stress: A contingency model explanation. *Journal of Personality and Social Psychology, 49,* 628–635.

Chemers, M. M., Rice, R. W., Sundstrom, E., & Butler, W. M. (1975). Leader esteem for the least preferred co-worker score, training, and effectiveness: An experimental examination. *Journal of Personality and Social Psychology, 31,* 401–409.

Chertkoff, J. M., & Esser, J. K. (1983). A review of experiments in explicit bargaining. In H. H. Blumberg, A. P. Hare, V. Kent, & M. F. Davies (Eds.), *Small groups and social interaction* (Vol. 2, pp. 145–161). Chichester, England: John Wiley.

Chertock, S. L. (1974). Effect of music on cooperative problem solving by children. *Perceptual and Motor Skills, 39,* 986.

Christie, R., & Geis, F. L. (Eds.). (1970). *Studies in Machiavellianism.* New York: Academic Press.

Cialdini, R. B., Bickman, L., & Cacioppo, J. T. (1979). An example of consumeristic social psychology: Bargaining tough in the new car showroom. *Journal of Applied Social Psychology, 9,* 115–126.

Cialdini, R. B., Braver, S. L., & Lewis, S. K. (1974). Attributional bias and the easily persuaded other. *Journal of Personality and Social Psychology, 30,* 631–637.

Cialdini, R. B., Cacioppo, J. T., Bassett, R., & Miller, J. A. (1978). Low-ball procedure for producing compliance: Commitment then cost. *Journal of Personality and Social Psychology, 36,* 463–476.

Cialdini, R. B., & Mirels, H. L. (1976). Sense of personal control and attributions about yielding and resisting persuasion targets. *Journal of Personality and Social Psychology, 33,* 395–402.

Cialdini, R. B., Vincent, J. E., Lewis, S. K., Catalon, J., Wheeler, D., & Darby, B. L. (1975). Reciprocal concessions procedure for inducing compliance: The door-in-the-face technique. *Journal of Personality and Social Psychology, 31,* 206–215.

Cini, M. A., Moreland, R. L., & Levine, J. M. (1993). Group staffing levels and responses to prospective and new group members. *Journal of Personality and Social Psychology, 65,* 723–734.

Clark, K. B., & Clark, M. P. (1947). Racial identification and preference in Negro children. In Society for the Psychological Study of Social Issues [T. M. Newcomb and E. L. Hartley] (Ed.), *Readings in social psychology* (pp. 169–178). New York: Holt.

Clark, M. L. (1983). Effect of confederate sex and status on competitive behavior of male and female college students. *Journal of Psychology, 113,* 191–198.

Clarke, B. B. (1993). Conflict termination: A rational model. *Studies in Conflict and Terrorism, 16,* 25–50.

Cline, R. W. (1989). The politics of intimacy: Costs and benefits determining disclosure intimacy in male-female dyads. *Journal of Social and Personal Relationships, 6,* 5–20.

Cohen, S. (1978). Environmental load and the allocation of attention. In A. Baum, J. E. Singer, & S. Valins (Eds.), *Advances in environmental psychology* (Vol. 1, pp. 1–29). Hillsdale, NJ: Erlbaum.

Cohen, S. L., Bunker, K. A., Burton, A. L., & McManus, P. D. (1978). Reactions of male subordinates to the sex-role congruency of immediate supervision. *Sex Roles, 4,* 297–311.

Condon, W. S., & Ogston, W. D. (1966). Sound film analysis of normal and pathological behavior patterns. *Journal of Nervous and Mental Disease, 143,* 338–347.

Conlon, D. E., & Ross, W. H. (1993). The effects of partisan third parties on negotiator behavior and outcome perceptions. *Journal of Applied Psychology, 78,* 280–290.

Cook, S. W. (1978). Interpersonal and attitudinal outcomes in cooperating interracial groups. *Journal of Research and Development in Education, 12,* 97–113.

Cooper, C. (1974). The house as symbol of the self. In J. Lang, C. Burnette, W. Moleski, & D. Vachon (Eds.), *Designing for human behavior; architecture and the behavioral sciences* (pp. 130–146). Stroudsburg, PA: Dowden, Hutchinson, & Ross.

Cooper, H. M. (1979). Statistically combining independent studies: A meta-analysis of sex differences in conformity research. *Journal of Personality and Social Psychology, 37,* 131–146.

Cottrell, N. B., Wack, D. L., Sekerak, G. J., & Rittle, R. H. (1968). Social facilitation of dominant responses by the presence of an audience and the mere presence of others. *Journal of Personality and Social Psychology, 9,* 245–250.

Cox, V. C., Paulus, P. B., & McCain, G. (1984). Prison crowding research: The relevance for prison housing standards and a general approach regarding crowding phenomena. *American Psychologist, 39,* 1148–1160.

Cull, J. G. (1976). The relationship between sex role and modification of judgments. *Journal of Psychology, 93,* 313–317.

Cummings, T. G. (1981). Designing effective work groups. In P. C. Nystrom & W. H. Starbuck (Eds.), *Handbook of organizational design* (Vol. 2, pp. 250–271). New York: Oxford University Press.

Cunningham, J. D. (1981). Self-disclosure intimacy: Sex, sex-of-target, cross-national, and "generational" differences. *Personality and Social Psychology Bulletin, 7,* 314–319.

Dansereau, F., Yammarino, F. J., & Markham, S. E. (1995). Leadership: The multiple-level approaches. *Leadership Quarterly, 6,* 251–263.

Darley, J. M., & Gilbert, D. T. (1985). Social psychological aspects of environmental psychology. In G. Lindzey & E. Aronson (Eds.), *Handbook of social psychology* (3rd ed., Vol. 2, pp. 949–992). New York: Random House.

Dashiell, J. F. (1930). An experimental analysis of some group effects. *Journal of Abnormal and Social Psychology, 25,* 190–199.

Davies, M. F., & Blumberg, H. H. (1988/1990). Attraction, friendship, and relationships: A classified bibliography 1974–1988. *Social and Behavioral Sciences Documents*, *18*(1), 15 [Ms. No. 2850, 41 pp].

Davis, J. D. (1976). Self-disclosure in an acquaintance exercise: Responsibility for level of intimacy. *Journal of Personality and Social Psychology*, *33*, 787–792.

Deaux, K. (1995). How basic can you be? The evolution of research on gender stereotypes. *Journal of Social Issues*, *51*(1), 11–20.

Deaux, K., Dane, F. C., & Wrightsman, L. S. (1993). *Social psychology in the '90s* (6th ed.). Pacific Grove, CA: Brooks/Cole.

Deaux, K., & Wrightsman, L. S. (1988). *Social psychology* (5th ed.). Pacific Grove, CA: Brooks/Cole.

de Guzman, J. (1979). Helping a lost passenger: An analysis of the number of bystanders and dependency of the victim in an urban and a rural community. *Philippine Journal of Psychology*, *12*, 10–16.

DeJong, W., & Musilli, L. (1982). External pressure to comply: Handicapped versus nonhandicapped requesters and the foot-in-the-door phenomenon. *Personality and Social Psychology Bulletin*, *8*, 522–527.

DePaulo, B. M., Tang, J., & Stone, J. I. (1987). Physical attractiveness and skill at detecting deception. *Personality and Social Psychology Bulletin*, *13*, 177–187.

Derlega, V. J., Wilson, M., & Chaikin, A. L. (1976). Friendship and disclosure reciprocity. *Journal of Personality and Social Psychology*, *34*, 578–582.

Deschamps, J.-C., & Doise, W. (1978). Crossed category memberships in intergroup relations. In H. Tajfel (Ed.), *Differentiation between social groups: Studies in the social psychology of intergroup relations* (pp. 141–158). London: Academic Press.

Deutsch, M. (1973). *The resolution of conflict: Constructive and destructive processes*. New Haven, CT: Yale University Press.

Deutsch, M. (1983). Conflict resolution: Theory and practice. *Political Psychology*, *4*, 431–453.

Deutsch, M. (1986). The malignant (spiral) process of hostile interaction. In R. K. White (Ed.), *Psychology and the prevention of nuclear war* (pp. 131–154). New York: New York University Press.

Deutsch, M. (1990). Cooperation, conflict, and justice. In S. A. Wheelan & E. A. Pepitone (Eds.), *Advances in field theory* (pp. 149–164). Newbury Park, CA: Sage.

Deutsch, M., & Gerard, H. B. (1955). A study of normative and informational social influences upon individual judgment. *Journal of Abnormal and Social Psychology*, *51*, 629–636.

Doise, W. (1978). *Groups and individuals: Explanations in social psychology*. Cambridge, England: Cambridge University Press.

Dollard, J., Doob, L. W., Miller, N. E., Mowrer, O. H., & Sears, R. R. (1939). *Frustration and aggression*. New Haven, CT: Yale University Press.

Doob, L. W. (1970). *Resolving conflict in Africa: The Fermeda workshop*. New Haven, CT: Yale University Press.

Drake, B. H., & Moberg, D. J. (1986). Communicating influence attempts in dyads: Linguistic sedatives and palliatives. *Academy of Management Review*, *11*, 567–584.

Duck, S. (1992). *Human relationships* (2nd ed.). London: Sage.

Duck, S. (Ed.). (1993). *Social context and relationships.* Newbury Park, CA: Sage. [Also, other volumes in this six-volume series on understanding relationship processes.]

Dunand, M., Berkowitz, L., & Leyens, J. P. (1984). Audience effects when viewing aggressive movies. *British Journal of Social Psychology, 21,* 69–76.

Duncan, S. (1969). Nonverbal communication. *Psychological Bulletin, 72,* 118–137.

Duncan, S., Brunner, L. J., & Fiske, D. W. (1979). Strategy signals in face-to-face interaction. *Journal of Personality and Social Psychology, 37,* 301–313.

Dyer, W. G. (1987). *Team building: Issues and alternatives* (2nd ed.). Reading, MA: Addison-Wesley.

Eagly, A. H. (1978). Sex differences in influenceability. *Psychological Bulletin, 85,* 86–116.

Eagly, A. H. (1983). Gender and social influence: A social psychological analysis. *American Psychologist, 38,* 971–981.

Eagly, A. H., & Carli, L. L. (1981). Sex of researchers and sex-typed communications as determinants of sex differences in influenceability: A meta-analysis of social influence studies. *Psychological Bulletin, 90,* 1–20.

Eagly, A. H., & Crowley, M. (1986). Gender and helping behavior: A meta-analytic review of the social psychological literature. *Psychological Bulletin, 100,* 283–308.

Eagly, A. H., & Johnson, B. T. (1990). Gender and leadership style: A meta-analysis. *Psychological Bulletin, 108,* 233–256.

Eagly, A. H., Makhijani, M. G., & Klonsky, B. G. (1992). Gender and the evaluation of leaders: A meta-analysis. *Psychological Bulletin, 111,* 3–22.

Eagly, A. H., & Steffen, V. J. (1986). Gender and aggressive behavior: A meta-analytic review of the social psychological literature. *Psychological Bulletin, 100,* 309–330.

Eagly, A. H., & Wood, W. (1982). Inferred sex differences in status as a determinant of gender stereotypes about social influence. *Journal of Personality and Social Psychology, 43,* 915–928.

Eagly, A. H., Wood, W., & Fishbaugh, L. (1981). Sex differences in conformity: Surveillance by the group as a determinant of male nonconformity. *Journal of Personality and Social Psychology, 40,* 384–394.

Eisenhardt, K. M., & Schoonhoven, C. B. (1990). Organizational growth: Linking founding team, strategy, environment, and growth among U. S. semiconductor ventures, 1978–1988. *Administrative Science Quarterly, 35,* 504–529.

Ekman, P. (1982). (Ed.). *Emotion in the human face* (2nd ed.). Cambridge, England: Cambridge University Press.

Ellsworth, P. C., Carlsmith, J. M., & Henson, A. (1972). The stare as a stimulus to flight in human subjects: A series of field experiments. *Journal of Personality and Social Psychology, 21,* 302–311.

Epley, S. W. (1974). Reduction of the behavioral effects of aversive stimulation by the presence of companions. *Psychological Bulletin, 81,* 271–283.

Epley, S. W., & Cottrell, N. B. (1977). Effect of presence of a companion on speed of escape from electric shock. *Psychological Reports, 40,* 1299–1308.

Epstein, Y. M. (1981). Crowding stress and human behavior. *Journal of Social Issues, 37*(1), 126–144.

Evans, G. W. (1978). Human spatial behavior: The arousal model. In A. Baum and Y. M. Epstein (Eds.), *Human response to crowding* (pp. 283–302). Hillsdale, NJ: Erlbaum.

Evans, G. W., & Jacobs, S. V. (1981). Air pollution and human behavior. *Journal of Social Issues, 37*(1), 95–125.

Exline, R. V., & Winters, L. C. (1965). Affective relations and mutual glances in dyads. In S. S. Tomkins & C. E. Izard (Eds.), *Affect, cognition, and personality: Empirical studies* (pp. 319–350). New York: Springer.

Farrell, M. P., Heinemann, G. D., & Schmitt, M. H. (1986). Informal roles, rituals, and styles of humor in interdisciplinary health care teams: Their relationship to stages of group development. *International Journal of Small Group Research, 2*, 143–162.

Ferguson, C. K., & Kelley, H. H. (1964). Significant factors in overevaluation of own-group's product. *Journal of Abnormal and Social Psychology, 69*, 223–228.

Fern, E. F., Monroe, K. B., & Avila, R. A. (1986). Effectiveness of multiple request strategies: A synthesis of research results. *Journal of Marketing Research, 23*(2), 144–152.

Festinger, L. (1954). A theory of social comparison processes. *Human Relations, 7*, 117–140.

Fiedler, F. E. (1967). *A theory of leadership effectiveness.* New York: McGraw-Hill.

Fiedler, F. E. (1978). Recent developments in research on the contingency model. In L. Berkowitz (Ed.), *Group processes.* New York: Academic Press.

Fiedler, F. E. (1987, September). When to lead, when to stand back. *Psychology Today, 21*(9), 26–27.

Fiedler, F. E., & Mahar, L. (1979). The effectiveness of contingency model training: A review of the validation of leader match. *Personnel Psychology, 32*, 45–62.

Fielding, L., Murray, J., & Steel, D. H. (1976). The influence of spectator reaction and presence during training on performance. *International Journal of Sport Psychology, 7*, 73–81.

Finholt, T., & Sproull, L. S. (1990). Electronic groups at work. *Organization Science, 1*, 41–64.

Fisher, D. V. (1984). A conceptual analysis of self-disclosure. *Journal for the Theory of Social Behaviour, 14*, 277–296.

Fisher, J. D., Nadler, A., & Whitcher-Alagna, S. (1982). Recipient reactions to aid. *Psychological Bulletin, 91*, 27–54.

Fisher, R. (1971). Fractionating conflict. In C. G. Smith (Ed.), *Conflict resolution: Contributions of the behavioral sciences* (pp. 157–169). Notre Dame, IN: University of Notre Dame Press. [Reprinted from Roger Fisher (Ed.), 1964, *International conflict and behavioral science: The Craigville papers* (pp. 91–109). New York: Basic Books.]

Fisher, R., & Ury, W. (1981). *Getting to yes: Negotiating agreement without giving in.* Boston: Houghton Mifflin.

Fisher, R., & Ury, W. (1991). *Getting to yes: Negotiating agreement without giving in* (new [3rd] ed.). London: Business Books.

Folkes, V. S. (1985). Mindlessness or mindfulness: A partial replication and extension of Langer, Blank, and Chanowitz. *Journal of Personality and Social Psychology, 48,* 600–604.

Follett, M. P. (1924). *Creative experience.* New York: Longmans, Green.

Forsyth, D. R., Schlenker, B. R., Leary, M. R., & McCown, N. E. (1985). Self-presentational determinants of sex differences in leadership behavior. *Small Group Behavior, 16,* 197–210.

Foss, R. D., & Dempsey, C. B. (1979). Blood donation and the foot-in-the-door technique: A limiting case. *Journal of Personality and Social Psychology, 37,* 580–590.

Foushee, H. C. (1984). Dyads and triads at 35,000 feet: Factors affecting group process and aircrew performance. *American Psychologist, 39,* 885–893.

Francis, D., & Young, D. (1979). *Improving work groups: A practical manual for team building.* San Diego: University Associates. [Also, rev. ed., 1992, San Diego: Pfeiffer.]

Freedman, J. L. (1979). Reconciling apparent differences between the responses of humans and other animals to crowding. *Psychological Review, 86,* 80–85.

Freedman, J. L., & Fraser, S. C. (1966). Compliance without pressure: The foot-in-the-door technique. *Journal of Personality and Social Psychology, 4,* 195–202.

French, J. R. P., Jr., & Raven, B. (1959). The bases of social power. In D. Cartwright (Ed.), *Studies in social power* (pp. 150–167). Ann Arbor: University of Michigan.

Friedman, V. J., & Lipshitz, R. (1992). Teaching people to shift cognitive gears: Overcoming resistance on the road to model II. *Journal of Applied Behavioral Science, 28,* 118–136.

Frieze, I. H., & Ramsey, S. (1976). Nonverbal maintenance of traditional sex roles. *Journal of Social Issues, 32*(3), 133–141.

Gaertner, S. L., Mann, J., Murrell, A., & Dovidio, J. F. (1989). Reducing intergroup bias: The benefits of recategorization. *Journal of Personality and Social Psychology, 57,* 239–249.

Gallupe, R. B., Dennis, A. R., Cooper, W. H., Valacich, J. S., Bastian III, L. M., & Nunamaker, J. F. (1992). Electronic brainstorming and group size. *Academy of Management Journal, 35,* 350–369.

Gamson, W. A. (1961). An experimental test of a theory of coalition formation. *American Sociological Review, 26,* 565–573.

Gastorf, J. W., Suls, J., & Sanders, G. S. (1980). Type A coronary-prone behavior pattern and social facilitation. *Journal of Personality and Social Psychology, 38,* 773–780.

Geen, R. G. (1989). Alternative conceptions of social facilitation. In P. B. Paulus (Ed.), *Psychology of group influence* (2nd ed., pp. 15–51). Hillsdale, NJ: Erlbaum.

Geen, R. G., & Gange, J. J. (1977). Drive theory of social facilitation: Twelve years of theory and research. *Psychological Bulletin, 84,* 1267–1288.

Geen, R. G., & Gange, J. J. (1983). Social facilitation: Drive theory and beyond.

In H. H. Blumberg, A. P. Hare, V. Kent, & M. F. Davies (Eds.), *Small groups and social interaction* (Vol. 1, pp. 141–153). Chichester, England: John Wiley.

Geis, F. L., & Moon, T. H. (1981). Machiavellianism and deception. *Journal of Personality and Social Psychology, 41,* 766–775.

Geller, D. M. (1978). Involvement in role-playing simulations: A demonstration with studies on obedience. *Journal of Personality and Social Psychology, 36,* 219–235.

Gersick, C. J., & Hackman, J. R. (1990). Habitual routines in task-performing groups. *Organizational Behavior and Human Decision Processes, 47,* 65–97.

Gilbert, D. T., Jones, E. E., & Pelham, B. W. (1987). Influence and inference: What the active perceiver overlooks. *Journal of Personality and Social Psychology, 52,* 861–870.

Gilbert, S. J. (1981). Another look at the Milgram obedience studies: The role of the gradated series of shocks. *Personality and Social Psychology Bulletin, 7,* 690–695.

Glance, N. S., & Huberman, B. A. (1994). The dynamics of social dilemmas. *Scientific American, 270*(3), 76–81.

Glaser, A. N. (1982). Drive theory of social facilitation: A critical reappraisal. *British Journal of Social Psychology, 21,* 265–282.

Gleason, J. M., Seaman, F. J., & Hollander, E. P. (1978). Emergent leadership processes as a function of task structure and Machiavellianism. *Social Behavior and Personality, 6,* 33–36.

Godfrey, D. K., Jones, E. E., & Lord, C. G. (1986). Self-promotion is not ingratiating. *Journal of Personality and Social Psychology, 50,* 106–115.

Golding, W. (1959). *Lord of the flies.* New York: Capricorn.

Goldman, M., Lewandowski, H. E., & Carrill, R. E. (1982). Altruistic behavior in rural and urban, residential and business areas. *Basic and Applied Social Psychology, 3,* 155–160.

Golembiewski, R. T. (1965). Small groups and large organizations. In J. G. March (Ed.), *Handbook of organizations* (pp. 87–141). Chicago: Rand McNally.

Gordon, W. J. J. (1961). *Synectics: The development of creative capacity.* New York: Collier Books.

Gottlieb, J., & Carver, C. S. (1980). Anticipation of future interaction and the bystander effect. *Journal of Experimental Social Psychology, 16,* 253–260.

Gove, W. R., Hughes, M., & Galle, O. R. (1979). Overcrowding in the home: An empirical investigation of its possible pathological consequences. *American Sociological Review, 44,* 59–80.

Griffitt, W. (1970). Environmental effects on interpersonal affective behavior: Ambient effective temperature and attraction. *Journal of Personality and Social Psychology, 15,* 240–244.

Griffitt, W., & Veitch, R. (1971). Hot and crowded: Influences of population density and temperature on interpersonal affective behavior. *Journal of Personality and Social Psychology, 17,* 92–98.

Grigsby, J. P., & Weatherley, D. (1983). Gender and sex-role differences in intimacy of self-disclosure. *Psychological Reports, 53,* 891–897.

Gudykunst, W. B. (1983). Toward a typology of stranger-host relationships. *International Journal of Intercultural Relations, 7,* 401–413.

Guerin, B. (1983). Social facilitation and social monitoring: A test of three models. *British Journal of Social Psychology, 22,* 203–214.

Guerin, B. (1986a). The effects of mere presence on a motor task. *Journal of Social Psychology, 126,* 399–401.

Guerin, B. (1986b). Mere presence effects in humans: A review. *Journal of Experimental Social Psychology, 22,* 38–77.

Guerin, B. (1993). *Social facilitation.* Cambridge: Cambridge University Press.

Guerin, B., & Innes, J. M. (1982). Social facilitation and social monitoring: A new look at Zajonc's mere presence hypothesis. *British Journal of Social Psychology, 21,* 7–18.

Guerin, B., & Innes, J. M. (1984). Explanations of social facilitation: A review. *Current Psychological Research and Reviews, 3,* 32–52.

Guillon, M., & Personnaz, B. (1983). Analyse de la dynamique des représentations des conflits minoritaire et majoritaire [Dynamic of representation of majority and minority conflicts]. *Cahiers de Psychologie Cognitive, 3,* 65–87.

Guzzo, R. A., & Dickson, M. W. (1996). Teams in organizations: Recent research on performance and effectiveness. *Annual Review of Psychology, 47,* 307–338.

Hacker, H. M. (1981). Blabbermouths and clams: Sex differences in self-disclosure in same-sex and cross-sex friendship dyads. *Psychology of Women Quarterly, 5,* 385–401.

Hall, E. T. (1966). *The hidden dimension.* New York: Doubleday.

Hall, J. A. (1984). *Nonverbal sex differences.* Baltimore: Johns Hopkins University Press.

Haney, C., Banks, C., & Zimbardo, P. (1973). Interpersonal dynamics in a simulated prison. *International Journal of Criminology and Penology, 1,* 69–97.

Hansen, W. B., & Altman, I. (1976). Decorating personal places: A descriptive analysis. *Environment and Behavior, 8,* 491–504.

Harada, J. (1985). Bystander intervention: The effect of ambiguity of the helping situation and the interpersonal relationship between bystanders. *Japanese Psychological Research, 27,* 177–184.

Harari, H., Harari, O., & White, R. V. (1985). The reaction to rape by American male bystanders. *Journal of Social Psychology, 125,* 653–658.

Hare, A. P. (1962). *Handbook of small group research.* [New York]: Free Press of Glencoe.

Hare, A. P. (1967). Small group development in the relay assembly testroom. *Sociological Inquiry, 37,* 169–182.

Hare, A. P. (1973). Group decision by consensus: Reaching unity in the Society of Friends. *Sociological Inquiry, 43,* 75–84.

Hare, A. P. (1976). *Handbook of small group research* (2nd ed.). New York: Free Press.

Hare, A. P. (1982). *Creativity in small groups.* Beverly Hills, CA: Sage.

Hare, A. P. (1983). A functional interpretation of interaction. In H. H. Blumberg, A. P. Hare, V. Kent, & M. F. Davies (Eds.), *Small groups and social interaction* (Vol. 2, pp. 429–447). Chichester, England: John Wiley.

Hare, A. P. (1989). New field theory: SYMLOG research 1960–1988. *Advances in Group Processes, 6,* 229–257.

Hare, A. P. (1992). *Groups, teams, and social interaction.* New York: Praeger.

Hare, A. P. (1993). Small groups in organizations. In R. T. Golembiewski (Ed.), *Handbook of organizational behavior* (pp. 61–89). New York: Marcel Dekker.

Hare, A. P., Blumberg, H. H., Davies, M. F., & Kent, M. V. (1994). *Small group research: A handbook.* Norwood, NJ: Ablex.

Hare, A. P., Borgatta, E. F., Bales, R. F. (Eds.). (1955). *Small groups: Studies in social interaction.* New York: Knopf.

Hare, A. P., Borgatta, E. F., Bales, R. F. (Eds.). (1965). *Small groups: Studies in social interaction* (rev. ed.). New York: Knopf.

Hare, A. P., & Naveh, D. (1985). Creative problem solving: Camp David Summit, 1978. *Small Group Behavior, 16,* 123–138.

Harkins, S. G. (1987). Social loafing and social facilitation. *Journal of Experimental Social Psychology, 23,* 1–18.

Harkins, S. G., & Szymanski, K. (1989). Social loafing and group evaluation. *Journal of Personality and Social Psychology, 56,* 934–941.

Harrison, A. A., & Connors, M. M. (1984). Groups in exotic environments. *Advances in Experimental Social Psychology, 18,* 49–87.

Hatfield, E. (1983). Equity theory and research: An overview. In H. H. Blumberg, A. P. Hare, V. Kent, & M. F. Davies (Eds.), *Small groups and social interaction* (Vol. 2, pp. 401–412). Chichester, England: John Wiley.

Hayduk, L. A. (1978). Personal space: An evaluative and orienting overview. *Psychological Bulletin, 85,* 117–134.

Hayduk, L. A. (1983). Personal space: Where we now stand. *Psychological Bulletin, 94,* 293–335.

Haythorn, W. W. (1953). The influence of individual members on the characteristics of small groups. *Journal of Abnormal and Social Psychology, 48,* 276–284.

Haythorn, W. W., Couch, A. S., Haefner, D., Langham, P., & Carter, L. F. (1956). The effects of varying combinations of authoritarian and equalitarian leaders and followers. *Journal of Abnormal and Social Psychology, 53,* 210–219.

Heilman, M. E. (1976). Oppositional behavior as a function of influence attempt intensity and retaliation threat. *Journal of Personality and Social Psychology, 33,* 574–578.

Heilman, M. E., Hornstein, H. A., Cage, J. H., & Herschlag, J. K. (1984). Reactions to prescribed leader behavior as a function of role perspective: The case of the Vroom-Yetton model. *Journal of Applied Psychology, 69,* 50–60.

Heller, J. F., Groff, B. D., & Solomon, S. H. (1977). Toward an understanding of crowding: The role of physical interaction. *Journal of Personality and Social Psychology, 35,* 183–190.

Hendrick, C. (Ed.). (1989). *Close relationships.* Newbury Park, CA: Sage. [*Review of Personality and Social Psychology,* Vol. 10.]

Henley, N. M. (1977). *Body politics: Power, sex, and nonverbal communication.* Englewood Cliffs, NJ: Prentice-Hall.

Herrick, N. Q. (1990). *Joint management and employee participation: Labor and management at the crossroads.* San Francisco: Jossey-Bass.

Hewstone, M. R. C., & Brown, R. J. (1986). Contact is not enough: An intergroup perspective on the "contact hypothesis." In M. Hewstone & R. Brown

(Eds.), *Contact and conflict in intergroup encounters* (pp. 1–44). Oxford: Blackwell.

Hiers, J. M., & Heckel, R. V. (1977). Seating choice, leadership, and locus of control. *Journal of Social Psychology, 103*, 313–314.

Hill, R. E. (1975). Interpersonal compatibility and workgroup performance. *Journal of Applied Behavioral Science, 11*, 210–219.

Hinkin, T. T., & Schriesheim, C. A. (1989). Development and application of new scales to measure the French and Raven (1959) bases of social power. *Journal of Applied Psychology, 74*, 561–567.

Hoffman, L. R. (1965). Group problem solving. *Advances in Experimental Social Psychology, 2*, 99–132.

Hogan, R., Curphy, G. J., & Hogan, J. (1994). What we know about leadership: Effectiveness and personality. *American Psychologist, 49*, 493–504.

Hogg, M. A. (1992). *The social psychology of group cohesiveness: From attraction to social identity*. London: Harvester Wheatsheaf.

Hogg, M. A., & Abrams, D. (1988). *Social identifications: A social psychology of intergroup relations and group processes*. London: Routledge.

Hogg, M. A., Cooper-Shaw, L., & Holzworth, D. W. (1993). Group prototypicality and depersonalized attraction in small interactive groups. *Personality and Social Psychology Bulletin, 19*, 452–465.

Hogg, M. A., & Moreland, R. L. (Eds.). (1993). *Social processes in small groups* (2 vols.). Leicester, England: British Psychological Society. [*British Journal of Social Psychology, 32* (1–2).]

Holahan, C. J. (1974). Experimental investigations of environment-behavior relationships in psychiatric facilities. *Man-Environment Systems, 4*(2), 109–113.

Hollander, E. P. (1958). Conformity, status, and idiosyncrasy credit. *Psychological Review, 65*, 117–127.

Hollander, E. P. (1985). Leadership and power. In G. Lindzey and E. Aronson (Eds.), *Handbook of social psychology* (3rd ed., Vol. 2, pp. 485–538). New York: Random House.

Hollander, E. P. (1992). The essential interdependence of leadership and followership. *Current Directions in Psychological Science, 1*, 71–75.

Hollander, E. P., Fallon, B. J., & Edwards, M. T. (1977). Some aspects of influence and acceptability for appointed and elected group leaders. *Journal of Psychology, 95*, 289–296.

Hollander, E. P., & Julian, J. W. (1970). Studies in leader legitimacy, influence and innovation. *Advances in Experimental Social Psychology, 5*, 33–69.

Hollander, E. P., & Yoder, J. D. (1980). Some issues in comparing women and men as leaders. *Basic and Applied Social Psychology, 1*, 267–280.

Hollingworth, L. S. (1942). *Children above 180 IQ Stanford-Binet: Origin and development*. Yonkers-on-Hudson: World Book.

Homans, G. C. (1950). *The human group*. New York: Harcourt, Brace/Random House.

Homans, G. C. (1958). Social behavior as exchange. *American Journal of Sociology, 63*, 597–606.

Homans, G. C. (1961). *Social behavior: Its elementary forms*. New York: Harcourt, Brace and World.

Hornstein, H. A., LaKind, E., Frankel, G., & Manne, S. (1975). Effects of knowledge about remote social events on prosocial behavior, social conception, and mood. *Journal of Personality and Social Psychology, 32*, 1038–1046.

Hovland, C. I., & Sears, R. R. (1940). Minor studies in aggression: VI. Correlation of lynchings with economic indices. *Journal of Psychology, 9*, 301–310.

Huse, E. F., & Cummings, T. G. (1985). *Organization development and change* (3rd ed.). St Paul: West Publishing. [Also, 4th ed., 1989, by Cummings & Huse.]

Huston, T. L., Ruggiero, M., Conner, R., & Geis, G. (1981). Bystander intervention into crime: A study based on naturally-occurring episodes. *Social Psychology Quarterly, 44*, 14–23.

Ickes, W., & Barnes, R. D. (1977). The role of sex and self-monitoring in unstructured dyadic interactions. *Journal of Personality and Social Psychology, 35*, 315–330.

Ickes, W., & Barnes, R. D. (1978). Boys and girls together—and alienated: On enacting stereotyped sex roles in mixed-sex dyads. *Journal of Personality and Social Psychology, 36*, 669–683.

Ickes, W. J., Schermer, B., & Steeno, J. (1979). Sex and sex-role influences in same-sex dyads. *Social Psychology Quarterly, 42*, 373–385.

Ingham, A. G., Levinger, G., Graves, J., & Peckham, V. (1974). The Ringelmann effect: Studies of group size and group performance. *Journal of Experimental Social Psychology, 10*, 371–384.

Innes, J. M., & Gordon, M. I. (1985). The effects of mere presence and a mirror on performance of a motor task. *Journal of Social Psychology, 125*, 479–484.

Insko, C. A., Smith, R. H., Alicke, M. D., Wade, J. & Taylor, S. (1985). Conformity and group size: The concern with being right and the concern with being liked. *Personality and Social Psychology Bulletin, 11*, 41–50.

Instone, D., Major, B., & Bunker, B. B. (1983). Gender, self confidence, and social influence strategies: An organizational simulation. *Journal of Personality and Social Psychology, 44*, 322–333.

Isgar, T., & Isgar, S. (1993). High-performing teams: A definition. In R. T Golembiewski (Ed.), *Handbook of organizational consultation* (pp. 417–421). New York: Marcel Dekker.

Jackson, J. M., & Latané, B. (1981). Strength and number of solicitors and the urge towards altruism. *Personality and Social Psychology Bulletin, 7*, 415–422.

Jacobs, R. C., & Campbell, D. T. (1961). The perpetuation of an arbitrary tradition through several generations of a laboratory microculture. *Journal of Abnormal and Social Psychology, 62*, 649–658.

Janis, I. L. (1982). *Groupthink: Psychological studies of policy decisions and fiascoes.* Boston: Houghton Mifflin.

Janis, I. L. (1983). Groupthink. In H. H. Blumberg, A. P. Hare, V. Kent, & M. F. Davies (Eds.), *Small groups and social interaction* (Vol. 2., pp. 39–46). Chichester, England: John Wiley.

Janis, I. L., & Mann, L. (1992). Cognitive complexity in international decision making. In P. Suedfeld & P. E. Tetlock (Eds.), *Psychology and social policy* (pp. 33–49). New York: Hemisphere (Taylor & Francis).

Jennings, L. B., & George, S. G. (1984). Group-induced distortion of visually perceived extent: The Asch effect revisited. *Psychological Record*, *34*, 133–148.

Johnson, C. (1992). Gender, formal authority, and leadership. In C. L. Ridgeway (Ed.), *Gender, interaction, and inequality* (pp. 29–49). New York: Springer-Verlag.

Johnson, D. W., Maruyama, G., Johnson, R., Nelson, D., & Skon, L. (1981). Effects of cooperative, competitive, and individualistic goal structures on achievement: A meta-analysis. *Psychological Bulletin*, *89*, 47–62.

Johnson, R. D., & Downing, L. L. (1979). Deindividuation and valence of cues: Effects on prosocial and antisocial behavior. *Journal of Personality and Social Psychology*, *37*, 1532–1538.

Jones, E. E., & Gerard, H. B. (1967). *Foundations of Social Psychology*. New York: John Wiley & Sons.

Jones, E. E., & Pittman, T. S. (1982). Toward a general theory of strategic self-presentation. In J. Suls (Ed.), *Psychological perspectives on the self* (Vol. 1, pp. 231–262). Hillsdale, NJ: Erlbaum.

Jones, E. E., Rhodewalt, F., Berglas, S., & Skelton, J. A. (1981). Effects of strategic self-presentation on subsequent self-esteem. *Journal of Personality and Social Psychology*, *41*, 407–421.

Jones, E. E., Wood, G. C., & Quattrone, G. A. (1981). Perceived variability of personal characteristics in in-groups and out-groups: The role of knowledge and evaluation. *Personality and Social Psychology Bulletin*, *7*, 523–528.

Jourard, S. M. (1971). *Self-disclosure: An experimental analysis of the transparent self*. New York: Wiley.

Julian, J. W., Bishop, D. W., & Fiedler, F. E. (1966). Quasi-therapeutic effects of intergroup competition. *Journal of Personality and Social Psychology*, *3*, 321–327.

Kahn, A., & Ryen, A. H. (1972). Factors influencing the bias towards one's own group. *International Journal of Group Tensions*, *2*(2), 33–50.

Karau, S. J., & Williams, K. D. (1995). Social loafing: Research findngs, implications, and future directions. *Current Directions in Psychological Science*, *4*, 134–140.

Katz, D., & Braly, K. (1933). Racial stereotypes of one hundred college students. *Journal of Abnormal and Social Psychology*, *28*, 280–290.

Katz, D., & Kahn, R. L. (1978). *The social psychology of organizations* (2d ed.). New York: Wiley.

Katz, I. (1970). Experimental studies of Negro-White relationships. *Advances in Experimental Social Psychology*, *5*, 71–117.

Katz, P. A., & Taylor, D. A. (Eds.). (1988). *Eliminating racism*. New York: Plenum.

Katzenbach, J. R., & Smith, D. K. (1993). The discipline of teams. *Harvard Business Review*, *71*(2), 111–120.

Kelley, H. H. (1951). Communication in experimentally created hierarchies. *Human Relations*, *4*, 39–56.

Kelley, H. H. (1984). The theoretical description of interdependence by means of transition lists. *Journal of Personality and Social Psychology*, *47*, 956–982.

Kelley, H. H., Berscheid, E., Christensen, A., Harvey, J. H., Huston, T. L., Levinger, G. McClintock, E., Peplau, L. A., & Peterson, D. R. (1983). *Close relationships*. New York: Freeman.

Kelley, H. H., & Schenitzki, D. P. (1972). Bargaining. In C. G. McClintock (Ed.), *Experimental social psychology* (pp. 298–337). New York: Holt, Rinehart & Winston.

Kelly, J. A., Wildman, H. E., & Urey, J. R. (1982). Gender and sex role differences in group decision-making social interactions: A behavioral analysis. *Journal of Applied Social Psychology, 12,* 112–127.

Kelman, H. C. (1958). Compliance, identification, and internalization: Three processes of attitude change. *Journal of Conflict Resolution, 2,* 51–60.

Kelman, H. C. (1992). Informal mediation by the scholar/practitioner. In J. Bercovitch & J. Z. Rubin (Eds.), *Mediation in international relations: Multiple approaches to conflict management* (pp. 64–96). New York: St. Martin's Press.

Kenny, D. A. (1996). The design and analysis of social interaction research. *Annual Review of Psychology, 47,* 59–86.

Kenny, D. A., & Zaccaro, S. J. (1983). An estimate of variance due to traits in leadership. *Journal of Applied Psychology, 68,* 678–685.

Kenrick, D. T., & Johnson, G. A. (1979). Interpersonal attraction in aversive environments: A problem for the classical conditioning paradigm? *Journal of Personality and Social Psychology, 37,* 572–579.

Kent, M. V. & Blumberg, H. H. (1988/1992a). Aggression and social interaction: A classified bibliography 1974–1990. *Social and Behavioral Sciences Documents, 18*(2), 36–37 [Ms. No. 2869, 66 pp.].

Kent, M. V., & Blumberg, H. H. (1988/1992b). Prosocial behavior and social interaction: A classified bibliography 1974–1990. *Social and Behavioral Sciences Documents, 18*(2), 37–38 [Ms. No. 2870, 69 pp.].

Kerr, S., & Slocom, J. W., Jr. (1981). Controlling the performances of people in organizations. In P. C. Nystrom & W. H. Starbuck (Eds.), *Handbook of organizational design* (Vol. 2, pp. 116–134). New York: Oxford University Press.

Kerwin, J., & Shaffer, D. R. (1994). Mock jurors versus mock juries: The role of deliberations in reactions to inadmissible testimony. *Personality and Social Psychology Bulletin, 20,* 153–162.

Kew, F. (1987). Contested rules: An explanation of how games change. *International Review for the Sociology of Sport, 22*(2), 125–135.

Kleinke, C. L. (1986). Gaze and eye contact: A research review. *Psychological Bulletin, 100,* 78–100.

Kohn, A. (1991). Group grade grubbing versus cooperative learning. *Educational Leadership, 48*(5), 83–87.

Komorita, S. S., & Kravitz, D. A. (1983). Coalition formation. In H. H. Blumberg, A. P. Hare, V. Kent, & M. F. Davies (Eds.), *Small groups and social interaction* (Vol. 2, pp. 189–197). Chichester, England: John Wiley.

Koneya, M. (1977). Privacy regulation in small and large groups. *Group and Organization Studies, 2,* 324–335.

Korte, C., Ypma, I., & Toppen, A. (1975). Helpfulness in Dutch society as a function of urbanization and environmental input level. *Journal of Personality and Social Psychology, 32,* 996–1003.

Kosower, E. (1987). The Shokuba Development Program: Japan's step beyond quality circles. *Organization Development Journal, 5,* 18–21.

Krackhardt, D., & Hansen, J. R. (1993). Informal networks: The company behind the chart. *Harvard Business Review, 71*(4), 104–111.

Krantz, D. S. (1979). A naturalistic study of social influences on meal size among moderately obese and nonobese subjects. *Psychosomatic Medicine, 41*(1), 19–27.

Kraut, R. E., & Johnston, R. E. (1979). Social and emotional messages of smiling: An ethological approach. *Journal of Personality and Social Psychology, 37,* 1539–1553.

Krech, D., Crutchfield, R. S., & Ballachey, E. L. (1962). *Individual in society.* New York: McGraw-Hill.

Kulik, J. A., & Mahler, H. I. (1989). Stress and affiliation in a hospital setting: Preoperative roommate preferences. *Personality and Social Psychology Bulletin, 15,* 183–193.

LaFrance, M. (1979). Nonverbal synchrony and rapport: Analysis by the cross-lag panel technique. *Social Psychology Quarterly, 42,* 66–70.

Lamb, T. A. (1981). Nonverbal and paraverbal control in dyads and triads: Sex or power differences? *Social Psychology Quarterly, 44,* 49–53.

Lane, I. M., & Messé, L. A. (1971). Equity and the distribution of rewards. *Journal of Personality and Social Psychology, 20,* 1–17.

Langer, E. J. (1978). Rethinking the role of thought in social interaction. In J. H. Harvey, W. J. Ickes, & R. F. Kidd (Eds.), *New directions in attribution research* (Vol. 2, pp. 35–58). Hillsdale, NJ: Erlbaum.

Langer, E. J. (1989). Minding matters: The consequences of mindlessness-mindfulness. *Advances in Experimental Social Psychology, 22,* 137–173.

Langer, E. J., Bashner, R. S., & Chanowitz, B. (1985). Decreasing prejudice by increasing discrimination. *Journal of Personality and Social Psychology, 49,* 113–120.

Langer, E. J., Blank, A., & Chanowitz, B. (1978). The mindlessness of ostensibly thoughtful action: The role of "placebic" information in interpersonal interaction. *Journal of Personality and Social Psychology, 36,* 635–642.

Langer, E. J., Chanowitz, B., & Blank, A. (1985). Mindlessness-mindfulness in perspective: A reply to Valerie Folkes. *Journal of Personality and Social Psychology, 48,* 605–607.

Langer, E. J., & Saegert, S. (1977). Crowding and cognitive control. *Journal of Personality and Social Psychology, 35,* 175–182.

Larson, C. E., & La Fasto, F. M. J. (1989). *Teamwork: What must go right, what can go wrong.* Newbury Park, CA: Sage.

Latané, B. (1981). The psychology of social impact. *American Psychologist, 36,* 343–356.

Latané, B., & Dabbs, J. M. (1975). Sex, group size and helping in three cities. *Sociometry, 38,* 180–194.

Latané, B., & Darley, J. M. (1968). Group inhibition of bystander intervention in emergencies. *Journal of Personality and Social Psychology, 10,* 215–221.

Latané, B., & Darley, J. M. (1970). *The unresponsive bystanders: Why doesn't he help?* New York: Appleton-Century Crofts.

Latané, B., & Jackson, C. (1994). *The spatial structure of electronic juries and the probability of "hanging."* Paper presented at the International Congress of Applied Psychology, Madrid, July.

Latané, B., & Nida, S. (1980). Social impact theory and group influence: A social engineering perspective. In P. B. Paulus (Ed.), *Psychology of group influence* (pp. 3–34). Hillsdale, NJ: Erlbaum.

Latané, B., & Nida, S. (1981). Ten years of research on group size and helping. *Psychological Bulletin, 89,* 308–324.

Latané, B., Nowak, A., & Liu, J. H. (1994). Measuring emergent social phenomena: Dynamism, polarization, and clustering as order parameters of social systems. *Behavioral Science, 39,* 1–24.

Latané, B., Williams, K., & Harkins, S. (1979). Many hands make light the work: The causes and consequences of social loafing. *Journal of Personality and Social Psychology, 37,* 822–832.

Latham, V. M. (1987). Task type and group motivation: Implications for a behavioral approach to leadership in small groups. *Small Group Behavior, 18,* 56–71.

Lay, C., Allen, M., & Kassirer, A. (1974). The responsive bystander in emergencies: Some preliminary data. *Canadian Psychologist, 15,* 220–227.

Leary, M. R., Robertson, R. B., Barnes, B. D., & Miller, R. S. (1986). Self-presentations of small group leaders: Effects of role requirements and leadership orientation. *Journal of Personality and Social Psychology, 51,* 742–748.

Leavitt, H. J. (1951). Some effects of certain communication patterns on group performance. *Journal of Abnormal and Social Psychology, 46,* 38–50.

Lecuyer, R. (1976). Social organization and spatial organization. *Human Relations, 29,* 1045–1060.

Lemyre, L., & Smith, P. M. (1985). Intergroup discrimination and self-esteem in the minimal group paradigm. *Journal of Personality and Social Psychology, 49,* 660–670.

Lenney, E. (1977). Women's self-confidence in achievement settings. *Psychological Bulletin, 84,* 1–13.

Leritz, L. (1987). *No-fault negotiating: A simple and innovative approach for solving problems, reaching agreements and resolving conflicts.* Portland, OR: Pacifica Press.

Levine, J. M., & Ruback, R. B. (1980). Reaction to opinion deviance: Impact of a fence straddler's rationale on majority evaluation. *Social Psychology Quarterly, 43,* 73–81.

Levinger, G. (1980). Toward the analysis of close relationships. *Journal of Experimental Social Psychology, 16,* 510–544.

Likert, R., & Likert, J. G. (1978). A method for coping with conflict in problem-solving groups. *Group and Organization Studies, 3,* 427–434.

Lippitt, R., & White, R. (1943). The social climate of children's groups. In R. G. Barker, J. Kounin, & H. Wright (Eds.), *Child behavior and development: A course of representative studies* (pp. 485–508). New York: McGraw-Hill.

Littlefield, L., Love, A., Peck, C., & Wertheim, E. H. (1993). A model for resolving conflict: Some theoretical, empirical and practical implications. *Australian Psychologist, 28,* 80–85.

Littlepage, G. E., & Pineault, M. A. (1985). Detection of deception of planned and spontaneous communications. *Journal of Social Psychology, 125,* 195–201.

Lockard, J. S., Fahrenbruch, C. E., Smith, J. L., & Morgan, C. J. (1977). Smiling and laughter: Different phyletic origins? *Bulletin of the Psychonomic Society*, *10*, 183–186.

Lord, R. G., & Alliger, G. M. (1985). A comparison of four information processing models of leadership and social perceptions. *Human Relations*, *38*, 47–65.

Lord, R. G., de Vader, C. L., & Alliger, G. M. (1986). A meta-analysis of the relation between personality traits and leadership perceptions: An application of validity generalization procedures. *Journal of Applied Psychology*, *71*, 402–410.

Lord, R. G., & Maher, K. J. (1990). Leadership perceptions and leadership performance: Two distinct but interdependent processes. In J. Carroll (Ed.), *Advances in applied social psychology: Business settings* (Vol. 4). Hillsdale, NJ: Erlbaum.

Maass, A., & Clark, R. D. (1983). Internalization versus compliance: Differential processes underlying minority influence and conformity. *European Journal of Social Psychology*, *13*, 197–215.

Maccoby, E. E., & Jacklin, C. N. (1974). *The psychology of sex differences*. Stanford, CA: Stanford University Press.

Mackie, D. M. (1987). Systematic and nonsystematic processing of majority and minority persuasive communication. *Journal of Personality and Social Psychology*, *53*, 41–52.

Magjuka, R. J., & Schmenner, R. (1993). Cellular manufacturing, group technology and human resource management: An international study. *Information & Management*, *10*, 405–412.

Mann, R. D. (1959). A review of the relationships between personality and performance in small groups. *Psychological Bulletin*, *56*, 241–270.

Manstead, A. S. R., & Semin, G. R. (1980). Social facilitation effects: Mere enhancement of dominant responses? *British Journal of Social and Clinical Psychology*, *19*, 119–136.

Manstead, A. S., Wagner, H. L., & MacDonald, C. J. (1984). Face, body, and speech as channels of communication in the detection of deception. *Basic and Applied Social Psychology*, *5*, 317–332.

Mantell, D. M., & Panzarella, R. (1976). Obedience and responsibility. *British Journal of Social and Clinical Psychology*, *15*, 239–245.

Markus, H. (1978). The effect of mere presence on social facilitation: An unobtrusive test. *Journal of Experimental Social Psychology*, *14*, 389–397.

Markus, H. (1981). The drive for integration: Some comments. *Journal of Experimental Social Psychology*, *17*, 257–261.

Martin, J., Lobb, B., Chapman, G. C., & Spillane, R. (1976). Obedience under conditions demanding self-immolation. *Human Relations*, *29*, 345–356.

Mathews, K. E., & Canon, L. K. (1975). Environmental noise level as a determinant of helping behavior. *Journal of Personality and Social Psychology*, *32*, 571–577.

McCann, J., & Galbraith, J. R. (1981). Interdepartmental relations. In P. C. Nystrom & W. H. Starbuck (Eds.), *Handbook of organizational design* (Vol. 2, pp. 60–84). New York: Oxford University Press.

McCarthy, D., & Saegert, S. (1978). Residential density, social overload, and social withdrawal. *Human Ecology*, *6*, 253–272.

McCarty, C., Turner, J. C., Hogg, M. A., David, B., & Wetherell, M. S. (1992).

Group polarization as conformity to the prototypical group member. *British Journal of Social Psychology, 31,* 1–20.

McClintock, C. G. (Ed.). (1972). *Experimental social psychology.* New York: Holt, Rinehart & Winston.

McDowall, J. J. (1978). Interactional synchrony: A reappraisal. *Journal of Personality and Social Psychology, 36,* 963–975.

McKenzie-Mohr, D., & Oskamp, S. (1995). Psychology and sustainability: An introduction. *Journal of Social Issues, 51*(4), 1–14.

McLaughlin, M. L., & Cody, M. J. (1982). Awkward silences: Behavioral antecedents and consequences of the conversational lapse. *Human Communication Research, 8,* 299–316.

McNeill, D. M. (1985). So you think gestures are nonverbal? *Psychological Review, 92,* 350–371.

Meeker, B. F., & Weitzel-O'Neill, P. A. (1977). Sex roles and interpersonal behavior in task-oriented groups. *American Sociological Review, 42,* 91–105.

Mehrabian, A. (1969). Significance of posture and position in the communication of attitude and status relationships. *Psychological Bulletin, 71,* 359–372.

Mehrabian, A., & Weiner, M. (1967). Decoding of inconsistent communications. *Journal of Personality and Social Psychology, 6,* 109–114.

Merei, F. (1949). Group leadership and institutionalisation. *Human Relations, 2,* 23–39.

Michaels, J. W., Blommel, J. M., Brocato, R. M., Linkous, R. A., & Rowe, J. S. (1982). Social facilitation and inhibition in a natural setting. *Replications in Social Psychology, 2,* 21–24.

Milgram, S. (1963). Behavioral study of obedience. *Journal of Abnormal and Social Psychology, 67,* 371–378.

Milgram, S. (1965). Some conditions of obedience and disobedience to authority. *Human Relations, 18,* 57–76.

Milgram, S. (1970). The experience of living in cities. *Science, 167,* 1461–1468.

Milgram, S. (1974). *Obedience to authority: An experimental view.* New York: Harper and Row.

Milgram, S. (1977). *The individual in a social world: Essays and experiments.* Reading, MA: Addison-Wesley.

Miller, A. G., Collins, B. E., & Brief, D. E.. (1995). Perspectives on obedience to authority: The legacy of the Milgram experiments. *Journal of Social Issues, 51* (3), 1–19.

Miller, C. E., & Anderson, P. D. (1979). Group decision rules and the rejection of deviates. *Social Psychology Quarterly, 42,* 354–363.

Miller, C. E., Jackson, P., Mueller, J., & Schersching, C. (1987). Some social psychological effects of group decision rules. *Journal of Personality and Social Psychology, 52,* 325–332.

Miller, D. T., & McFarland, C. (1987). Pluralistic ignorance: When similarity is interpreted as dissimilarity. *Journal of Personality and Social Psychology, 53,* 298–305.

Miller, L. C., Berg, J. H., & Archer, R. L. (1983). Openers: Individuals who elicit intimate self-disclosure. *Journal of Personality and Social Psychology, 44,* 1234–1244.

Miller, N., & Brewer, M. B. (Eds.) (1984). *Groups in contact: The psychology of desegregation.* New York: Academic Press.

Miller, N., Brewer, M. B., & Edwards, K. (1985). Cooperative interaction in desegregated settings: A laboratory analogue. *Journal of Social Issues, 41*(3), 63–79.

Miner, J. B. (1992). *Industrial-organizational psychology.* New York: McGraw-Hill.

Misavage, R., & Richardson, J. T. (1974). The focusing of responsibility: An alternative hypothesis in help-demanding situations. *European Journal of Social Psychology, 4,* 5–15.

Mishra, P. K., & Das, B. K. (1983). Group size and helping behavior: A comprehensive review. *Perspectives in Psychological Researches, 6*(2), 60–64.

Moch, M., & Seashore, S. E. (1981). How norms affect behaviors in and of corporations. In P. C. Nystrom & W. H. Starbuck (Eds.), *Handbook of organizational design* (Vol. 1, pp. 210–237). New York: Oxford University Press.

Molm, L. D. (1985). Relative effects of individual dependencies: Further tests of the relation between power imbalance and power use. *Social Forces, 63,* 810–837.

Montgomery, R. L., Hinkle, S. W., & Enzie, R. F. (1976). Arbitrary norms and social change in high- and low-authoritarian societies. *Journal of Personality and Social Psychology, 33,* 698–708.

Moore, D. L., & Baron, R. S. (1983). Social facilitation: A psychophysiological analysis. In J. T. Cacioppo & R. E. Petty (Eds.), *Social psychophysiology: A sourcebook* (pp. 434–466). New York: Guilford Press.

Moore, D. L., Byers, D. A., & Baron, R. S. (1981). Socially mediated fear reduction in rodents: Distraction, communication, or mere presence? *Journal of Experimental Social Psychology, 17,* 485–505.

Moreland, R. L. (1985). Social categorization and the assimilation of "new" group members. *Journal of Personality and Social Psychology, 48,* 1173–1190.

Moreland, R. L., & Levine, J. M. (1982). Socialization in small groups: Temporal changes in individual-group relations. *Advances in Experimental Social Psychology, 15,* 137–192.

Moriarty, T. (1975). Crime, commitment, and the responsive bystander: Two field experiments. *Journal of Personality and Social Psychology, 31,* 370–376.

Morris, W. N., Worchel, S., Bois, J. L., Pearson, J. A., Rountree, C. A., Samaha, G. M., Wachtler, J., & Wright, S. L. (1976). Collective coping with stress: Group reactions to fear, anxiety, and ambiguity. *Journal of Personality and Social Psychology, 33,* 674–679.

Moscovici, S. (1976). *Social influence and social change.* London: Academic Press.

Moscovici, S. (1980). Towards a theory of conversion behavior. *Advances in Experimental Social Psychology, 13,* 209–239.

Moscovici, S. (1985). Social influence and conformity. In G. Lindzey and E. Aronson (Eds.), *Handbook of social psychology* (3rd ed., Vol 2, pp. 347–412). New York: Random House.

Moscovici, S., & Faucheux, C. (1972). Social influence, conformity bias, and the study of active minorities. *Advances in Experimental Social Psychology, 6,* 149–202.

Moscovici, S., Lage, E., & Naffrechoux, M. (1969). Influence of a consistent minority on the responses of a majority in a color-perception task. *Sociometry*, 32, 365–380.

Moscovici, S., & Paicheler, G. (1983). Minority or majority influences: Social change, compliance, and conversion. In H. H. Blumberg, A. P. Hare, V. Kent, & M. Davies (Eds.), *Small groups and social interaction* (Vol. 1, pp. 215–224). Chichester, England: John Wiley.

Moscovici, S., & Personnaz, B. (1980). Studies in social influence: V. Minority influence and conversion behavior in a perceptual task. *Journal of Experimental Social Psychology*, 16, 270–282.

Mowen, J. C., & Cialdini, R. B. (1980). On implementing the door-in-the-face compliance technique in a business context. *Journal of Marketing Research*, 17, 253–258.

Mugny, G. (1984a). Compliance, conversion and the Asch paradigm. *European Journal of Social Psychology*, 14, 353–368.

Mugny, G. (1984b). Complaisance et conversion dans le "paradigme de Asch" [Compliance and conversion in "Asch's paradigm"]. *Bulletin de Psychologie*, 38, 49–61.

Mugny, G., & Perez, J. A. (1991). *The social psychology of minority influence*. Cambridge: Cambridge University Press.

Murray, E. J., & Vincenzo, J. (1976). Bystander intervention in a mild need situation. *Bulletin of the Psychonomic Society*, 7(2), 133–135.

Myers, D. G., & Lamm, H. (1976). The group polarization phenomenon. *Psychological Bulletin*, 83, 602–627.

Nagata, Y. (1980). [Status as a determinant of conformity to and deviation from the group norm]. *Japanese Journal of Psychology*, 51, 152–159.

Nemeth, C. J. (1981). Jury trials: Psychology and law. *Advances in Experimental Social Psychology*, 14, 309–367.

Nemeth, C. J. (1983). Reflections on the dialogue between status and style: Influence processes of social control and social change. *Social Psychology Quarterly*, 46, 70–74.

Nemeth, C. J. (1986). Differential contributions of majority and minority influence. *Psychological Review*, 93, 23–32.

Nemeth, C. J., & Chiles, C. (1988). Modelling courage: The role of dissent in fostering independence. *European Journal of Social Psychology*, 18, 275–280.

Nemeth, C., Endicott, J., & Wachtler, J. (1976). From the '50s to the '70s: Women in jury deliberations. *Sociometry*, 39, 293–304.

Nemeth, C. J., & Kwan, J. L. (1985). Originality of word associations as a function of majority vs. minority influence. *Social Psychology Quarterly*, 48, 277–282.

Nemeth, C. J., & Kwan, J. L. (1987). Minority influence, divergent thinking and detection of correct solutions. *Journal of Applied Social Psychology*, 17, 788–799.

Nemeth, C. J., & Staw, B. M. (1989). The tradeoffs of social control and innovation in groups and organizations. *Advances in Experimental Social Psychology*, 22, 175–210.

Nemeth, C. J., & Wachtler, J. (1974). Creating the perceptions of consistency and confidence: A necessary condition for minority influence. *Sociometry*, 37, 529–540.

Nemeth, C. J., Wachtler, J., & Endicott, J. (1977). Increasing the size of the minority: Some gains and some losses. *European Journal of Social Psychology,* 7, 15–27.

Newman, J., & McCauley, C. (1977). Eye contact with strangers in city, suburb, and small town. *Environment and Behavior,* 9, 547–558.

Newman, O. (1972). *Defensible space: Crime prevention through urban design.* New York: MacMillan.

Norman, W. T. (1963). Toward an adequate taxonomy of personality attributes: Replicated factor structure in peer nomination personality ratings. *Journal of Abnormal and Social Psychology,* 66, 574–583.

Nyquist, L. V., & Spence, J. T. (1986). Effects of dispositional dominance and sex role expectations on leadership behaviors. *Journal of Personality and Social Psychology,* 50, 87–93.

Oakes, P. J., & Turner, J. C. (1980). Social categorization and intergroup behavior: Does minimal intergroup discrimination make social identity more positive? *European Journal of Social Psychology,* 10, 295–301.

O'Connell, M. J., Cummings, L. L., & Huber, G. P. (1976). The effects of environmental information and decision unit structure on felt tension. *Journal of Applied Psychology,* 61, 493–500.

O'Donnell, A. M., & O'Kelly, J. (1994). Learning from peers: Beyond the rhetoric of positive results. *Educational Psychology Review,* 6, 321–349.

Offermann, L. R., & Schrier, P. E. (1985). Social influence strategies: The impact of sex, role and attitudes toward power. *Personality and Social Psychology Bulletin,* 11, 286–300.

Ofshe, R., & Lee, M. T. (1981). Reply to Greenstein. *Social Psychology Quarterly,* 44, 383–385.

O'Hair, H. D., Cody, M. J., & McLaughlin, M. L. (1981). Prepared lies, spontaneous lies, Machiavellianism, and nonverbal communication. *Human Communication Research,* 7, 325–339.

O'Leary, V. E. (1974). Some attitudinal barriers to occupational aspirations in women. *Psychological Bulletin,* 81, 809–826.

Olmsted, M. S. (1959). *The small group.* New York: Random House.

Olmsted, M. S., & Hare, A. P. (1978). *The small group* (2nd ed.). New York: McGraw-Hill/Random House.

O'Reilly, C. A. (1991). Organizational behavior: Where we've been, where we're going. *Annual Review of Psychology,* 42, 427–458.

Osgood, C. E. (1962). *An alternative to war or surrender.* Urbana: University of Illinois Press.

Osgood, C. E., Suci, G. J., & Tannenbaum, P. H. (1957). *The measurement of meaning.* Urbana: University of Illinois Press.

Osmond, H. (1957). Function as the basis of psychiatric ward design. *Mental Hospitals,* 8, 23–30.

Paicheler, G. (1977). Norms and attitude change: II. The phenomenon of bipolarization. *European Journal of Social Psychology,* 7, 5–14.

Parry, G. (1990). *Coping with crises.* Exeter, England: BPCC Wheatons.

Patchen, M. (1987). Strategies for eliciting cooperation from an adversary: Laboratory and internation findings. *Journal of Conflict Resolution,* 31, 164–185.

Patten, T. H., Jr. (1988). Team building, Part I: Designing the intervention. In

W. B. Reddy & K. Jamison (Eds.), *Team building: Blueprints for productivity and satisfaction* (pp. 15–24). Alexandria, VA: NTL Institute for Applied Behavioral Science. San Diego: University Associates.

Patterson, M. L. (1976). An arousal model of interpersonal intimacy. *Psychological Review, 83,* 235–245.

Patterson, M. L. (1982). A sequential functional model of nonverbal exchange. *Psychological Review, 89,* 231–249.

Paulus, P. B. (1980). Crowding. In P. B. Paulus (Ed.), *Psychology of group influence* (pp. 245–289). Hillsdale, NJ: Erlbaum.

Paulus, P. B., Seta, C. E., & Baron, R. A. (1995). *Effective human relations: A guide to people at work* (3rd ed.). Boston: Allyn and Bacon.

Peabody, D., & Goldberg, L. R. (1989). Some determinants of factor structures from personality-trait descriptors. *Journal of Personality and Social Psychology, 57,* 552–567.

Pendleton, M. G., & Batson, C. D. (1979). Self-presentation and the door-in-the-face technique for inducing compliance. *Personality and Social Psychology Bulletin, 5,* 77–81.

Personnaz, B. (1981). Study in social influence using the spectrometer method: Dynamics of the phenomena of conversion and covertness in perceptual responses. *European Journal of Social Psychology, 11,* 431–438.

Peters, L. H., Hartke, D. D., & Pohlmann, J. T. (1985). Fiedler's contingency theory of leadership: An application of the meta-analysis procedures of Schmidt and Hunter. *Psychological Bulletin, 97,* 274–285.

Pettigrew, T. F. (1958). Personality and sociocultural factors in intergroup attitudes: A cross-national comparison. *Journal of Conflict Resolution, 2,* 29–42.

Pettigrew, T. F. (1971). *Racially separate or together?* New York: McGraw Hill.

Petty, R. E., & Cacioppo, J. T. (1981). *Attitudes and persuasion: Classic and contemporary approaches.* Dubuque, IA: William C. Brown.

Petty, R. E., & Cacioppo, J. T. (1986). The elaboration likelihood model of persuasion. *Advances in Experimental Social Psychology, 19,* 123–205.

Petty, R. E., Cacioppo, J. T., & Harkins, S. G. (1983). Group size effects on cognitive effort and attitude change. In H. H. Blumberg, A. P. Hare, V. Kent, & M. F. Davies (Eds.), *Small groups and social interaction* (Vol. 1). Chichester, England: John Wiley.

Petty, R. E., Williams, K. D., Harkins, S. G., & Latané, B. (1977). Social inhibition of helping yourself: Bystander response to a cheeseburger. *Personality and Social Psychology Bulletin, 3,* 575–578.

Piliavin, J. A., Dovidio, J. F., Gaertner, S. L., & Clark, R. D., III. (1981). *Emergency intervention.* New York: Academic Press.

Plous, S. (1987). Perceptual illusions and military realities: Results from a computer-simulated arms race. *Journal of Conflict Resolution, 31,* 5–33.

Podsakoff, P. M., & Schriescheim, C. A. (1985). Field studies of French and Raven's bases of power: Critique, reanalysis, and suggestions for future research. *Psychological Bulletin, 97,* 387–411.

Polley, R. B. (1989). Coalition, mediation, and scapegoating: General principles and cultural variation. *International Journal of Intercultural Relations, 13,* 165–181.

Poole, M. S., & DeSanctis, G. (1992). Microlevel structuration in computer-supported group decision making. *Human Communication Research, 19*, 5–49.

Porras, J. I., & Silvers, R. C. (1991). Organization development and transformation. *Annual Review of Psychology, 42*, 51–78.

Prentice-Dunn, S., & Rogers, R. W. (1989). Deindividuation and the self-regulation of behavior. In P. B. Paulus (Ed.), *Psychology of group influence* (2nd ed., pp. 89–109). Hillsdale, NJ: Erlbaum.

Price, K. H., & Garland, H. (1981a). Compliance with a leader's suggestions as a function of perceived leader/member competence and potential reciprocity. *Journal of Applied Psychology, 66*, 329–336.

Price, K. H., & Garland, H. (1981b). Influence mode and competence: Compliance with leader suggestions. *Personality and Social Psychology Bulletin, 7*, 117–122.

Pruitt, D. G. (1983a). Achieving integrative agreements. In M. H. Bazerman & R. J. Lewicki (Eds.), *Negotiating in organizations* (pp. 35–50). Beverly Hills, CA: Sage.

Pruitt, D. G. (1983b). Experimental gaming and the goal/expectation hypothesis. In H. H. Blumberg, A. P. Hare, V. Kent, & M. F. Davies (Eds.), *Small groups and social interaction* (Vol. 2, pp. 107–121). Chichester, England: John Wiley.

Pruitt, D. G., & Lewis, S. A. (1975). Development of integrative solutions in bilateral negotiation. *Journal of Personality and Social Psychology, 31*, 621–633.

Pugh, M. D., & Wahrman, R. (1983). Neutralizing sexism in mixed-sex groups: Do women have to be better than men? *American Journal of Sociology, 88*, 746–762.

Quattrone, G. A. (1986). On the perception of a group's variability. In S. Worchel & W. G. Austin (Eds.), *The psychology of intergroup relations* (2nd ed., pp. 25–48). Chicago: Nelson-Hall.

Rabbie, J. M., & Bekkers, F. (1978). Threatened leadership and intergroup competition. *European Journal of Social Psychology, 8*, 9–20.

Rabbie, J. M., & DeBrey, J. H. C. (1971). The anticipation of intergroup cooperation and competition under private and public conditions. *International Journal of Group Tensions, 1*, 230–251.

Rabbie, J. M., & Horwitz, M. (1969). Arousal of ingroup-outgroup bias by a chance win or loss. *Journal of Personality and Social Psychology, 13*, 269–277.

Rehm, J., Steinleitner, M., & Lilli, W. (1987). Wearing uniforms and aggression: A field experiment. *European Journal of Social Psychology, 17*, 357–360.

Reis, H. T., Senchak, M., & Solomon, B. (1985). Sex differences in the intimacy of social interaction: Further examination of potential explanations. *Journal of Personality and Social Psychology, 48*, 1204–1217.

Rice, R. W. (1978). Construct validity of the Least Preferred Co-worker score. *Psychological Bulletin, 85*, 1199–1237.

Rice, R. W., Bender, L. R., & Vitters, A. G. (1980). Leader sex, follower attitudes toward women, and leadership effectiveness: A laboratory experiment. *Organizational Behavior and Human Performance, 25*, 46–78.

Rice, R. W., & Kastenbaum, D. R. (1983). The contingency model of leadership: Some current issues. *Basic and Applied Social Psychology*, 4, 373–392.

Ridgeway, C. L. (1981). Nonconformity, competence, and influence in groups: A test of two theories. *American Sociological Review*, 46, 333–347.

Ridgeway, C. L. (1982). Status in groups: The importance of motivation. *American Sociological Review*, 47, 76–88.

Ridgeway, C. L., & Jacobson, C. K. (1977). Sources of status and influence in all female and mixed sex groups. *Sociological Quarterly*, 18, 413–425.

Riecken, H. W. (1958). The effect of talkativeness on ability to influence group solutions to problems. *Sociometry*, 21, 309–321.

Riggio, R. E., Tucker, J., & Throckmorton, B. (1987). Social skills and deception ability. *Personality and Social Psychology Bulletin*, 13, 568–577.

Rittle, R. H. (1981). Changes in helping behavior: Self- versus situational perceptions as mediators of the foot-in-the-door effect. *Personality and Social Psychology Bulletin*, 7, 431–437.

Robey, D. (1986). *Designing organizations* (2nd ed.). Homewood, IL: Irwin. [Also, 4th ed., 1994, Burr Ridge, IL: Irwin.]

Rodin, J., Solomon, S. K., & Metcalf, J. (1978). Role of control in mediating perceptions of density. *Journal of Personality and Social Psychology*, 36, 988–999.

Roethlisberger, F. J., & Dickson, W. J. (1939). *Management and the worker*. Cambridge, MA: Harvard University Press.

Rofé, Y. (1984). Stress and affiliation: A utility theory. *Psychological Review*, 91, 235–250.

Rofé, Y., & Lewin, I. (1986). Affiliation in an unavoidable stressful situation: An examination of the utility theory. *British Journal of Social Psychology*, 25, 119–127.

Rogers, C. R. (1982). A psychologist looks at nuclear war: Its threat, its possible prevention. *Journal of Humanistic Psychology*, 22(4), 9–20.

Rokeach, M. (1960). *The open and closed mind: Investigations into the nature of belief systems and personality systems*. New York: Basic Books.

Rokeach, M., & Mezei, L. (1966). Race and shared belief as factors in social choice. *Science*, 151, 167–172.

Rosch, E., Mervis, C. B., Gray, W. D., Johnson, D. M., & Boyes-Braem, P. (1976). Basic objects as natural categories. *Cognitive psychology*, 8, 382–439.

Rotton, J., Barry, T., Frey, J., & Soler, E. (1978). Air pollution and interpersonal attraction. *Journal of Applied Social Psychology*, 8, 57–71.

Rotton, J., Frey, J., Barry, T., Mulligan, M., & Fitzpatrick, M. (1979). The air pollution experience and physical aggression. *Journal of Applied Social Psychology*, 9, 397–412.

Rubin, J. Z. (1980). Experimental research on third-party intervention in conflict: Toward some generalizations. *Psychological Bulletin*, 87, 379–391.

Rubin, J. Z. (1981). Psychological traps. *Psychology Today*, 15(3), 52–63.

Rubin, J. Z. (1983). Negotiation: An introduction to some issues and themes. *American Behavioral Scientist*, 27, 135–147. (From *Psychological Abstracts*, 1984, 71, Abstract No. 23077)

Rubin, Z. (1970). Measurement of romantic love. *Journal of Personality and Social Psychology*, 16, 265–273.

Rubin, Z. (1975). Disclosing oneself to a stranger: Reciprocity and its limits. *Journal of Experimental Social Psychology, 11,* 233–260.

Rubin, Z., & Shenker, S. (1978). Friendship, proximity, and self-disclosure. *Journal of Personality, 46,* 1–22.

Rucker, M. H., & King, D. C. (1985). Reactions to leadership style as a function of locus of control and ascendancy of subordinates. *Social Behavior and Personality, 13,* 91–107.

Ruscher, J. B., Fiske, S. T., Miki, H., & Van Manen, S. (1991). Individuating processes in competition: Interpersonal versus intergroup. *Personality and Social Psychology Bulletin, 17,* 595–605.

Rutkowski, G. K., Gruder, C. L., & Romer, D. (1983). Group cohesiveness, social norms, and bystander intervention. *Journal of Personality and Social Psychology, 44,* 545–552.

Rutter, D. R., & Stephenson, G. M. (1979). The functions of looking: Effects of friendship on gaze. *British Journal of Social and Clinical Psychology, 18,* 203–205.

Ryen, A. H., & Kahn, A. (1975). Effects of intergroup orientation on group attitudes and proxemic behavior. *Journal of Personality and Social Psychology, 31,* 302–310.

Saegert, S. (1973). Crowding: Cognitive overload and behavioral constraint. In W. F. E. Preiser (Ed.), *Environmental design research: Vol. 2. Symposia and workshops* [Proceedings of the Fourth International Environmental Design Research Conference] (pp. 254–260). Stroudsburg, PA: Dowden, Hutchinson, & Ross.

Sanders, G. S. (1981a). Driven by distraction: An integrative review of social facilitation theory and research. *Journal of Experimental Social Psychology, 17,* 227–251.

Sanders, G. S. (1981b). Toward a comprehensive account of social facilitation: Distraction/conflict does not mean theoretical conflict. *Journal of Experimental Social Psychology, 17,* 262–265.

Sanders, G. S. (1983). Attentional processes and social facilitation: How much, how often, how long-lasting? In H. H. Blumberg, A. P. Hare, V. Kent, & M. F. Davies (Eds.), *Small groups and social interaction* (Vol. 1, pp. 155–163). Chichester, England: John Wiley.

Sanders, G. S. (1984). Self-presentation and drive in social facilitation. *Journal of Experimental Social Psychology, 20,* 312–322.

Sanders, G. S., & Baron, R. S. (1975). Motivating effects of distraction on task performance. *Journal of Personality and Social Psychology, 32,* 956–963.

Sanders, G. S., Baron, R. S., & Moore, D. L. (1978). Distraction and social comparison as mediators of social facilitation effects. *Journal of Experimental Social Psychology, 14,* 291–303.

Sanford, F. H. (1950). *Authoritarianism and leadership: A study of the follower's orientation to authority.* Philadelphia: Institute for Research in Human Relations.

Schachter, S. (1951). Deviation, rejection, and communication. *Journal of Abnormal and Social Psychology, 46,* 190–207.

Schachter, S. (1959). *The psychology of affiliation: Experimental studies of the sources of gregariousness.* Stanford, CA: Stanford University Press.

Scherer, K. R. (1986). Vocal affect expression: A review and model for further research. *Psychological Bulletin, 99,* 143–165.

Schmidt, D. E., & Keating, J. P. (1979). Human crowding and personal control: An integration of the research. *Psychological Bulletin, 86,* 680–700.

Schmitt, B. H., Gilovich, T., Goore, N., & Joseph, L. (1986). Mere presence and social facilitation: One more time. *Journal of Experimental Social Psychology, 22,* 242–248.

Schneider, D., Hastorf, A., & Ellsworth, P. (1979). *Person perception* (2nd ed.). Reading, MA: Addison-Wesley.

Schneider, W., & Shiffrin, R. M. (1977). Controlled and automatic human information processing. 1. Detection, search and attention. *Psychological Review, 84,* 1–66.

Schneier, C. E., & Goktepe, J. R. (1983). Issues in emergent leadership: The contingency model of leadership, leader sex, and leader behavior. In H. H. Blumberg, A. P. Hare, V. Kent, & M. F. Davies (Eds.), *Small groups and social interaction* (Vol. 2, pp. 413–421). Chichester, England: John Wiley.

Schopler, J., & Stockdale, J. E. (1977). An interference analysis of crowding. *Environmental Psychology and Nonverbal Psychology, 1,* 81–88.

Schreiber, E. (1979). Bystanders' intervention in situations of violence. *Psychological Reports, 45,* 243–246.

Schutz, W. C. (1958). *FIRO: A three dimensional theory of interpersonal behavior.* New York: Rinehart.

Sebba, R., & Churchman, A. (1983). Territories and territoriality in the home. *Environment and Behavior, 15,* 191–210.

Seligman, C., Bush, M., & Kirsch, K. (1976). Relationship between compliance in the foot-in-the-door paradigm and size of first request. *Journal of Personality and Social Psychology, 33,* 517–520.

Seligman, M. E. P. (1975). *Helplessness: On depression, development, and death.* San Francisco: Freeman.

Seta, J. J. (1982). The impact of comparison processes on coactors' task performance. *Journal of Personality and Social Psychology, 42,* 281–291.

Shaplin, J. T. (1964). Toward a theoretical rationale for team teaching. In J. T. Shaplin & H. F. Olds (Eds.), *Team teaching* (pp. 57–98). New York: Harper & Row.

Shaver, P., & Klinnert, M. (1982). Schachter's theories of affiliation and emotion: Implications of developmental research. In L. Wheeler (Ed.), *Review of personality and social psychology* (Vol. 3, pp. 37–72). Beverly Hills, CA: Sage.

Shaw, M. E. (1954). Some effects of problem complexity upon problem solution efficiency in different communication nets. *Journal of Experimental Psychology, 48,* 211–217.

Shaw, M. E. (1964). Communication networks. *Advances in Experimental Social Psychology, 1,* 111–147.

Shaw, M. E. (1971). *Group dynamics, the psychology of small group behavior.* New York: McGraw-Hill.

Shaw, M. E. (1976). *Group dynamics: The psychology of small group behavior* (2nd ed.). New York: McGraw-Hill.

Shaw, M. E. (1981). *Group dynamics: The psychology of small group behavior* (3rd ed.). New York: McGraw-Hill.

Sheehan, J. J. (1979). Conformity prior to the emergence of a group norm. *Journal of Psychology, 103*, 121–127.

Shepperd, J. A. (1995). Remedying motivation and productivity loss in collective settings. *Current Directions in Psychological Science, 4*, 131–134.

Sherif, M. (1935). A study of some social factors in perception. *Archives of Psychology, 27* (187), 1–60.

Sherif, M. (1966). *In common predicament: Social psychology of intergroup conflict and cooperation.* Boston: Houghton Mifflin. [Also in 1967 as *Group conflict and co-operation.*]

Sherif, M. (1967). *Group conflict and co-operation.* London: Routledge and Kegan Paul. [Also in 1966 as *In common predicament . . .*]

Sherif, M., Harvey, O. J., White, B. J., Hood, W. R., & Sherif, C. W. (1961). *Intergroup conflict and cooperation: The Robber's Cave experiment.* Norman, OK: University Book Exchange.

Sherif, M., & Sherif, C. W. (1964). *Reference groups: Explorations into conformity and deviation of adolescents.* New York: Harper and Row.

Sherrod, D. R., & Downs, R. (1974). Environmental determinants of altruism: The effects of stimulus overload and perceived control on helping. *Journal of Experimental Social Psychology, 10*, 468–479.

Shotland, R. L., & Heinold, W. D. (1985). Bystander response to arterial bleeding: Helping skills, the decision-making process, and differentiating the helping response. *Journal of Personality and Social Psychology, 49*, 347–356.

Shotland, R. L., & Huston, T. L. (1979). Emergencies: What are they and do they influence bystanders to intervene? *Journal of Personality and Social Psychology, 37*, 1822–1834.

Shotland, R. L., & Straw, M. K. (1976). Bystander response to an assault: When a man attacks a woman. *Journal of Personality and Social Psychology, 34*, 990–999.

Shuter, R. (1976). Proxemics and tactility in Latin America. *Journal of Communication, 26*(3), 46–52.

Sieber, S. D. (1974). Toward a theory of role accumulation. *American Sociological Review, 39*, 567–578.

Siegel, S., & Fouraker, L. E. (1960). *Bargaining and group decision making.* New York: McGraw-Hill.

Simon, B., & Brown, R. (1987). Perceived intragroup homogeneity in minority-majority contexts. *Journal of Personality and Social Psychology, 53*, 703–711.

Sinclair, A. (1992). The tyranny of a team ideology. *Organization Studies, 13*, 611–626.

Singh, R., Bohra, K. A., & Dalal, A. K. (1979). Favourableness of leadership situations studied with information integration theory. *European Journal of Social Psychology, 2*, 253–264.

Sistrunk, F., & McDavid, J. W. (1971). Sex variable in conforming behavior. *Journal of Personality and Social Psychology, 17*, 200–207.

Slater, P. E. (1966). *Microcosm: Structural, psychological and religious evolution in groups.* New York: Wiley.

Slavin, R. E. (1991). Synthesis of research on cooperative learning. *Educational Leadership, 48*(5), 71–82.

Snyder, M., & Cunningham, M. R. (1975). To comply or not comply: Testing the self-perception explanation of the "foot-in-the-door" phenomenon. *Journal of Personality and Social Psychology, 31,* 64–67.

Solomon, L. Z., Solomon, H., & Maiorca, J. (1982). The effects of bystander's anonymity, situational ambiguity, and victim's status on helping. *Journal of Social Psychology, 117,* 285–294.

Solomon, L. Z., Solomon, H., & Stone, R. (1978). Helping as a function of number of bystanders and ambiguity of emergency. *Personality and Social Psychology Bulletin, 4,* 318–321.

Sommer, R. (1969). *Personal space: The behavioral basis of design.* Englewood Cliffs, NJ: Prentice-Hall.

Sommer, R. (1983). Spatial behavior. In H. H. Blumberg, A. P. Hare, V. Kent, & M. F. Davies (Eds.), *Small groups and social interaction* (Vol. 1, pp. 9–15). Chichester, England: John Wiley.

Sommer, R. & Becker, F. D. (1969). Territorial defense and the good neighbor. *Journal of Personality and Social Psychology, 11,* 85–92.

Sorrels, J. P., & Kelley, J. (1984). Conformity by omission. *Personality and Social Psychology Bulletin, 10,* 302–305.

Sorrentino, R. M., & Boutillier, R. G. (1975). The effect of quantity and quality of verbal interaction on ratings of leadership ability. *Journal of Experimental Social Psychology, 11,* 403–411.

Sorrentino, R. M., & Field, N. (1986). Emergent leadership over time: The functional value of positive motivation. *Journal of Personality and Social Psychology, 50,* 1091–1099.

Sparkes, K. K. (1991). Cooperative and competitive behavior in dyadic game-playing: A comparison of Anglo-American and Chinese children. *Early Child Development and Care, 68,* 37–47.

Staub, E. (1974). Helping a distressed person: Social, personality, and stimulus determinants. *Advances in Experimental Social Psychology, 7,* 293–341.

Staub, S. & Green, P. (Eds.). (1992). *Psychology and social responsibility: Facing global challenges.* New York: New York University Press.

Steblay, N. M. (1987). Helping behavior in rural and urban environments: A meta-analysis. *Psychological Bulletin, 102,* 346–356.

Stein, R. T. (1975). Identifying emergent leaders from verbal and nonverbal communications. *Journal of Personality and Social Psychology, 32,* 125–135.

Stein, R. T., & Heller, T. (1983). The relationship of participation rates to leadership status: A meta-analysis. In H. H. Blumberg, A. P. Hare, V. Kent, & M. F. Davies (Eds.), *Small groups and social interaction* (Vol. 1, pp. 401–406). Chichester, England: John Wiley.

Steinzor, B. (1950). The spatial factor in face-to-face discussion groups. *Journal of Abnormal and Social Psychology, 45,* 552–555.

Stephan, W. G. (1977). Cognitive differentiation in intergroup perception. *Sociometry, 40,* 50–58.

Stephan, W. G., & Brigham, J. C. (1985). Intergroup contact: Introduction. *Journal of Social Issues, 41*(3), 1–8.

Stier, D. S., & Hall, J. A. (1984). Gender differences in touch: An empirical and theoretical review. *Journal of Personality and Social Psychology, 47,* 440–459.

Stogdill, R. M. (1948). Personal factors associated with leadership: A survey of the literature. *Journal of Psychology, 25,* 35–71.

Stogdill, R. M. (1974). *Handbook of leadership.* New York: Free Press.

Stokes, J. P., Childs, L., & Fuehrer, A. (1981). Gender and sex roles as predictors of self-disclosure. *Journal of Counseling Psychology, 28,* 510–514.

Stokols, D. (1972). On the distinction between density and crowding: Some implications for future research. *Psychological Review, 79,* 275–278.

Stokols, D., Rall, M., Pinner, B., & Schopler, J. (1973). Physical, social, and personal determinants of the perception of crowding. *Environment and Behavior, 5,* 87–115.

Strodtbeck., F., & Hook, L. H. (1961). The social dimensions of a 12–man jury table. *Sociometry, 24,* 397–415.

Stroebe, W., & Diehl, M. (1994). Why groups are less effective than their members: On productivity losses in idea-generating groups. *European Review of Social Psychology, 5,* 271–303.

Strube, M. J., & Garcia, J. E. (1981). A meta-analytic investigation of Fiedler's contingency model of leadership effectiveness. *Psychological Bulletin, 90,* 307–321.

Stryker, S. (1972). Coalition behavior. In C. G. McClintock (Ed.), *Experimental Social Psychology* (pp. 338–380). New York: Holt, Rinehart & Winston.

Sundstrom, E., & Altman, I. (1989). Physical environments and work-group effectiveness. *Research in Organizational Behavior, 11,* 175–209.

Sundstrom, E., Herbert, R. K., & Brown, D. W. (1982). Privacy and communication in open-plan offices. *Environment and Behavior, 14,* 379–392.

Susman, G. I. (1990). Work groups: Autonomy, technology, and choice. In P. S. Goodman & L. S. Sproull (Eds.), *Technology and organizations* (pp. 87–108). San Francisco: Jossey-Bass.

Tajfel, H. (1970, November). Experiments in intergroup discrimination. *Scientific American, 223*(5), 96–102.

Tajfel, H. (Ed). (1978). *Differentiation between social groups: Studies in the social psychology of intergroup relations.* London: Academic Press.

Tajfel, H. (1982). Social psychology of intergroup relations. *Annual Review of Psychology, 33,* 1–39.

Tajfel, H., Billig, M. G., Bundy, R. P., & Flament, C. (1971). Social categorization and intergroup behaviour. *European Journal of Social Psychology, 1,* 149–178.

Tajfel, H., & Turner, J. C. (1979). An integrative theory of intergroup conflict. In W. G. Austin & S. Worchel (Eds.), *The social psychology of intergroup relations* (pp. 33–53). Monterey, CA: Brooks/Cole.

Tajfel, H., & Wilkes, A. L. (1963). Classification and quantitative judgment. *British Journal of Psychology, 54,* 101–114.

Tannenbaum, S. I., & Yukl, G. (1992). Training and development in work organizations. *Annual Review of Psychology, 43,* 399–441.

Taylor, D. A., & Altman, I. (1983). Environment and interpersonal relationships: Privacy, crowding, and intimacy. In H. H. Blumberg, A. P. Hare, V. Kent, & M. F. Davies (Eds.), *Small groups and social interaction* (Vol. 1, pp. 17–41). Chichester, England: John Wiley.

Taylor, F. W. (1903). Group management. *Transactions of the American Society of Mechanical Engineers, 24*, 1337–1480.

Tesser, A., Campbell, J., & Mickler, S. (1983). The role of social pressure, attention to the stimulus, and self-doubt in conformity. *European Journal of Social Psychology, 13*, 217–233.

Thelen, H. A. (1949). Group dynamics in instruction: Principle of least group size. *School Review, 57*, 139–148.

Thibaut, J. W., & Kelley, H. H. (1959). *The social psychology of groups*. New York: Wiley.

Thompson, L. (1990). Negotiation behavior and outcomes: Empirical evidence and theoretical issues. *Psychological Bulletin, 108*, 515–532.

Thornton, R., & Nardi, P. M. (1975). The dynamics of role acquisition. *American Journal of Sociology, 80*, 870–885.

Tice, D. M., & Baumeister, R. F. (1985). Masculinity inhibits helping in emergencies: Personality does predict the bystander effect. *Journal of Personality and Social Psychology, 49*, 420–428.

Tichy, N. M. (1981). Networks in organizations. In P. C. Nystrom & W. H. Starbuck (Eds.), *Handbook of organizational design* (Vol. 2, pp. 225–249). New York: Oxford University Press.

Tindale, R. S., & Davis, J. H. (1983). Group decision making and jury verdicts. In H. H. Blumberg, A. P. Hare, V. Kent, & M. F. Davies (Eds.), *Small groups and social interaction* (Vol. 2, pp. 9–37). Chichester, England: John Wiley.

Tubbs, S. L. (1995). *A systems approach to small group interaction* (5th ed.). New York: McGraw-Hill.

Tuckman, B. W. (1965). Developmental sequence in small groups. *Psychological Bulletin, 63*, 384–399.

Turner, J. C. (1980). Fairness or discrimination in intergroup behavior? A reply to Branthwaite, Doyle and Lightbown. *European Journal of Social Psychology, 10*, 131–147.

Turner, J. C. (1981). Some considerations in generalizing experimental social psychology. In G. M. Stephenson & J. H. Davies (Eds.), *Progress in applied social psychology* (Vol. 1, pp. 3–34). Chichester, England: John Wiley.

Turner, J. C. (1985). Social categorization and the self-concept: A social-cognitive theory of group behavior. *Advances in Group Processes, 2*, 77–121.

Turner, J. C. (1991). *Social Influence*. Milton Keynes, England: Open University Press.

Unger, R. K., & Crawford, M. (1992). *Women and gender: A feminist psychology*. New York: McGraw-Hill.

Valenti, A., & Downing, L. (1974). Six versus twelve member juries: An experimental test of the Supreme Court assumption of functional equivalence. *Personality and Social Psychology Bulletin, 1*, 273–275.

Valenti, A. C., & Downing, L. L. (1975). Differential effects of jury size on verdicts following deliberation as a function of the apparent guilt of a defendant. *Journal of Personality and Social Psychology, 32*, 655–663.

Valentine, M. E. (1980). The attenuating influence of gaze upon the bystander intervention effect. *Journal of Social Psychology, 111*, 197–203.

Valentine, M. E., & Ehrlichman, H. (1979). Interpersonal gaze and helping behavior. *Journal of Social Psychology, 107*, 193–198.

Vanbeselaere, N. (1987). The effects of dichotomous and crossed social categorizations upon intergroup discrimination. *European Journal of Social Psychology, 17,* 143–156.

Van Buskirk, W., & McGrath, D. (1993). Culture-focused T group: Laboratory learning from the interpretive perspective. In R. T. Golembiewski (Ed.), *Handbook of organizational consultation* (pp. 731–742). New York: Marcel Dekker.

Van de Vliert, E., & Euwema, M. C. (1994). Agreeableness and activeness as components of conflict behaviors. *Journal of Personality and Social Psychology, 66,* 674–687.

Virk, J., Aggarwal, Y. P., & Bhan, R. N. (1983). Similarity *versus* complementarity in clique formation. *Journal of Social Psychology, 120,* 27–34.

von Baeyer, C. L., Sherk, D. L., & Zanna, M. P. (1981). Impression management in the job interview: When the female applicant meets the male (chauvinist) interviewer. *Personality and Social Psychology Bulletin, 7,* 45–51.

Wagner, H. L., MacDonald, C. J., & Manstead, A. S. R. (1986). Communication of individual emotions by spontaneous facial expressions. *Journal of Personality and Social Psychology, 50,* 737–743.

Wahrman, R., & Pugh, M. D. (1972). Competence and conformity: Another look at Hollander's study. *Sociometry, 35,* 376–386.

Wahrman, R., & Pugh, M. D. (1974). Sex, nonconformity and influence. *Sociometry, 37,* 137–147.

Walster [Hatfield], E., Walster, G. W., & Berscheid, E. (1978). *Equity: Theory and research.* Boston: Allyn & Bacon.

Webster, M., & Driskell, J. E. (1983). Processes of status generalization. In H. H. Blumberg, A. P. Hare, V. Kent, & M. F. Davies (Eds.), *Small groups and social interaction* (Vol. 1, pp. 57–67). Chichester, England: John Wiley.

Wegner, D. M., & Schaefer, D. (1978). The concentration of responsibility: An objective self-awareness analysis of group size effects in helping situations. *Journal of Personality and Social Psychology, 36,* 147–155.

Whitcher, S. J., & Fisher, J. D. (1979). Multidimensional reaction to therapeutic touch in a hospital setting. *Journal of Personality and Social Psychology, 37,* 87–96.

White, R. K., & Lippitt, R. (1960). *Autocracy and democracy.* New York: Harper.

Wicker, A. W., Kirmeyer, S. L., Hanson, L., & Alexander, D. (1976). Effects of manning levels on subjective experiences, performance, and verbal interaction in groups. *Organizational Behavior and Human Performance, 17,* 251–274.

Wiersema, M. F., & Bantel, K. A. (1992). Top management team demography and corporate strategic change. *Academy of Management Journal, 35,* 91–121.

Wilcox, B. L., & Holahan, C. J. (1976). Social ecology of the megadorm in university student housing. *Journal of Educational Psychology, 68,* 453–458.

Wilder, D. A. (1977). Perception of groups, size of opposition, and social influence. *Journal of Experimental Social Psychology, 13,* 253–268.

Wilder, D. A. (1984). Intergroup contact: The typical member and the exception to the rule. *Journal of Experimental Social Psychology, 20,* 177–194.

Wilder, D. A. (1986). Social categorization: Implications for creation and reduction of intergroup bias. *Advances in Experimental Social Psychology, 19*, 291–355.

Wilke, H. A., de Boer, K. L., & Liebrand, W. B. (1986). Standards of justice and quality of power in a social dilemma situation. *British Journal of Social Psychology, 25*, 57–65.

Williams, J. M. (1984). Assertiveness as a mediating variable in conformity to confederates of high and low status. *Psychological Reports, 55*, 415–418.

Williams, K. B. & Williams, K. D. (1983). Social inhibition and asking for help: The effect of number, strength and immediacy of potential help givers. *Journal of Personality and Social Psychology, 44*, 67–77.

Williams, S., & Taormina, R. J. (1993). Unanimous versus majority influences on group polarization in business decision making. *Journal of Social Psychology, 133*, 190–205.

Williams, T. P., & Sogon, S. (1984). Group composition and conforming behavior in Japanese students. *Japanese Psychological Research, 26*, 231–234.

Wilson, J. P., Aronoff, J., & Messé, L. A. (1975). Social structure, member motivation, and group productivity. *Journal of Personality and Social Psychology, 32*, 1094–1098.

Winstead, B. A., & Derlega, V. J. (1993). Gender and close relationships: An introduction. *Journal of Social Issues, 49*(3), 1–9.

Winter, D. G. (1987). Leader appeal, leader performance and the motive profiles of leaders and followers: A study of American presidents and elections. *Journal of Personality and Social Psychology, 52*, 196–202.

Wolf, S., & Latané, B. (1981). If laboratory research doesn't square with you, then Qube it: The potential of interactive TV for social psychological research. *Personality and Social Psychology Bulletin, 7*, 344–352.

Wolpert, L., & Richards, A. (1988). *A passion for science.* Oxford: Oxford University Press.

Wood, W. (1987). Meta-analytic review of sex differences in group performance. *Psychological Bulletin, 102*, 53–71.

Wood, W., Polek, D., & Aiken, C. (1985). Sex differences in group task performance. *Journal of Personality and Social Psychology, 48*, 63–71.

Worchel, S., Andreoli, V. A., & Folger, R. (1977). Intergroup cooperation and intergroup attraction: The effect of previous interaction and outcome of combined effort. *Journal of Experimental Social Psychology, 13*, 131–140.

Worchel, S., & Norvell, N. (1980). Effect of perceived environmental conditions during cooperation on intergroup attraction. *Journal of Personality and Social Psychology, 38*, 764–772.

Worchel, S., & Teddlie, C. (1976). The experience of crowding: A two-factor theory. *Journal of Personality and Social Psychology, 34*, 30–40.

Worchel, S., Wood, W., & Simpson, J. A. (Eds.). (1991). *Group process and productivity.* Newbury Park, CA: Sage.

Worringham, C. J., & Messick, D. M. (1983). Social facilitation of running: An unobtrusive study. *Journal of Social Psychology, 121*, 23–29.

Yarczower, M., & Daruns, L. (1982). Social inhibition of spontaneous facial expressions in children. *Journal of Personality and Social Psychology, 43*, 831–837.

Yarnold, P. R., Grimm, L. G., & Mueser, K. T. (1986). Social conformity and the Type A behavior pattern. *Perceptual and Motor Skills, 62,* 99–104.

Yinon, Y., Sharon, I., Gonen, Y., & Adam, R. (1982). Escape from responsibility and help in emergencies among persons alone or within groups. *European Journal of Social Psychology, 12,* 301–305.

Yoder, J. D. (1981). The effects of disagreement on the continuation of an interpersonal relationship. *Human Relations, 34,* 195–205.

Zaccaro, S. J., Foti, R. J., & Kenny, D. A. (1991). Self-monitoring and trait-based variance in leadership: An investigation of leadership flexibility across multiple group situations. *Journal of Applied Psychology, 76,* 308–315.

Zajonc, R. B. (1965). Social facilitation. *Science, 149,* 269–274.

Zajonc, R. B. (1980). Feeling and thinking: Preferences need no inferences. *American Psychologist, 35,* 151–175.

Zajonc, R. B., & Sales, S. M. (1966). Social facilitation of dominant and subordinate responses. *Journal of Experimental Social Psychology, 2,* 160–168.

Zimbardo, P. G. (1970). The human choice: Individuation, reason, and order versus deindividuation, impulse, and chaos. In W. J. Arnold & D. Levine (Eds.). *Nebraska symposium on motivation, 1969* (Vol. 17, pp. 237–307). Lincoln: University of Nebraska Press.

Zimbardo, P. G. (1973). On the ethics of intervention in human psychological research: With special reference to the Stanford prison experiment. *Cognition, 2,* 243–256.

Author Index

Subject Index

Notes about Ourselves

A. PAUL HARE is a Professor of Sociology at Ben Gurion University of the Negev in Israel. He received a doctorate from the University of Chicago. His writing on social interaction in small groups includes *Small Groups: Studies in Social Interaction* (edited by Hare, Borgatta, and Bales, 1955 and 1965), *Small Groups and Social Interaction* (co-edited with Blumberg, Kent, and Davies) published in 1983, and the *Handbook of Small Group Research* (1962 and 1976), plus *Small Group Research: A Handbook* (by Hare, Blumberg, Davies, and Kent, 1994). His books *Creativity in Small Groups* (1982) and *Social Interaction as Drama: Applications from Conflict Resolution* (1985) provide the first outlines of the dramaturgical perspective, developed into the textbook *Dramaturgical Analysis of Social Interaction* by Hare and Blumberg (1988). He is also the author or editor of other books, the author of many journal articles, and the founder and editor of a journal on social science research. One of his most recent books on small groups is *Groups, Teams, and Social Interaction: Theories and Applications* (1992).

HERBERT H. BLUMBERG lectures at Goldsmiths College, University of London. He has been a Visiting Scholar in Psychology at Harvard University (1988 and 1989) and Visiting Professor of Psychology at Haverford College (1992–1993). He wrote the chapter on group processes in Eysenck and Wilson's *Textbook of Human Psychology* (1976). Besides collaborating on books on small groups, he has co-edited (with Paul Hare) three volumes on nonviolence, peace, and justice (related to applied group processes), and has written articles in various areas of social psychology. He has also edited two volumes with Chris French—*Peace: Abstracts of the*

Psychological and Behavioral Literature (published by the American Psychological Association, 1994) and *The Persian Gulf War: Views from the Social and Behavioral Sciences* (1994).

MARTIN F. DAVIES is a Senior Lecturer in Psychology at Goldsmiths College, University of London. He was Visiting Professor of Psychology at the University of Texas at Austin in 1985. His research interests cover a wide area of experimental social psychology. He has published numerous articles on the self and social cognition as well as coauthored books and chapters on small groups. From 1989 to 1994 he was an Associate Editor of the *British Journal of Social Psychology*.

M. VALERIE KENT is a Visiting Fellow in the Psychology Department at Goldsmiths College, University of London, where she was a Lecturer for many years, specializing in social psychology. Her particular research interests are in social development and in the social psychology of health. She was Joint Director (with Martin F. Davies) of a project—funded by the Health Education Authority—on the development of social interaction routines in the heterosexual encounters of young people. In 1992 she was a Development Fellow of the Association of Commonwealth Universities at the University of the West Indies in Trinidad. She explored parents' perceptions of, and strategies for influencing, children's behavior. She is currently completing a project in Tobago on psychological aspects of the self-management of diabetes. She has jointly edited and authored works small groups with A. Paul Hare, Herbert H. Blumberg, and Martin F. Davies.

ISBN 0-275-94896-X

9 780275 948962

HARDCOVER BAR CODE